"From Aristotle to John Locke to Karl Marx t
LGBTQIA+ struggles and Black Lives Matter,
the pressing question, through an interrogation (
and evaluate values—revealing what she calls th
and values: What, in the end, are we worth? Th
lated by Cooper more than a century ago, drives this well-written, poi-
gnant, and careful study of the normative and economic dimensions and
beyond of building democratic society and the political challenges and re-
sponsibilities such a project embodies. A genuine work of *political* thought,
Claiming Value brings political reality to the fore with clarity, precision,
and scholarly breadth."

Lewis R. Gordon, *author of* Freedom,
Justice, and Decolonization

C000001601

"In *Claiming Value* Alena Wolflink skillfully traces the tension between
the material/economic and ethical/aspirational senses of "value." Revealing the slippage between and entwinement of these senses of value, she
shows the political benefits of attending to the polyvalence of "value" and
the injustice that arises from failing to do so. This graceful work about an
ascendant and persistent political language—used by both the "Black Lives
Matter" movement and the "values voter"—offers an original and timely
way of articulating how any successful political struggle must simultaneously attend to the necessary interrelation between material needs and
structures and the ethical character of collective life."

Shalini Satkunanandan,
University of California, Davis

"This book is a novel treatment of the problem of value. Its methodology
is sound and well-justified, and it brings together an array of thinkers and
writers who are rarely found in the same books or anthologies. Its scope
is ambitious, and its topic is an important one for democratic life in late
capitalism."

Emily Nacol, *University of Toronto*

"*Claiming Value* makes an important contribution to political theory, political philosophy, race, gender and sexuality studies, and also theories of
political economy."

Kevin Bruyneel, *Babson College*

Claiming Value

Value is typically theorized from the frameworks of economic theory or of moral/ethical theory, but we need to instead think about value foremost as political. Alena Wolflink uncovers a tension in value discourses between material and aspirational life. As she shows, erasing this tension, as has been the historical tendency, can entrench existing configurations of power and privilege, while acknowledging the tension is a vital part of democratic practice. Using genealogical, conceptual-historical, and interpretive approaches, and drawing from such diverse sources as Aristotle, Anna Julia Cooper, Michael Warner, Alicia Garza, and Patrisse Khan-Cullors, Wolflink argues that abstractions of value discourse in both economic theory and moral philosophy have been complicit in devaluing the lives of women, queer people, and people of color. Yet she further argues that value claims nonetheless hold democratic potential as a means of asserting and defining priorities that center the role of political economy in the making of political communities.

With many real-world examples vividly portrayed, *Claiming Value* is an unusually accessible work of political theory accessible to students in courses on political theory, moral philosophy, social theory, economic theory, democracy, social inequality, and more.

Alena Wolflink is Assistant Professor of Political Science at the University of Denver. She is a political theorist of democratic agency and identity. Her current research examines the construction of narratives about democracy and citizenship through analyses of the undercurrents of race, gender, and sexuality discourses in the language of political economy. Wolflink's work has been published in such venues as *Theory & Event*, *Critical Philosophy of Race*, and *Philosophy and Global Affairs*.

Claiming Value

The Politics of Priority from Aristotle to
Black Lives Matter

Alena Wolflink

Routledge
Taylor & Francis Group

NEW YORK AND LONDON

Cover image: Lightspring, Business consulting vision idea and investment financial guidance with 3D render elements.

First published 2023
by Routledge
605 Third Avenue, New York, NY 10158

and by Routledge
4 Park Square, Milton Park, Abingdon, Oxon OX14 4RN

Routledge is an imprint of the Taylor & Francis Group, an informa business

© 2023 Taylor & Francis

Library of Congress Cataloging-in-Publication Data
Names: Wolflink, Alena, author.
Title: Claiming value : the politics of priority from Aristotle to
Black Lives Matter / Alena Wolflink.
Description: New York, NY : Routledge, 2022. |
Includes bibliographical references and index.
Identifiers: LCCN 2022008962 | ISBN 9781032302782 (hardback) |
ISBN 9781032302775 (paperback) | ISBN 9781003304302 (ebook)
Subjects: LCSH: Values—Political aspects. | Political ethics. |
Political sociology.
Classification: LCC JA79 .W655 2022 |
DDC 172—dc23/eng/20220701
LC record available at https://lccn.loc.gov/2022008962

ISBN: 9781032302782 (hbk)
ISBN: 9781032302775 (pbk)
ISBN: 9781003304302 (ebk)

DOI: 10.4324/9781003304302

Typeset in Bembo
by codeMantra

Contents

Acknowledgments

The most urgent gratitude goes to my students over the years for needing me to be a responsible grown-up. My efforts to match the maturity they assumed of me have assisted my development as a writer more than anything else I could do. Plus, without their enthusiasm, insight, resilience, and critical engagement in class and office hours, none of the ideas in here would ever have been generated, let alone put to paper.

An enormous thank you to Dean Mathiowetz, Jane Gordon, Megan Thomas, and Mark Anderson, who have all provided inspiration, intellectual exchange, and sound advice over the years, and far more of the latter than called for by their job descriptions. Each of them has pushed me to be a more rigorous and compassionate political thinker. Liz Beaumont and Vanita Seth also supported my work at the University of California Santa Cruz in subtle but indispensable ways. At Goucher College, Eric Singer, Abhishek Chatterjee, Nina Kasniunas, Nelly Lahoud, Janet Shope, and Rachel Templer were so brilliant that I shaped my life around trying to be just like them. Kevin Bruyneel, Lewis Gordon, Emily Nacol, and Shalini Satkunanandan all provided rich engagement, kind advice, and insightful feedback at key moments in the development of this book. Thanks to the tremendous patience of numerous co-panelists, participants, and audience members at the annual meetings of the Association for Political Theory, the Western Political Science Association, and the American Political Science Association, and to the faculty and graduate students in the University of Connecticut Political Theory workshop, many of the worst ideas have been cut from this text. I was able to travel to receive this essential feedback thanks to funding from the American Political Science Association, the University of California at Santa Cruz, and Beloit College. An earlier version of Chapter 4 was originally published by *Critical Philosophy of Race* and I am grateful to be able to reproduce it here. My University of Denver writing accountability group kept me sane during the final round of editing. I am enormously grateful to Dean Birkenkamp for believing in the book and shepherding it to quick publication, and I am thrilled we can connect in Colorado.

I am delighted to have colleagues who are also friends, role models, and mentors in Jesse Acevedo, Sara Chatfield, Phil Chen, Lisa Conant, Seth

Masket, Chiara Piovani, Liz Sperber, Darlene Squires, Alison Staudinger, Jing Sun, Nancy Wadsworth, and Josh Wilson at the University of Denver and before them in Beth Dougherty, Rachel Ellett, Pablo Toral, and Ron Watson at Beloit College. I am also deeply indebted to the intelligence, company, and good humor of Dustin Albertson, Trina Barton, Dashell Fittry, Covina Kwan, Joe Lehnert, Ada Lin, Inem Newsome, Scott Newsome, Martín Ordóñez, Jasleen Pannu, Daria Pugh, Alejandra Rodriguez, Jeff Sherman, Gabe Stuart-Sikowitz, Abigail Swisher, Kate Watkins, and Jess Whatcott. John Prosise taught me about the architecture of writing and personality, and in the wake of his loss Olga Mikhnyuk helped me figure out who to be. My life is enriched every single day by the friendship of Juan Diego Prieto, Megan Simon, and Liz Wilson.

I have the rare pleasure of a family that I would choose. Carmen Isasi and Lorre Wolf get a particular thanks for modeling excellence in academia and for always making me laugh. Thanks to Ellis Flink for political humor, to Phil Simkowitz for historical grounding, and to Bill Wolf for boldness and radical skepticism. Evan and Matt Simkowitz consistently inspire me with their political awareness, sensitivity, and activism. Thanks to my in-laws Beth Swallow and John Swallow, to the Swallows for weekly Zoom fun, and to the Arnaizes for always sending me home with a week's groceries. I often forget that April and Paul Keyes are my relatives through marriage rather than blood. An *in memoriam* thank you to Elisabeth Flink, Steve Flink, and Jess Wolf. Dorothy Wolf's spirit and audacity are what I strive for (with limited success) in every class I teach and in every argument I make. She is sorely missed.

To my immediate family, with so much love: thank you to Erik Wolflink for his unique and constructive contrarianism, to Fred Wolflink for curiosity and imagination, and to Stephanie Wolflink for teaching me to play with words. Jack Wolflink is somehow both audacious and measured, and has endless creativity, knowledge, kindness, patience, insight, wisdom, empathy, and wit. He surprises me every day.

1 Introduction

Recovering Our Political Values

Imagine opening your mailbox and finding a "Special Offer for Valued Customers." On some level you know that the invitation's suggestion that you are "valued" is deceitful. An inner cynic reminds you that to the company you have been algorithmically flagged as an occasional consumer likely to develop brand loyalty in response to personalized solicitations. You know that the sender does not care about your prosperity, quality of life, hopes and dreams, or even whether you save the invitation or immediately cast it aside.

There is nevertheless something honest and frank about the lettering on the mailer—those who sent it *do* value you. They have determined a price point for their goods, considered the likelihood of your continued consumption—both with and without an additional nudge—and deemed you worth the processing costs of targeted mailing. In this sense you have in fact been valued by this company, and likely estimated to be worth an expenditure of about $0.13 in printing materials.

This choice of word, *valued*, somehow still resonates on a deeper level. It implies something more personal than a monetary transaction. The connotations of 'valued' exceed the frank notification that you are being estimated for your profitability; they also convey messages like "you are important to us," and "we care about you." Still, try as this mailer might, it cannot convince you that its company values you in the same way that your grandparent or best friend values you.

The concept of value is pervasive in our language. It is the *sine qua non* of economic and normative theory alike. The word is used to describe everything from individual convictions to the power of a currency. Economies and economic development are visualized in long chains of "value-adding" processes, and sales advertise "great value" at low prices. We often discuss value as something that is "added" for the consumer, but when we speak of 'values' we say (or we hope) that we share the same ones. We then worry about "clashes of values," and proceed to mobilize in defense of American values, Christian values, and occasionally even democratic values.

Part of what is at stake in these diverse uses of value discourse is an ambiguity at the heart of this concept. The term 'value' perplexingly partakes

DOI: 10.4324/9781003304302-1

of both the realm of cultural norms, morality, and understandings of the "good," and of ostensibly neutral descriptions of the mechanisms of prices and transactions.[1] Claims about value can certainly serve the purposes of flagging our principal concerns, explaining motivations, or justifying actions—of signaling what we care about, and what is important to us. However, as the example of the mailer shows, distilling a message to importance alone actually dilutes the political content of value claims. There are, after all, a number of types of value, and cares and concerns are not always accompanied by deeper material processes of prioritization. For instance, one can receive a bounty of certain types of valuation absent other types. Many purportedly benevolent hierarchies have precisely this quality—those with power provide a form of care to those below them, but not the respect or reciprocity that would demonstrate both parties being equally valued in many of the ways that matter. The concept of value thereby exposes unstable boundaries between human needs and desires, and our entanglements with one another.

There is also an opaque relationship between what exists already that people want and what is produced for the market. When one looks at a piece of real estate, it is unclear whether its value is intrinsic and evident, or something that must be verified through careful comparison of price points. On some level one may feel that the value of a property is ultimately determined by individual utility calculations. But a shrewd buyer also knows that market incentivization can render individual preferences moot. Regardless of my personal aesthetics, I know that a brand-new condo in a major metropolis is more valuable to the market than a fix-me-up atop a Superfund site. Value, in its economic expression, can be both objective and subjective, and simultaneously within and outside of our immediate control.

We may erroneously believe that moral imperatives—that *values*—offer the way out of this mess. When we read daily stories about poverty, food deserts, and homelessness, we are reminded that society at large does not value many communities as much as it could (if at all). But this is even as egalitarian values fail to transform the incentive structures sustaining the prison-industrial complex, enabling predatory insurance schemes, and blocking access to integrated neighborhoods and well-funded school districts. A moral claim to values in human life and dignity does not automatically carry with it the material investment necessary to transform perverse social distributions of valuation.

Value's economic and moral dimensions can even work against each other. That human bodies are valuable to the mass-incarceration industry, forming a surplus population from whom resources can be drawn, directly denies the moral values of life and livelihood. But the two logics of value are not always at odds, and their relationship can be a harmonious one. For instance, extracting surplus value from enslaved people has historically coincided with the enshrinement of racist values.

Two logics of value thus stand in peculiar tension with each other: economic form (value) on the one hand, and moral or ethical pluralization (values) on the other. While advertisements sometimes treat *value* as something that one ought to maximize in pursuit of one's economic self-interests, claiming to act on one's *values* instead delinks rationality from material gain in favor of action on the basis of a higher purpose. This tension can present itself in a variety of forms. Someone might, for example, purchase discounted sneakers, but later return them upon discovering that they were made with sweatshop labor. Similarly, one might initially support a ballot measure to cut taxes, but renege after finding out that those taxes support a local theater program. Then again, one might also invest in a sustainable energy company that posts impressive returns, a case in which economic and moral values remain fully aligned.

This dissonance between these two logics of value raises the questions of how we view what politics is, and of whether we have the language to do politics effectively. Perplexingly, the concept of value is used to say that things alternately are and are not political. We do not argue about the relative value of our currency, which we take to be an objective rather than normative consideration. But we readily disagree about values, or what we take to be good or just.

As I will show throughout this book, efforts to either separate or to collapse economic and moral framings of value have the effect of depoliticizing discourse. I further argue that ignoring or collapsing their tension supports projects of political closure rather than democratic claim-making. If we want value to be a resource for democratic action and for prioritizing morality over economics, then we must ground our analysis of the relationship between value and values upon an open acknowledgment of their tension.[2]

Though tension usually has a negative connotation, bringing to mind unresolved and simmering conflicts between incompatible parties, it can also be used productively. Putting tension into metal or fiber wires is the basis for the whole genus of stringed instruments, from guitars to qin. Stretching a string between two points, so that tension is present but not overwhelming, creates beautiful music (according to the skill of the player). Likewise, value discourse requires its economic and moral dimensions be held in tension—a tension that opens up rather than forecloses the possibility of different relationships between material and aspirational life.

As I will show, the persistent reappearance of the language of value and values at the center of activism by and for people of color, women, and queer communities indicates an urgent need for theorizing value today. However, the ways this language can be used by marginalized people as a means of reclaiming power and agency are also a reminder that regardless of how one navigates the tension between these discourses of value, there is always an assumed community involved in contestation over value. It is for this reason that I proceed from a perspective on value and valuation that conceives of this concept as primarily, and even paradigmatically, political.

Value Claims as Political Claims

To say that value is political may seem an empty platitude—it is fairly obvious that if we disagree about values then they are political. However, I argue that value claims are political in the sense that they are always based in judgments about particular people and communities.[3] Moreover, I argue that claims about value sneak different images of human material interdependence into assessments about people.

Politics, I argue, is contestation over the relationship between the political, economic, and aspirational demands of life. The tension between different discourses of value shows us that there are moments when these relationships are actively challenged, contested, and fought over. However, there are also many moments, perhaps even the vast majority of moments, when sedimented versions of these relationships are institutionalized, normalized, and policed, and consequently a certain naturalism is attached to otherwise contingent constructions of value.[4] Whenever the tension between different discourses of value appears in contemporary political life, democratic politics requires noticing the tension and being mindful of how it can conceal prejudice and oppression. Democratic politics further requires that we not try to resolve the tension but rather let it remain active, and let it guide our actions in the face of unresolved dilemmas. This is not to say that an institutionalization of particular values or ways of conceiving of the relationship between value and values is always deficient or pernicious. It is simply to demand that institutionalization remain open to future contestation and challenge. Trying to achieve reification of a particular relationship between value and values by ignoring the distance between the two, or else by refusing to note their congruity, can create and sustain all kinds of hierarchies and exclusions.

Value claims, at their core, are a kind of productive contestation about the very basis of politics. Specifically, I argue that our uses of value discourse implicate particular visions of community, in terms of both which people and which activities are prioritized as parts of that community, and in which ways. When we value things, we define who we are. This means that it will never be possible to make a choice that benefits all, because by describing our values we implicitly define who the "all" is in one particular way. The "we" that does the valuing is, in other words, limited by the "what" that is valued.

Of course, all language presents a certain picture of the world at the expense of other possibilities, and therefore contains political ambiguities. Even the supposedly democratic claim "all power to the people" still begs the question: "which people?" My argument is not simply that value claims do productive work; rather, it is that the concept of value at its root contains a form of contestation over the very boundaries of politics, even if individuals or groups who speak about values do not necessarily experience it in this way. Because of this dimension of the concept, I argue, value claims both delineate what it means to be a member of a body politic and arbitrate the boundaries of human interdependence and material interconnectedness.

Value does not require language to exist.[5] The presence of a politics of value can be seen in expansive suburban lawns, well-funded school districts, and campaign spending, and its absence felt in boarded-up blocks, school shootings, prison recidivism, and avoidable epidemics. Since claims to and about value also play a vital role in constructing political communities, I look at linguistic appeals to value as a way into evaluating some of the commonsense assumptions that reify broader structures of valuation. Though my argument treats claims about value as a productive mode of contestation, the rhetorical power of value does not diminish the force of the material relationships of value—the language of value is another among the material relationships of value. Rather, looking to the illocutionary force of value claims can importantly reveal some of the moments in which aspirations for distinction collide with connections to communities— when our values and value collide, it is an indication to us that our personal priorities may have a tense relationship with the broader political and economic systems that structure our lives.

Several things occur whenever someone uses the language of value(s): first, a value claim is a provocation to evaluate someone or something. Oftentimes, this can inspire a shift in how the subject being evaluated is perceived. A value claim also imagines a particular configuration of the public. In some cases, using the language of value or values requires a reconsideration of the extent to which our agency is materially determined, depending upon whether the term's material or aspirational qualities are emphasized. To put this concretely: if I say I value queerness, then I implicitly call for others to consider or evaluate the relative importance of queer cultural norms as opposed to straight ones. I call for a reimagining of the public as one divided between values in heteronormativity and queerness. In doing so, I also draw implicitly from a particular logic of value, whether economic or moral, or some fusion of the two. I will discuss many examples of how value claims imply different understandings of the material dimensions of human agency in the following pages. For now, it is simply worth noting that when I invoke the concept of value throughout this book, what I have in mind is a way of defining a body politic with and through a particular set of political-economic or moral or ethical capacities. Practically, what this means is that any account of value, even represented as an abstract and neutral assessment of the worth of a particular good, is also an account of the value of the people involved in the exchange.

My focus on who is being valued in any value claim, as an integral component of understanding what is being valued, requires revisiting the roles of race, gender, and sexual politics in political-economic discourse. Looking at how classical political economists on the one hand, and at how theorists and activists from marginalized communities on the other hand mobilize the language of value, I will show that value discourse, deployed uncritically, hides sources of political injury or injustice, but, when deployed with purpose and attention to nuance, can reveal the exclusionary dimensions of various images of human interdependence. Value claims also draw boundaries around the people and activities that constitute the public. My effort, then, will be to unsettle exclusions in discourses that conceive of value as an abstract and objective property by arguing that what we value is also an indication of who we value.

Value's Political Genealogy

Throughout this book, I engage tensions in value discourse and consider the various ways that ignoring them has hidden the contingency of particular constructions of political communities and action. Tracing value discourses genealogically, and thus uncovering their biopolitical dimensions, I look at the shifting senses of value in the ancient and early modern debates from which we inherit a refraction of commercial activities in moral language. The subjects of these debates pertained to needs, monopolies, marriage, and food reserves, as portrayed in Aristotelian political thought, medieval just price discourses, and English legal history from the turn of the seventeenth century. In exploring this history, I argue that our abstraction of the concept of value(s) from these contexts; in which the biopolitical stakes were evident, comes with the consequence that conflicts over the uses of power and its rightful wielders that are deeply ingrained in the history of the concept are repressed in modern uses of the term. Erasure of these origins presents value as intrinsic and apparent, rather than as a means of impressing particular political commitments, community boundaries, and visions of politics upon others.

This book therefore illuminates how claims to value can be a source of democratic action as they reveal choices to be made about the limits of both our attachments to the material world and of our political communities—ones that we ignore at the expense of avoiding or even discouraging political contestation. Drawing from examples of value discourse used by Black feminists, queer theorists, and early twenty-first-century social movements, I suggest furthermore that the concept can be used for a certain category of democratic claims—ones that are distinctly not about equality, or even necessarily about justice. I suggest that value claims are best understood as claims about importance and priority, and thus play a critical role in disputes about the bounds and boundaries of our needs, and our communal self-understandings.[6]

I further show that value and values are neither independent of one another nor indistinct but are rather in a productive tension. Treating these two logics as entirely distinct or indistinct, I show, helped stave off the political problems of addressing when and how ideas about who we are as a people rest uneasily with the material realities of our lives, and especially how both are often constructed in ways that privilege particular perspectives and experiences. I also claim that the tension between moral and economic discourses of value is fruitful for recognizing how different images of human interdependence are at play in present-day mobilizations of the language of value and values.

Before proceeding further, a brief note on why I use the language of 'claims' is in order.[7] My goal in using the language of claims is to draw together more closely the contestable and linguistic with the political-economic dimensions of value discourses since the word 'claim' is also connected to material and aspirational politics.[8] We say 'claim' when talking about property, but we also use this word to make an, as-of-yet, unadjudicated statement of affairs, thereby setting contestation in motion. When we use a claim to argue something that we believe to be a truth but know that others might doubt, we are understood to be making something more substantial than an assertion, yet less grounded than an argument. When we go to claim our baggage after a flight, it is to collect property that is unquestionably ours. But land claims are often considered to be more provisional and highly contested. Value too has a deep connection to questions about truth and propriety—since we talk about it as if it is evident, but also as something that we construct and produce. The language of claiming therefore draws out some of the ambiguities of value, so I use this language of claiming as a way of emphasizing the contestation involved in any argument about value.

Overall, I argue that concepts like value and values smuggle into political discourse particular images of what sorts of matters are pertinent to political life. I also argue that construing value as exclusively either economic or moral, or as uncomplicatedly both, has obstructed our ability to think democratically about both material and aspirational politics. I suggest that an examination of the concept of value itself can help move beyond those accounts. I will now attempt to lay out the requirements of such a reinvestigation and the stakes for diverse normative political theories. In the following sections, I detail the efforts I make over the course of this book to unpack the various political dimensions of value.

Navigating Material and Aspirational Life

To understand why someone would want economic and moral or ethical logics of value to be considered as separate, one need only look at uses of value discourse by the now-notorious "family values" voters of the late twentieth century. This voting bloc's arguments about family values represent a troubling means of pretending that value and values are entirely distinct. However, prioritizing morality and keeping economic value at bay, as I will argue, also offers resources for appropriations of values voting discourse by the left, as exemplified in more recent immigration debates. Looking at these diverse examples, I will show why it is important to be mindful of the tension between value and values, and how keeping the potential for their separation alive can be appealing.

While the language of "values voting" has been used by many movements, its most prominent adoption was by the Christian Right in the 1970s in their presentation of "values voters" as a fully-realized political force.[9] Value claims were carefully deployed by leaders like Jerry Falwell, Phyllis Schlafly, and Anita Bryant to appeal to a coalition of conservative Christians and to link this coalition to the Republican Party.[10] The goal in using this slogan was to present the Christian Right as a unified voice, despite significant internal disagreements, and to cast a very narrow version of political evangelicalism as "a widely held belief."[11] This brand of evangelicalism is infamous for merging a vision of scripture with conservative and reactionary politics, and it has played a key role in shifting political rhetoric from a politics of equality (in the discourse of equal rights) to a politics of value.[12]

"Values voters" rely on a hazy picture of value: at times they frame moral or ethical values as entirely distinct from economic value, and at other times they treat economic value as a mere product of the moral or ethical choices we make. This movement is especially infamous for using value discourse as a vehicle for conservative white American opposition to the welfare state, civil rights, and desegregation.[13] As Seth Dowland shows, the language was part of a carefully crafted political message; in the 1980s and 1990s, the image of "family values" was of a "breadwinning father, stay-at-home mother, and well-tended children."[14] In support of these purported values, the evangelical right continues to mobilize around a variety of issues from abortion to gay marriage.[15]

Though the movement claims that "values voters" are guided to the polling booth by a higher purpose, the practice of values voting actually succumbs to a sort of value relativism. Indeed, this title has stuck despite overwhelming evidence both that the supposed values issues of traditional families and abortion have not played a significant role in recent elections, and that economic issues consistently take prominence instead.[16] The language of "values voting" has instead served a covert political agenda. For instance, like Richard Nixon's "politics of decency," this language was a dog whistle that triggered nostalgia for a time when racial lines were more clearly demarcated.[17]

Values voters cast obvious doubts on the aspiration that we can set our values free from historical patterns of valuation. The idea that values voters truly vote for moral principles rather than the economic benefits of white supremacy, patriarchy, and heteronormativity is suspicious at best.[18]

However, the claim this group makes about the importance of moral or ethical values in politics is not to be discarded so easily—there is certainly something enticing about the idea that we can vote on something other than economic interests, and that our principles might surpass even economic rationality. Lest we assume that it is impossible to imagine how the world might look from outside of our own immediate material needs, we have to take this part of their argument seriously.

Values voters are not the only ones who have something at stake in this distinction between economic and moral value. To see this, one need only look to the way the language of values is oftentimes used in contrast to the language of interests. As the commonsense economic logic goes, if something is valuable, then obtaining it is in our interests. By contrast, the language of values is used to explain behavior on the basis of concerns about justice, equality, virtue, and shared life with others—to suggest that we are motivated not by the kind of zero-sum conflict over resources connoted by the idea of self-interest, but rather by altruism and selflessness.[19] One might use the language of values, for instance, to advocate against policies that give one preferential treatment.

At the same time, conceiving of values as the remedy for "baser" material interests is only a relatively recent phenomenon. As Albert Hirschman has shown, early arguments for capitalism actually did nearly the opposite— they framed economic interests as a rational motive for human enterprise, displacing the assumption that irrational "passions" such as greed, avarice, and lust otherwise drove human behavior in the marketplace.[20] Narrowly pursuing economic value, in other words, was perceived to be a judicious action, whereas people were deeply suspicious of action on behalf of sentiments. The incentives embedded in economic behavior were assumed throughout the seventeenth and eighteenth centuries to quell the insidious desires intrinsic to human nature. In the value–values dichotomy, this logic is flipped on its head. Instead of the pursuit of value being viewed as a higher form of rationality above acting on behalf of our "passions," value-maximizing behavior is treated as synonymous with self-interested action, and oftentimes even selfishness. In sum: we inherit, via classical liberalism, the seventeenth- and eighteenth-century assumption that economic behavior is an antidote to moral bankruptcy. However, we also inherit the ideal of a world of unbounded choice untethered by material processes of production, evident whenever anyone claims to vote on their moral or ethical values alone. In other words, we think that bad *values* can be remedied through the pursuit of economic *value*. Yet we also think that good values remedy the evils of economic value narrowly construed. These competing images of the relationship between economic and moral discourses of value are indications of the tensions at the heart of value discourse.

Though flying the flag of "values" is often done to conceal selfish motivations, doing so still reminds us that there are foundations of decision-making that go beyond material power. When someone says, "that goes against my values," they can do two contradictory things. They assert the importance of their own view of the world, but they can also choose to affirm or to deny a connection between their values and their self-interest. In the case of denial, they also express that their standpoint comes from a place beyond their individualized acquisition of utility—that it comes from, perhaps, a norm, or another type of shared connection with others.

Updating Family Values

More recently, the 2016 presidential election marked the widespread appropriation of the language of values by a variety of voting blocs. The category of "values voters" has since been described as expanding to include all American voters. For instance, George Lakoff commented that today, "voters don't vote their self-interest, they vote their values."[21] Hillary Clinton used the language of value in her response to the 2016 election results by encouraging her supporters to continue to "fight" for their own "values."[22] Nancy Pelosi's insistence that Trump's border wall was "immoral" and not "wasteful" or something that "wouldn't work," for instance, also exemplifies this form of value-based claim-making.[23]

Legislative initiatives in particular have capitalized upon this language, such as in the pointedly titled California Values Act, which made California a sanctuary state.[24] Announcing his office's support for the law, Attorney General Xavier Becerra said that the state had a:

> Right to determine how it will provide for the safety and general welfare of its residents and to safeguard their constitutional rights... fearmongering and falsehoods will not intimidate our state into compromising our *values*.[25]

State Senator Kevin de León, who introduced the legislation, described the state as "moving forward some progressive values," and went on to say, "we're here to defend our values—family values—because no government should separate mothers from their children and children from their fathers."[26] Others too began to ask questions like, "so where is the pro-life movement now that children are being hurt?" with the suggestion that "people who said...that they cared so much about traditional religious values" ought to be concerned about this issue as well.[27] The clash here is not between different values, but between different interpretations of what the same professed values ("family values") even entail. This use of language furthermore raises both the question of how to measure whether "family" values are what they are purported to be, and the possibility that values voters have misunderstood or misrepresented their own values.

It is also notable that for both values voters and those appropriating this language, economic value is treated as beside the point. The language of the California Values Act treats political contestation as something that can be carried out without considering material interests, or even at their explicit exclusion. Voting one's values, whether those values be purportedly Christian ones, centrist ones, or pro-immigration ones, is framed as a matter of conscience or principle rather than as one of economic value. Here, value, or material need, enters the conversation only in the sense of an abstract need for justice or sanctity—this despite the possibility that material needs certainly *could* be part of the conversation. In the case of the California Values Act, for instance, the argument could be made that repatriation often comes at the cost of physical security, or that we need immigrants to thrive as a nation.

This position that sanctuary is a problem of values rather than value diverges from the argument made by the Black Lives Matter movement, for which aspirations and material needs are deeply entangled. While arguments about values voting frame needs and aspirations as separable, the Black Lives Matter movement treats them as intrinsically bound together. In claiming that Black lives "matter," they raise Black devaluation both as an economic consideration (to the extent that mattering is material), and as a moral priority (what matters). Supporters of sanctuary state legislation and Black Lives Matter activists both mobilize value discourse, and in support of causes that are largely complementary. However, they do so in very different ways. The former, in appropriating the language used by "values voters," distinguishes 'values' from 'value', and thereby asserts that a choice between material value and moral values is even possible. The argument that Blacks lives "matter," by contrast, does not propose such a distinction.

I will return to these diverse framings of political dilemmas in terms of one or both discourses of value throughout the book. However, for now, it is imperative only to note that viewing these dilemmas with attention to the tension between economic and moral discourses of value brings into focus how the use of the language of values (as opposed to value) represents a particular choice. The choice is not only about how to represent a political position, but also about how to represent politics.

Navigating Contested Language

Anything valuable is necessarily valuable to someone or for some purpose. Yet understanding how things come to have value, whether on or outside of the market, and for whom they have it, requires thinking about the implications of the word 'value' itself.[28] In particular, navigating the rhetoric of family values voting and sanctuary state legislation alike requires thinking about the way language functions as a vehicle of political disagreement.

Language is an essential constitutive dimension of "our feelings, our goals, our social relations, and our practices," and the site through which identities are expressed and mediated.[29] When we talk about value, the language we use discloses particular images of the good or the just and implicit assumptions about who "we" even are. A linguistic analysis of value is thus critical to understanding the content and force of value claims today. I therefore organize my analysis around a genealogical approach and put language at the center of my inquiry. Given the dominance of materialist studies of value, it is important to note here that I proceed from the position that speech acts are not merely cultural expressions of material conditions; rather, they are integral to the production of material culture.[30] Because we formulate ideas through language, terms and the networks of other words in which they are enmeshed play an important role in changing the terms of debate and "channeling" political thought and actions "in certain directions."[31] Ludwig Wittgenstein's demonstration that the assumptions of language can hide in plain view could not be more pertinent to the problem of value discourse. Both economic and moral uses of the language of value treat the word as having reference points in the world with uncontested meanings. Economics and moral philosophy thereby lend credibility to claims to value that might otherwise be contestable.[32] Empirical investigation, as Hanna Pitkin puts it, "presupposes conceptual definition." Yet economists and moral philosophers have consistently launched straight into empirical investigation without examining the construction of the categories they deploy in their investigation.

In response to the realization that many of the central concepts of political studies are themselves the sites of political contestation, a movement within political theory and philosophy has attempted to provide conceptual-historical mappings of keywords. These studies of the political purposes for which concepts were mobilized at earlier historical junctures, and of the various views of power they were used to underpin, ultimately aim to lend analytical purchase to their present-day uses.[33] Surprisingly, value has been all but exempt from this type of analysis, absent in Raymond Williams's *Keywords*, the recent *Keywords for Radicals*, and all of the major works that Melvin Richter cites as engaging in this type of inquiry from *Geschichtliche Grundbegriffe* to its French-language analog.[34] The word 'value' does appear in *New Keywords*, but in a departure from Williams's original format, the entry deals primarily with the term's diverse meanings as though they were the same across history, rather than detailing the moments at which particular uses emerged, disappeared, changed, or evolved.[35] This route is taken even despite the fact that Raymond Williams's *Keywords* was originally produced for the explicit purpose of seeing how contemporary uses either "bound together certain ways of seeing culture and society" or "open up issues and problems," both features that he argued could only be uncovered in historical perspective.[36] In fact, uncovering the ways past values live on in present uses of various words is a central goal of keywords scholarship.[37]

Philosophical mappings of the concept of value have attempted to grapple with this problem, though they do so for very different purposes.[38] The tendency in philosophical studies has been to argue for returning to value's original definitions. In his entry for 'value' in *The Encyclopedia of Philosophy*, William Frankena laments the passing of the days when value meant simply "the worth of a thing," and writes that it is now "the generic noun for all kinds of critical or pro and con predicates." The term, he explains, is used "like 'temperature' to cover the whole range of a scale."[39] Other philosophical studies have taken a less prescriptivist stance on linguistic evolution and have embraced an expansive set of understandings of value, but at the expense of identifying historical change in the way that the language of value and values has evolved. W. J. T. Mitchell's entry in *New Keywords* dismisses Frankena's account of value's simpler origins and in doing so avoids the trap of imagining a moment in which the word was uncontested. Mitchell harkens back to Plato and Aristotle, writing that the word 'value' is connected with "questions of justice, morality, virtue, pleasure, utility, and happiness," and with the three chief domains of philosophy: the true, the good, and the beautiful.[40] As a result of these broader debates, Mitchell argues, the term contains tensions between "normative and descriptive statements, objective and subjective judgments, absolute and relative values, qualitative and quantitative assessments"—distinctions that, he writes, "tend to break down in practice."[41] While Frankena seeks to reduce value's plurality, Mitchell embraces it, yet implies that the same multiplicity of meanings and uses has persisted across time and space.

In compiling broad keywords and encyclopedic entries, these diverse linguistic studies demonstrate that the concept of value is contested. At the same time, they each erase the concept's history of contestation in their own way. My genealogical orientation toward this kind of conceptual study, by contrast, takes the contested terrain of language as indicative of the modalities of power that the concept mobilizes and represents, and analyzes how these modalities shift over time.[42] In fact, the differences between past and present uses that Frankena identifies have had different bearings on its contradictory uses today. Yet precisely how historical uses resonate today is a problem that none of these accounts of the concept tackle.

Part of the issue is that conceptual-historical analyses trace the concept to broad debates about truth, goodness, and beauty in Ancient Greek philosophy, despite the word's actual etymological origins, which I locate in Latin. The term's root, *valor*, was the Roman word for 'power,' and particularly a sort of personal power in the sense of 'courage,' 'strength,' or good health.[43] Though modern English speakers tend to think of 'value' in economic discourse as connoting the worth or price of a good, in Latin, the closest concepts to modern notions of value were *aestimatio* and *pretium*, and *aestimatio* was used to signify worth, while *pretium* was used to refer to price. *Valere* (the root of 'value') meant power, might, bravery, and physical vigor.[44] Seneca, for instance, used the adjectival form of the word *valere* in order to describe people favorably, in what modern English speakers might understand to be remarks about their 'valor' and 'valience'. He described the "resolution and value" of Hercules and depicted his subjects as having "as much worth and value as a medicine" when he intended to showcase their heroic qualities.[45] These senses also linger in the cognates for value in Spanish and French (*valor* and *valeur*), which continue to be used to describe bravery, courage, and import.[46]

I argue that this concept's evolution from these earlier senses can be tracked to changing conceptions of the marketplace. That the word 'value' was initially used to talk about the power of a particular person or sort of person, rather than as a way of abstractly conceptualizing how money changes hands, is critical to understanding its later uses in political–economic discourse. Why the term has come to take on such a different set of resonances, in other words, requires an examination of the uses of this earlier form, in which the political dimension—namely the concept's relation to power or strength—was more evident. As I will show, value's shift to the later economic and moral senses came only with the transition from Middle to Modern English.[47] This change came in the immediate wake of significant discourse and debate about human needs, and later about just prices, and pertained to disagreements over effective pricing mechanisms. The ways these disagreements were settled normalized particular modes of commercial decision-making and played a critical role in shaping the arguments that would succeed them, namely those of classical political economy, in ways that denied the political core of value discourse.

Organization of Chapters

The first part of this book is historical, to the extent that it treats episodes in the conceptual history of the concept of value. In Chapter 2, I look at how the naturalizing language of value and values came to replace an overtly political discourse about needs in the transference of ideas between Aristotelian political thought and the early Roman Empire. Revisiting the supposed origins of value discourse in Ancient Greek thought, I examine Aristotle's concepts of use and exchange, which are often read as precursors to modern political economy's concepts of use value and exchange value. Yet Aristotle, I will show, did not write primarily about value, but about needs. Moreover, he wrote about needs in order to make a critical claim about democratic citizenship—namely that needs are based in systems of material interdependence that are always contestable. In doing so, I destabilize modern value discourse by highlighting an important disjuncture in the history of the concept.

Chapter 3 traces the emergence of value discourse in ancient, medieval, and early modern theories of exchange. It looks at the origin of value discourse in Ancient Rome to argue that the concept is biopolitical—that it is used to produce and define individual and social bodies. Yet, I argue, we can use value claims to do the important democratic work of identifying and embracing political tensions, so long as we recognize this biopolitical dimension. Tracing the term 'value' etymologically, I examine this concept's root in the Ancient Roman lexicon, especially in legal terminology, as a way to assess the power and sovereignty of individuals. I then look at the term's use in medieval debates about just prices, which reflected concerns about problems of fairness in exchange. I highlight an unacknowledged feature of the just price debates, provoked by their Latin inheritance of ideas about sovereign control over currency—and it is a biopolitical quality that generates a distinct social hierarchy. As I argue, we inherit this unacknowledged dimension of just price debates in modern value discourses through narratives of economic liberalism. Consequently, a highly authoritarian vision of power is embedded in the ideological foundations of economic liberalism because the originators of economic discourses of value assumed that all value was determined by a monarch.

I then turn to the moment when the concept emerged in modern discourse and examine the shifting senses of value and values as they evolved over the course of early modern British debates about individual worth. Looking at the ways value was imagined in relation to earlier vulnerable populations uncovers a logic of valuation that is deeply invested in measurements of the worth of bodies. I argue that the ways in which bodies were put at the center of political–economic discourses reveal a logic of valuation hidden within the writings of classical political economy that continues to be biopolitical.

At the midpoint of the book, I shift my narrative focus to discuss appropriations of value discourse by Black feminists and queer theorists. Chapter 4 picks up the problems posed by the biopolitical elements of value discourse and uses this perspective to begin to think about race in the United States. I look at Anna Julia Cooper's political-economic thought in her essay "What Are We Worth" [1892], in order to explore the racialization and gendering of value discourse. Wrestling with the relationship between political economy and Black devaluation in the immediate aftermath of slavery, Cooper considers the problems of human 'worth' and 'material' as ways of measuring value, and ultimately uses her discussion of these concepts to provide critical insight into the ways competing systems of value in economic and moral discourses reflect similar disregard for Black women's lives and livelihood. Cooper reverses discourses that conceive of value as abstract and ahistorical through a parodic treatment of the concepts of worth and material as they are deployed in commonsense economic discourse and in the work of John Locke and Adam Smith. In response, she argues for a radical shift in how value is conceived, measured, and nurtured.[48]

The final two chapters look at diverse uses of value discourses by more recent social movements, as part of activists' efforts to revalue the lives and livelihoods of marginalized communities. Handing off the insight of my historical evaluations of value discourse to these efforts, I especially take to heart Cooper's perspective. Her points about the unacknowledged dominance of particular discourses of value in standard historical narratives are an indication that treatments of value must be conducted through a critical lens.

In Chapter 5, I argue that a tension between discourses of moral value on the one hand, and economic value on the other, enables different representations of the relationship between political economy and the boundaries of political communities. I explore this dimension of value discourse in a discussion of Michael Warner's writing on late twentieth-century New York City queer culture in *The Trouble with Normal: Sex, Politics, and the Ethics of Queer Life* [1999]. In this text, Warner argues that LGBTQIA+ communities should refocus activism from gay marriage to claiming and transforming public space and promoting cultures of sex positivity. I show that his argument relies on an imagination of politics as based both in contestation over economic resources and in a practice of aspirational world-building. Drawing from this example, I argue that a tension between value and its pluralization in 'values' is fruitful for recognizing how different images of human interdependence are at play in present-day mobilizations of this concept.

In the final chapter, I draw out my claims about the politics of value by looking at the writing of Black Lives Matter movement founders. I argue that the value claims that animate this movement, evident in the language of 'mattering', acknowledge tensions between material and aspirational systems of human interdependence. I read Patrisse Khan-Cullors's *When They Call You a Terrorist: A Black Lives Matter Memoir* [2018] as a text that articulates the political vision of this movement. I also draw extensively from Alicia Garza's "A Herstory of the Black Lives Matter Movement" [2014] and the platform of the Movement for Black Lives. I argue that the tension between value and values enables not only a choice between two imaginations of our relationship to the material world, but also a choice of two means of self-representation in struggles for inclusion. Value claims, such as those made by the Black Lives Matter movement, I demonstrate, embrace political contestation in a way that is deeply intersectional. This movement's claims about prioritization and distinction, I therefore argue, are paradoxically offered as a way of achieving equality.

In a more holistic way, my argument is divided into two parts. First, in tracing value genealogically, chapters 2 and 3 seek to demonstrate that value is primarily political. Chapter 2 does so by highlighting an erasure in the typical historical account of this concept. I demonstrate that the concept's purported origins rest upon a selective memory of Aristotelian theory, which forgets the ways that this earlier political–economic discourse was enmeshed in political contestation. I denaturalize this origin story, yet nevertheless call for a re-grounding of value in the model of embracing political contestation that this alternative path represents. Chapter 3 locates the more accurate historical origins of value discourse in Ancient Rome. It tracks the concept's transformation in medieval debates about the just price and the reverberations of these debates in early modern European economic legislation and classical political-economic theory. It then argues that this history reflects a gradual concealment of value's biopolitical qualities behind the fracturing of value into separate language for its moral and economic dimensions. My overall aim is to expose the implicit political projects that value discourse has been used in while simultaneously showing what it would mean to truly acknowledge and even prioritize value's political qualities.

The second part of my argument picks up this thread from the perspective of people who have often been the subjects of devaluations—namely Black, feminist, and queer activists and writers. In doing so, I turn directly to the tension between economic and moral discourses of value, and in chapters 4, 5, and 6, I begin to show the opportunities that being mindful of their tension (without seeking to erase it) can open up for thinking about value politically. Chapter 4 explores the injustices that bringing these two dimensions of value discourse together can expose, as Cooper demonstrates their complementarity in gendered and racialized violence. Chapter 5, by contrast, explores the way Warner pries these two logics of value apart, and in so doing offers opportunities for imagining other possible communities (particularly queer and trans communities) that might be valued. Finally, in Chapter 6, I show how Black Lives Matter activists bring the two discourses of value together while maintaining their tension—thus fully realizing the democratic possibilities of value discourse without forgetting their biopolitical history.

Notes

1 I draw this insight in part from George Henderson's discussion of this dynamic in Marx's writing. See *Value in Marx: The Persistence of Value in a More-Than-Capitalist World* (Minneapolis MN: University of Minnesota Press, 2013).

2 Here I am inspired by a way of navigating tensions developed by Hanna Pitkin throughout her work, but perhaps best exemplified in her text on slippages in Bentham's discussions of utility. See Hannah Fenichel Pitkin, "Slippery Bentham: Some Neglected Cracks in the Foundation of Utilitarianism," *Political Theory* 18, no. 1 (1990).

3 I conceive of politics as a practice of making judgments and taking actions in a world that is complex and heterogeneous, and that is revealed as such whenever those judgments are contested. On the argument that value always involves judgment, see Linda Zerilli, *A Democratic Theory of Judgment* (University of Chicago Press, 2016). John Dewey also connected value to judgment. As he wrote: "The term 'value' has two quite different meanings. On the one hand, it denotes the attitude of prizing a thing, finding it worthwhile, for its own sake, or intrinsically. This is a name for a full or complete experience. To value in this sense is to appreciate. But to value also means a distinctively intellectual act—an operation of comparing and judging—to valuate." John Dewey, *Democracy and Education: An Introduction to the Philosophy of Education* (New York NY: The Macmillan Company, 1916), 248–249. However, my

argument is that value claims are not only judgments about what is good, but also about which people are worthy or worthwhile.

4 On the point about naturalism, see Judith Shklar, *Political Theory and Ideology* (New York NY: The Macmillan Company, 1966). On how people naturalize particular values, see Mariana Mazzucato, *The Value of Everything: Making and Taking in the Global Economy* (New York NY: PublicAffairs, 2018). See also Karl Marx, "Economic and Philosophic Manuscripts of 1844," in Robert C. Tucker, ed., *The Marx-Engels Reader* (New York NY: W.W. Norton & Company, 1978).

5 Geoffrey Harpam, *Language Alone: The Critical Fetish of Modernity* (Abingdon UK: Routledge, 2002).

6 As Michael Freeden shows, thinking politically always entails assigning significance—to the extent that it involves that which is crucial, urgent, important. And, as he points out, "significance is almost always distributed unequally." Because significance is "a scarce resource and an expression of the preferences and evolutions in which we all engage" it will unavoidably "entail ranking." Michael Freeden, *The Political Theory of Political Thinking* (Oxford University Press, 2013), 132

7 Here it is useful to pause and differentiate between claims and demands. As Ernesto Laclau argues, 'demand' is a notion that is ambiguous in English—it can mean a request, but also a claim (in the sense of, for instance, demanding an explanation). However, this ambiguity, he argues, is useful for understanding how political arguments move from mere requests to their more potent form in claims. Ernesto Laclau, *On Populist Reason* (London UK: Verso, 2007), 73.

8 On the linguistic dimensions of contestation see Karen Zivi, *Making Rights Claims: A Practice of Democratic Citizenship* (Oxford University Press, 2011). Drawing from performative theories of language, Zivi argues that "rights claiming is a practice that allows us to question and reconstitute the very meaning of what is common or sensible and what is not" and to "shape as well as reflect our identity, our communities, and our understanding of politics." Ibid., 7 and 1.

9 Seth Dowland, *Family Values and the Rise of the Christian Right* (Philadelphia PA: University of Pennsylvania Press, 2015), 8. See also Melinda Cooper, *Family Values: Between Neoliberalism and the New Social Conservatism* (New York NY: Zone Books, 2017).

10 Dowland, "Family Values and the Rise," 17.

11 Ibid., 15.

12 Ibid., 17 and 10.

13 Ibid., 3–4.

14 Ibid., 9.

15 They mobilized first around issues connected to children, with early campaigns focused on homeschooling, textbooks, and creating Christian schools. They next shifted attention to motherhood, agitating against the Equal Rights Amendment and abortion, and finally turned to instantiating a vision of masculinity in the male figurehead of this trinity by advocating for militarization and against gay rights.

16 Amelia Thomson-DeVeaux, "The Values that 'Values Voters' Care About Most are Policies, Not Character Traits," November 20, 2017, https://fivethirtyeight.com/features/the-values-that-values-voters-care-about-most-are-policies-not-character-traits/.

17 As Dowland shows, values voters championed a family structure and style of living kept out of the reach of most non-white Americans. For instance, this

movement saw the Los Angeles riots as an example of youth troublemaking caused by absent fathers and neglectful mothers. Values voters understood these actions not as a form of political struggle grounded in legitimate grievances, but as the unfortunate consequence of the absence of family values from Black communities. Dowland, "Family Values and the Rise," 6–7.

18 See also Wendy Brown's evidence that values voters have transformed their appeals into a generalized argument for authoritarianism. Wendy Brown, *In the Ruins of Neoliberalism: The Rise of Anti-Democratic Politics in the West* (New York NY: Columbia University Press, 2019).

19 For such a critique of self-interest, see Stephen G. Engelmann, *Imagining Interest in Political Thought: Origins of Economic Rationality* (Durham NC: Duke University Press, 2003).

20 Albert O. Hirschman, *The Passions and the Interests: Political Arguments for Capitalism Before Its Triumph* (Princeton University Press, 1977).

21 Daphne White, "Berkeley Author George Lakoff Says, 'Don't Underestimate Trump,'" Berkeleyside, May 2, 2016, http://www.berkeleyside.com/2017/05/02/berkeley-author-george-lakoff-says-dont-underestimate-trump/.

22 Elliot Hannon, "In First Public Appearance, Hillary Clinton Says 'Fight for Our Values…America Is Worth It'," *Slate Magazine*, November 16, 2016, http://www.slate.com/blogs/the_slatest/2016/11/16/hillary_clinton_says_fight_for_our_values_america_is_worth_it_in_first_public.html.

23 Michel Martin, "The Moral Question of Trump's Border Wall," National Public Radio, January 27, 2019, https://www.npr.org/2019/01/27/689191255/the-morality-question-of-trump-s-border-wall.

24 Katy Murphy, "California's 'Sanctuary State' Bill Clears Hurdle, Moves to Senate," *The Mercury News*, March 13, 2017, http://www.mercurynews.com/2017/03/13/californias-sanctuary-state-bill-clears-hurdle-moves-to-senate/.

25 Carrie Johnson, "Justice Department Warns 'Sanctuary Cities,' With Grant Money At Risk," National Public Radio, April 21, 2017, http://www.npr.org/2017/04/21/525072689/justice-department-warns-sanctuary-cities-with-grant-money-at-risk, emphasis added.

26 Jessica Yellin, "Under Trump, California Goes Its Own Way," National Public Radio, May 25, 2017, http://www.npr.org/podcasts/510053/on-point-with-tom-ashbrook.

27 Robert Scheer, "A Community Terrorized: Immigration Crackdown Could Destroy The Social Fabric Of The U.S.," *Huffington Post*, April 2, 2017, http://www.huffingtonpost.com/entry/a-community-terrorized-immigration-crackdown-could_us_58e1222de4b0d804fbbb73fd.

28 There is an important distinction to be drawn here between a concept and a discourse. Though both are composed of a set of practices (linguistic and non-linguistic), I draw from Michel Foucault's understanding of discourse to think of it as encompassing concepts, but also as extending to a broader set of interpretive frameworks for understanding the world and our relation to it. See Michel Foucault, *The Order of Things: An Archaeology of the Human Sciences* (Abingdon UK: Routledge, 1994). Another way of putting this would be to say that I envision concepts such as value as essentially contested, and discourses as ways of imagining that contestation is not there. We might therefore be using the concept of value when we describe ourselves as shopping for the "best value," or describe ourselves as "values voters." But our use of value discourse would involve these activities, but also the various practices involved in valuation—selling or purchasing a good, deciding which ethical argument we find to be most consistent with our understandings of morality,

and so on. Though these practices depend on the concept of value, they do not require that we use the word, nor do they depend only on our understanding of the concept of value. Throughout this book, whenever I use the word 'concept' I am talking about language use, whereas my use of the word 'discourse' pertains to the broader systems of production that value drives—and of which concept use is only a part. For a more limited understanding of discourse that restricts it to linguistic practice, yet also views it as a wider context within which language use occurs, see Catherine Belsey's comment that "a discourse is a domain of language-use, a particular way of talking (and writing and thinking). A discourse involves certain shared assumptions which appear in the formulations that characterize it." Catherine Belsey, *Critical Practice* (Abingdon UK: Routledge, 1980).

29 Charles Taylor, *Human Agency and Language* (Cambridge University Press, 1985), 273; Ludwig Wittgenstein, *The Philosophical Investigations*, G. E. M. Anscombe, trans. (Hoboken NJ: Blackwell Publishers, 1953), 8, 11.

30 I am in strong concurrence with Ernesto Laclau and Chantal Mouffe's rejection of the discursive/non-discursive distinction. See Ernesto Laclau and Chantal Mouffe, *Hegemony and Socialist Strategy: Towards a Radical Democratic Politics* (New York NY: Verso, 2001), 107, 97, and 108.

31 This point is in many ways a Husserlian one—that language, like other cultural tools, does not gesture to external objects in the world, but is rather a constitutive part of the world. See Charles Taylor, *Human Agency and Language* (Cambridge University Press, 1985), 257–259; Charles Taylor, "The Hermeneutics of Conflict," in James Tully, ed., *Meaning and Context: Quentin Skinner and His Critics* (Princeton NJ: Princeton University Press, 1988). See also Quentin Skinner. "'Social Meaning' and the Explanation of Social Action," in James Tully, ed., *Meaning & Context: Quentin Skinner and his Critics* (Princeton University Press, 1988); Raymond Williams, *Keywords: A Vocabulary of Culture and Society* (Oxford University Press, 1985); Paul Ziff, *Semantic Analysis* (Ithaca NY: Cornell University Press, 1960).

32 Here I have in mind Connolly's discussion of essentially contested concepts. William Connolly, *The Terms of Political Discourse* (Princeton University Press, 1993).

33 Reinhardt Koselleck, "Begriffsgeschichte and Social History," in *Futures Past: On the Semantics of Historical Time* (New York NY: Columbia University Press, 2004); J. G. A. Pocock, *Politics and Time: Essays on Political Thought and History* (University of Chicago Press, 1989); Melvin Richter, *The History of Social and Political Concepts* (Oxford University Press, 1995); Quentin Skinner, *Liberty Before Liberalism* (Cambridge University Press, 1998).

34 Kelly Fritsch, Clare O'Connor, and A. K. Thompson, *Keywords for Radicals: The Contested Vocabulary of Late Capitalist Struggle* (Oakland CA: AK Press, 2016); Richter, "The History of Social." The absence of 'value' in any of the German keywords collections is likely a result of the lack of Germanic cognates. The nearest term, *wert* (worth) does appear in those volumes.

35 W. J. T. Mitchell, "Value," in Tony Bennett, Lawrence Grossberg, and Meaghan Morris, eds., *New Keywords: A Revised Vocabulary of Culture and Society* (Malden MA: Blackwell Publishing, 2005).

36 Williams, "Keywords: A Vocabulary," 15. For instance, the word 'natural' today bounds together a causal description and an implicit value judgment. Likewise, 'reason' combines the contingent associations of Enlightenment thinking with the neutral procedure of evaluating situations unemotionally. But a historical treatment of either term might show them to have once had very different senses.

37 Needless to say, a look to past values is complicated when investigating the concept of value itself. Though its problems, like those of many other key-words, are, as Williams writes, "inextricably bound up with the problems it was being used to discuss," value also has a way of serving as the concept against which all the other concepts are measured. Williams, "Keywords: A Vocabulary," 15. As Williams puts it, in a discussion of the applications of his method to other keywords: "when we come to say 'we just don't speak the same language' we mean…that we have different immediate values or different kinds of valuation." Ibid., 11. What he means by this statement is not entirely clear—though he is writing generally about the ways people assign meaning to events, the term value's very ambiguity with respect to economic and moral analysis betrays him a bit here, indicating that the term 'value' itself requires similar scrutiny.

38 Their purposes are most often to provide a comprehensive and authoritative definition of concepts, rather than an historical account of them.

39 William Frankena, "Value," in P. Edwards, ed., *The Encyclopedia of Philosophy* (New York NY: Macmillan, 1967), 229. As Frankena elaborates, "behind this widespread usage lies the covert assumption that nothing really has objective value," he argues, and "in using the terms [value and valuation], one should choose a clear and systematic scheme and use it consistently because of the ambiguity and looseness that the terms often engender, it would seem advisable to use them in their narrower senses or not at all." Ibid., 230. Frankena thus calls for precision, which he envisions as a restriction of value to its earlier, narrower uses. Yet what these narrower senses are, and how they have changed, is unclear in this account.

40 Mitchell, "Value," 365–366.

41 Ibid., 366.

42 To this end, this study is inspired both substantively and methodologically by similar work on the concept of interest in Dean Mathiowetz, *Appeals to Interest: Language, Contestation, and the Shaping of Political Agency* (University Park PA: The Pennsylvania State University Press, 2011).

43 Barbara Cassin (ed.), *Dictionary of Untranslatables: A Philosophical Lexicon* (Princeton University Press, 2014).

44 Different words were used to speak about morality as well.

45 Lucius Seneca, *On Benefits*, trans. Thomas Lodge (1614), 26, 33, 111, and 140 respectively.

46 See, for instance, Derrida's translation of *valeur* as "import" in Jacques Derrida, "Signature Event Context" in *Limited Inc.* (Chicago IL: Northwestern University, 1988).

47 As detailed in the *Middle English Dictionary*.

48 I engage a political-theoretical method of reading Cooper alongside classical political–economic discourse that she is responding to what Jane Gordon terms "creolizing" the canon. Jane Anna Gordon, *Creolizing Political Theory: Reading Rousseau Through Fanon* (New York NY: Fordham University Press, 2014).

2 Revaluing Need

Aristotle, Commercial Exchange, and Necessity

To understand how the concept of value has shaped and been shaped by modern discourse, one must look not only to value's roots and origins, but also to the discourse it replaced. In this chapter I look to the Ancient Greek tradition of political theorizing, to which the origin of the concept of value is typically attributed.[1] I turn specifically to the work of Aristotle, considered the quintessential value theorist because of his conjoined reflections on ethics and economics, and frequently hailed as the originator of the concepts of use and exchange value.[2]

However, as a closer reading of Aristotle shows, though the field of political economy claims to derive its categories of use and exchange value from Aristotle, reading the concept of value into his writing is anachronistic. Needless to say, Aristotle did not in fact use the word 'value' in his writing—no word or cognate for 'value' existed in Ancient Greek.[3] As I will show in Chapter 3, value discourse as we use it in modern economic and moral thought was a classical Roman invention. This prolepsis, I argue, reveals that modern political economy conceptualizes the categories of use and exchange value as having a much more harmonious relationship with one another than Aristotle might have theorized had he actually written about these concepts.

My perspective in this chapter is consequently genealogical. Looking to this moment in the typical origin story of value discourse, I follow Michel Foucault's call to look at concepts without fixating on "founding moments" or reducing complex histories to a single narrative.[4] In doing so, I show that modern value discourse, whose emergence I explore in Chapter 3, represents a significant departure from an earlier form of needs discourse that kept politics front and center.[5] Reading Aristotle as a theorist of needs avoids slippage into liberal economic categorizations of material life, and sheds light on an important disjuncture in the development of value discourse.[6] Though I remain agnostic on the question of whether Aristotle had much to say about value writ large or more broadly construed (insofar as it is connected to truth and goodness), I argue that the specific senses of value we inherit today do not come from Aristotle.

My ultimate goal in this chapter is to show that we must think about material constraints alongside democratic politics.[7] I draw out this critical

DOI: 10.4324/9781003304302-2

point in a reading of the political-economic language in the first book of Aristotle's *Politics*. As I demonstrate, Aristotle shows "bad" needs to be those that are endless and that cannot be satisfied, as exemplified by the ailment of *pleonexia*.[8] "Good" needs, by contrast, cannot be universally defined, but can still be bounded. However, because they cannot be universally defined, we also have something of a 'need' for deliberation or political contestation.[9] Through deliberation, we can realize the natural ends of our needs.

My reading of Aristotle thus builds on others' accounts of his political-economic thinking. However, it grounds his arguments on necessity and exchange more firmly in Aristotle's concern with bringing together abstract debates about justice and concrete concerns about distribution under the banner of democratic citizenship—democratic to the extent that he conceives this practice as about sharing responsibility and communal self-actualization. As I show, what has been taken as Aristotle's characterization of use values is actually his concept of "good" needs, or as he puts it, "necessary needs." But this concept is more complicated than typical treatments of his economic thought suggest, because Aristotle imagines needs as available for contestation and political struggle, rather than as a prerequisite to deliberation.[10] He required that citizens have a certain threshold of material resources to enable their participation in politics, *and* that that threshold be determined by nothing other than deliberative politics.

Examining the relationship between needs and citizenship from the perspective of democratic theory rather than political economy, I argue, reveals contestation about the boundaries of need to be at the core of political activity. Though 'need' signifies an imperative—that which is compulsory, unavoidable, or required—political economists have predominantly mediated their analyses through the enigmatic terrain of value discourse. Needs, whether imagined as material or psychological, historical or universal, are always treated as concrete, and a boundary is drawn between what constitutes a need and what does not. Value is, by contrast, more abstract, and represents a way of conceptualizing how importance is determined, and how that line is drawn.[11]

To really understand the politics of value, we must have a solid understanding of needs and their relationship to democratic action. Dissociating value discourse from needs discourse comes at the expense of seeing how contestation over resources is predicated on a political delineation of priority. Moreover, thinking of needs narrowly rather than expansively (as Aristotle did) jeopardizes political projects that are ostensibly founded in concerns about justice—concerns shared with Aristotle, who believed that understanding human needs play a key role in determining justice. For instance, arguing for a politics of redistribution without attention to the contingency of needs reduces politics to technical adjustment rather than an expansive means of altering human capacities and renegotiating, deepening, and transforming our relationships.

Moreover, I argue that readings of Aristotelian economics that ignore the connection between his claims about household economics and acquisition and his necessarily open-ended picture of deliberation reduce the complexity of his conceptions of freedom and slavery. They relegate his economic thinking to one sphere and his political thinking to another, discursively replicating an artificial division between public and private spheres—a division that value discourse upholds, maintains, and even occasionally buttresses. By contrast, a closer scrutiny of Aristotle's writings about the use and exchange of commodities demonstrates that needs are messy because they are diverse and unavoidably plural, but also because they are never private. After all, how I define my needs has consequences for you. This is a dimension of political–economic discourse of value that we must acknowledge, if we are to avoid uncritically reproducing the exclusions made possible by its departure from needs discourse.

Faulty Origins of Value Discourse

Economic historians frequently trace the concept of value back to Ancient Greece in the fifth century B.C.E., if not earlier. These historians locate early versions of modern value theory in Aristotelian thought, describing him as everything from a proto-Marxist to an early theorist of utility theory.[12] However, despite conflicting interpretations of the quality of his ideas about value, very few readers dispute the claim that Aristotle *was* an early thinker of economic categories of value. Karl Marx and Joseph Schumpeter both famously attributed the concepts of use and exchange value to Aristotle, and Schumpeter took the appearance of arguments about use and exchange values in Aristotle's writing as evidence that he believed money to be worth only as much as the metals it was made from.[13] Schumpeter also read a *laissez-faire* attitude into Aristotle's understandings of exchange value.[14] Others have taken issue with reading Aristotle's discussions of value as permissive of unequal exchange, and instead argued that the Marxian transformation of C–M–C into M–C–M are theorized clearly in Aristotle.[15] Ironically, both Schumpeter and Marx, whose perspectives rarely aligned, were in full agreement that Aristotle's concepts of use and exchange value were vastly undertheorized. For instance, Marx wrote that Aristotle's insights for value theory amounted to nothing more than "a mere statement of the accounting function of money," while Schumpeter described the very same discussion of money in Aristotle as "decorous, pedestrian, slightly mediocre, and slightly pompous common sense."[16] Despite these thinkers' shared attribution of economic value theory to Aristotle, neither held his views on the matter in high esteem.

Meanwhile, attributions of value theory to Aristotle do not stop with discussions of trade, money, and utility—many scholars also read Aristotle as a theorist of moral and/or ethical values. Philosopher William Frankena and "keywords" theorist W. J. T. Mitchell both date the concept of value back to Aristotle, connecting it to both the economic concept concerning the "worth of the thing" and questions about beauty and virtue.[17] Mitchell even draws from Raymond Williams to note that the concept is at the heart of a variety of Ancient Greek debates about everything from justice and morality to pleasure and happiness.[18] While political economists treat Aristotle as the originator of both use and exchange value (even as they are less impressed with his analyses of these concepts), keywords scholarship traces the origins of moral or ethical value theory to Aristotle.

Yet there is something misplaced about all of these arguments. The word 'value' was not a part of the Ancient Greek lexicon; in nearly every Aristotelian passage cited by readers enthused about his value theory, the concept that recurs is 'need'. However, the concept of need contains its own challenges. Aristotle's writing brings us to a central paradox of needs: we need other people to meet our needs, but we also have needs to begin with because of other people. This paradox stymies pinpointing a precise boundary around needs because it shows us that political life causes our needs to expand and change.[19]

This key oversight is part of why Aristotle's understandings of needs and necessity, as they are articulated in the very first book of his *Politics*, have presented a variety of problems for those who attempt to draw together his discussions of economics and politics into an uncomplicated picture of political freedom.[20] Frequently, Aristotle's discussions of public deliberation are championed while his discussions of acquisition are excluded.[21] Alternatively, his economic thought is treated as a crude precursor to the more refined understanding of use and exchange value developed in early modern Europe alongside the emergence of a capitalist economy.[22] The former approaches ignore the role of material need in Aristotelian thought, while the latter reduce citizenship to economic analysis. By contrast, exploring the democratic entanglements of Aristotelian thought on household economics allows a reopening of the political life of needs discourse, and a way of reading his political-economic work as critical to his understanding of citizenship and deliberation. Seeing this synthesis of political and economic thought in Aristotle's writing requires returning to *Politics I,* which deals with the relationship between material needs and the composition of the city.

Locating Needs in the Polis

Though Aristotle's philosophy is arranged to pave a road to the ultimate end of happiness, he builds that road in the city, beginning his text on *Politics* with an account of the people and animals that inhabit the city and their diverse relationships with one another. In this book, Aristotle argues that the city exists to guarantee that people's needs are met, and subsequently tackles how people who differ by occupation, status, or gender each approach the various activities involved in needs-meeting.

Approaching politics in this way, he details the activities of acquisition that are required to realize contemplation, the good life, and ultimately, happiness. The activities of needs-meeting function as the prerequisites for all of these higher values, and it is therefore against this backdrop that he begins his discussions of politics.

Aristotle initially sets household production and maintenance on the one hand, and commerce on the other, as two types of acquisitive activities. Household management, Aristotle explains, is concerned with the acquisition of useful goods, and meets a definite limit:

> it would seem to be these things that make up genuine wealth. For sufficiency in possessions of this sort with a view to a good life is not limitless, as Solon asserts it to be in his poem: "of wealth no boundary lies revealed to men."[23]

Aristotle argues, contra Solon, that genuine wealth is made up of possessions aimed at the good life, of which we only need so many. However, this is not the only type of acquisitive activity that Aristotle discusses. A second one involves wealth acquisition, which he argues has no limit and leads to the malaise of *pleonexia*, or unbounded desire.[24] He therefore bifurcates the realm of necessity into the essential (things that are useful), and the treacherous extension of the action of needs-meeting in "the art of getting goods." Noting a dramatic difference between meeting needs and exceeding them, he argues that the latter type of activity has a tendency to take priority over civic virtue.[25] In this distinction between "household management" and "commerce," he is quite critical of those who, he argues, take the action of needs-meeting too far in the practice of "money-making," or "the *unnecessary* sort of getting goods."[26] That "it is impossible to live without sustenance" does not, for him, justify the limitless accumulation that he describes as the inevitable result of exchange.[27]

For Aristotle, those who engage in non-necessary acquisition orient all activities toward money-making, losing sight of their needs along with the ultimate priority of deliberation.[28] He writes that those whose desire is "without limit" and who pursue money and acquisition are "serious about living, but not about living well."[29] Living well, for him, consists of political participation through deliberation about justice (what he describes alternatively as "ruling and being ruled" and "partaking in decision and office") and practicing *leisure*—things for which profit-seekers simply do not have time. He underscores this point in his connection of citizen activity with "self-generated work" to supply "sustenance."[30] For those who take this route, he writes, time is spent "in the manner that need [together with pleasure] compels them to," and Aristotle deems this practice of meeting needs without succumbing to *chrēmatistikē* (excess accumulation of goods and money) both gratifying and virtuous.[31] Aristotle thus cordons off a space for one particular sort of good, which is *anagkaion*—necessary or non-negotiable needs—arguing that these needs in particular must be met to facilitate citizen engagement in deliberation.[32]

This boundary between needs and desire has long been a problem for democratic theory and the utility of Aristotle's distinction bears out in a number of ways. Although I remain ambivalent about the utility of collapsing unruly concepts into one another throughout this book, I do so in this chapter in order to cast light on a different, if deeply connected, tension than the one between needs and desires—the tension between needs and values. I do so in part because the line between needs and desires is not one that Aristotle seems to linger on very much (if at all) in this text, so I find it in many ways to be an anachronistic way into his own distinction between needs and *unbounded* desire. This approach, I believe, is useful for uncovering the political dimension of these concepts, as it pays less attention to the slippery definitions of needs or desires and focuses instead on the problems of *whose* needs are fulfilled, overinflated, hindered, or violated.

Democratizing Need

Material needs pose a difficult problem for the Aristotelian tradition of citizenship theory. His republican citizenship offers an enticing vision of deliberative community action.[33] However, unlike liberalism, republican theory does not seek to base a conception of citizenship on a fraught imagination of all-inclusive citizenship as membership; instead, it grounds its image of citizenship in ongoing struggles over boundaries and resources.[34] These struggles include ones over needs, which Aristotle finds to be paradoxically both dangerous and vital.[35] A certain degree of economic activity facilitates collective sovereignty, but Aristotelian citizens also need leisure time, and thus some way to externalize the problem of securing material goods in order to create it.[36]

Naturally, Aristotle's image of participatory citizenship sits uneasily (for modern readers) with its reliance on slaves.[37] Some treat Aristotle's requirement that "daily recurrent needs" be met as one that renders citizenship an exclusive privilege because of the labor that must be committed to guaranteeing that these needs are met.[38] The claim here is that the mandate that citizenship be carried out in leisure requires the existence of a working class to underpin the leisure of a citizen class, thereby confining certain people to subservient roles in the household.[39] To be sure, Aristotelian slavery is neither an unambiguous need nor an unmitigated good.[40] He goes to great lengths to dismiss the legal and institutional foundations of slavery in Athens and to reground it in activity and virtue.[41] As Jill Frank argues, Aristotle is firm that eligibility is determined by citizen activity rather than nature, implying that people are only justly slaves, and their disposition for slavery thus revealed, through the activities of citizenship.[42]

Here it is useful to read Aristotle with a view to the present. Precisely because Aristotle is unwilling to fully condemn slavery and is unapologetic in his defenses of certain uses of slavery, his writing is a useful guide for identifying modern exclusions from citizenship—particularly when they are sublimated, disavowed, or glorified on the bases of appeals to either necessity or freedom. Aristotle's unwillingness to condemn slavery as an institution even as he criticizes its practical implementation and his insistence that slavery is both natural and beneficial are both sticking points for modern readers, and for good reason. However, his stubbornness about the value of slavery is also a reminder to look for some of the forms of oppression that can persist even when exclusion is disowned. For instance, we might look at how modern definitions of needs are supported by the labor and oppression of some for the benefit of others, and at how people are excluded from deliberation about the extent and distribution of human needs and the forms of labor we valorize. In Chapter 4 I will return to this problem of exclusions that are renounced even as they are reinforced when I look at Anna Julia Cooper's writing about the invisibility of Black women's labor, and again in Chapter 6 when I discuss willful ignorance as a mechanism of white supremacy. For now, it needs to be noted only that Aristotle's discussions of slavery are morally dubious but descriptively useful in their reminder that systems of oppression, exclusion, marginalization, and inequality are nurtured when their existence is something we overlook or ignore.

What is distinctive about Aristotle's understanding of politics is his insistence on the role of material interconnectedness in freedom. Whereas liberal notions of freedom tend to prioritize negative freedom, whether from necessity or even from political participation, Aristotle's overall understanding of freedom is as something that is realized *in* politics.[43] Aristotle's argument therefore strikes at the core of modern liberal imaginations of freedom. Whereas market fundamentalism imagines a straightforward relationship between acquiring money and satisfying needs, Aristotle shows the connection to be opaque. This opacity is also the critical point from which the deliberative roots of needs emerge. One particular way of defining needs, or even sustenance, cannot be an unequivocal human requirement because for Aristotle, things are defined as "necessary" not by nature, but by politics.

Aristotle's concept of the "necessary" was not developed in relation to an ideal baseline requirement of sustenance. Whenever he invokes the concept of *anagkaion*, or "necessary needs," Karl Polanyi shows, it is not a vague deployment of the concept of need, but a reference to the "rations" or "the commonly stored staples" of the *polis*—to what, in other words, had *already* been decided through public deliberation was necessary for survival.[44] Moreover, according to Jill Frank, Aristotle conceives of the 'necessary' as accidental, or that which only "happened to happen," and thus historically contingent. His understanding of needs is therefore not universal, but historical.[45] His references to necessary needs reflect past

decisions by citizens about what is required, rather than intrinsic charac-
teristics of the world. Aristotle is concerned both with a certain threshold
of material needs *and* with a political basis for their determination, as if
saying, "it is up to the citizens to decide the bounds of our needs…and
here is what they have decided."[46]

Whereas modern readers of Aristotle's economic thought treat "use values" as a private determination and "exchange values" as either a public
good or problem, Aristotle sees the problem of use as itself political, and as
a problem of justice. This is why the question of what constitutes necessity
is ultimately one that Aristotle refuses to settle on his own. From here it
follows that for Aristotle, any claim about need at all is unsettled and must
be determined through public deliberation. One can even read his own
references to the need for sustenance as a form of participation in this kind
of debate, in favor of a particular view of justice. References to sustenance
and rations insist on the value of speech from a particular position—in
his case, speaking rather prosaically as a consumer of food—rather than a
search for a neutral one.[47] Still, that needs are always political is for Aristotle not a sign of conceptual weakness, but of democratic potential. After
all, he believes engagement in political life is a virtuous action, and surely
the only actual route toward happiness and a good life. This centricity of
citizen activity to the problem of needs moreover indicates that a metaphysical reading of Aristotle's discussions of needs can address some of the
problems raised by a reading that attempts to think only in terms of needs
or sustenance as a category and never as an activity.[48]

The Needs Paradox: Aristotle and the Necessity of Politics

There is no denying the tension between the importance of needs and
the fear of *pleonexia* in Aristotle's account of politics. Even as Aristotle
attempts to distance needs from citizenship, he nevertheless argues that
certain needs simply must be priorities, staking his whole argument on
the possibility that there are specific things humans require. Herein lies
the trouble. Aristotle tries to hold space for addressing needs, even as he
finds their definition to be impossible to pin down. Yet by focusing on
the perils of commerce and leaving needs themselves obscure, Aristotle
does not stake a claim about the limitations of citizenship—about, for instance, what sorts of skills slaves would be obligated to have or how many
slaves might be committed to help meet each need. This connection between the definition of needs and the activities of slavery is critical because
Aristotle's writing indicates that needs are never private, and that how we
conceive of our needs has consequences for other people.

For Aristotle, needs are in many ways the essence of politics. It is no accident that he opens his discussion of household acquisition with the argument
that men and women, masters and slaves, are conjoined "of necessity."[49]
However, it is important to be clear that part of what is counterintuitive

about my way of reading him is that Aristotelian politics is also, importantly, about justice and freedom. He does not want needs-meeting to crowd out politics, which is why he seeks to reserve space for leisure and deliberation. Aristotle is unwilling to draw the boundary between needs and freedom on his own—and perhaps even believes that part of living the good life is participating in the creation of this boundary.[50]

This perspective emerges in the ways Aristotle avoids providing a precise definition of necessary needs. For instance, Aristotle sometimes defines needs as "sustenance." [51] However, he tells us, sustenance is defined differently from species to species and even within human communities:

> There are indeed many kinds of sustenance, and therefore many ways of life both of animals and of human beings. For it is impossible to live without sustenance, so that the differences in sustenance have made the ways of life of animals differ. The same is the case for human beings as well; for there are great differences in their ways of life.[52]

The general need for sustenance collides here with the problem of specificity.[53] As Aristotle details the ways categories of animals differ, he shows that bodily and cultural diversity render needs infinitely plural. Observing that carnivores, herbivores, and omnivores need different sustenance, he writes that "the same is the case for human beings as well; for there are great differences in their ways of life."[54] Just as animals are differentiated by the diverse nature of their needs, so are humans.

As his argument shifts from animals to humans, however, politics begin to sneak in. Aristotle elaborates about these different "ways of life" as follows:

> The idlest are nomads: they derive sustenance from tame animals... others live from hunting, and different sorts from different sorts of hunting. Some, for example, live from brigandage; others from fishing...but the type of human being that is most numerous lives from the land and from cultivated crops.[55]

Aristotle argues that people derive sustenance from a wide variety of sources and activities, even if they are most commonly engaged in organized agriculture. In this passage, Aristotle does not have an obvious preference for one lifestyle.[56] Writing that "there must of necessity be a conjoining of persons who cannot exist without one another," the city, he tells us, is "by nature prior to the household and to each of us" and is necessary for human flourishing.[57] Thus nomads, hunters, fishers, farmers, and even brigands are already part of communities—even as he describes the farmer as typical of most people, he imagines him not as a yeoman but rather as a citizen whose life is already deeply intertwined with the lives of others in his community.[58]

Classical liberalism has deployed this image in another way. Updating the brigand into the highwayman, John Locke imagines a solitary state of nature in which individuals are occasionally beset by the excesses of others—a condition Locke also imagines as existing prior to society.[59] But Aristotle's complicated depiction of the relationship between necessity and political life, and his introduction of politics as happening first and foremost in the city, flags a different perspective. As he writes:

> The city is thus prior by nature to the household and to each of us. For the whole must of necessity be prior to the part; for if the whole body is destroyed there will not be a foot or a hand, unless in the sense that the term is similar (as when one speaks of a hand made of stone), but the thing itself will be defective.[60]

The city is, in other words, more fundamental to our flourishing than anything we acquire in the household. Necessity itself arises not from the part, but from the whole. Aristotle's brigand and farmer are not billiard balls who occasionally collide, but two people (or communities, really) who are inextricably bound to one another, and their relationship has much room for change and growth.[61] This perspective on interdependence is critical, because these lines follow Aristotle's reminder that other people cause us to have needs but can also help us to meet them.

This view of the role of dynamic systems of material interdependence in Aristotle's thinking clarifies why some of discussions of needs and acquisition are opaque. "Self-sufficiency," Aristotle tells us, "is having everything available and being in need of nothing." However, he explains, it is harder to identify this in practice, as he writes that it is complicated "to give an account of [acquiring] property and what is involved in being well off in terms of possessing it." The complications herein arise on account of there being "many disputes in connection with this investigation on account of those who invite us toward either sort of excess in our way of life—the ones toward penury, the others toward luxury."[62] Contestation over what constitutes necessary acquisition and what constitutes "excess" is inevitable, he shows, as we do not all share the same view on these matters. Observing use helps to identify whether an item in question is needed; but use is also contextual. These ambiguities of needs are ultimately why, Aristotle explains, some "invite us" to live in poverty, while others "invite us" to live in luxury. Though it is clear that Aristotle is uninterested in either invitation, he does not go so far as to delineate a boundary between necessity and excess on his own. Instead, he merely identifies the possibility of competing perspectives on this issue and leaves their resolution up to deliberation.

The problem of needs is only a definitional one if we think about distinctions as existing in nature. However, Aristotle clearly does not think that they do, and thus the problem is with modern readings of Aristotle's text that treat needs as defined categories. By contrast, Aristotle argues that our needs and desires are adjusted, and sometimes even produced by our deliberation. As he puts it, "when we have reached a judgment as a result of deliberation, we desire in accordance with our deliberation."[63] Aristotle makes a similar point about the ways citizens delineate necessity together. Elaborating on the concept of acquisition, he argues that:

> This [activity] is the one that is concerned with the arts without which a city cannot be inhabited (though of these arts only some must exist of necessity, while others are directed toward luxury or living finely).[64]

Though one tendency might be to set luxury and fine living against necessity, because Aristotle conjoins luxury and living finely with an "or" he also urges readers to wonder whether these two are necessarily synonymous. Perhaps, he implies, it is possible to live finely yet avoid luxury, or to live with luxury, but without the kind of security and happiness connoted by living 'finely'. His indication that all three of these aims—necessity, luxury, and living finely—are arts without which cities cannot exist suggests that delineating the very boundaries of necessity, luxury, and living finely are the critical activity in which citizens must participate.

What is useful about this ambiguity pertaining to needs and excess in Aristotle's writing is that it opens up space for political discussion about needs. It raises, for instance, the possibility that there are a variety of ways that needs can be disputed. You can say that your needs take priority over mine, and I can claim that my needs take priority over yours. But you can also say that I have misunderstood my needs—that at least some of what I think of as my needs are not really my needs. Aristotle's mention of the paradoxical necessity of luxury and/or living finely also attempts to preserve some ground for priorities beyond needs. We could also say in our disputes about our needs that needs ought not to take precedence over moral imperatives, opening up space for the discussion of concerns that extend beyond our needs, or perhaps even for values that we hold despite their incompatibility with what we take to be our needs.[65] Ultimately, Aristotle refuses to settle these debates. He is unwilling to defend a specific claim about basic needs (other than that they exist), or to articulate a picture of the good life on his own, simply because he does not think it is possible to imagine any life on one's own.

To ground this position, Aristotle immediately complicates any a priori assignment of needs one might reasonably offer. This complication appears later in the text, in a curious discussion about situations in which those with enormous purchasing power do not always have their needs met:

> Money seems to be something nonsensical and to exist altogether by convention, and in no way by nature, because when changed by its users it is worth nothing and is not useful with a view to any of the

necessary things; and it will often happen that one who is wealthy in money will go in want of necessary sustenance.[66]

Money, he tells us, is not intrinsically useful. Those who have it, one might assume, can still use it to acquire necessary things. But this is not always so. Lest one think that this passage simply indicates that the rich do not spend their money wisely, he continues:

> It would be absurd if wealth were something one could have in abundance and die of starvation—like the Midas of the fable, when everything set before him turned into gold on account of the greediness of his prayer.[67]

Obviously, the rich do manage to feed themselves, he explains. They are not characters in a fable, but real people with physical urges that compel them to acquire food, and the financial means to do so. However, his argument that rich people nevertheless "often" do not have the capacity to acquire "necessary sustenance" indicates that they might be starved of something else.[68] The household, he states, is "the community constituted by nature for the needs of daily life."[69] This he contrasts with the "complete community" where we engage in politics, implying that the needs met in the household do not constitute *all* of our needs, but only those of "daily life." To meet *all* of our needs, we must instead turn to citizenship—after all, it is not necessarily exclusively out of *economic* necessity that people join together.

Aristotle's remarks on these different ways of acquiring sustenance are a reminder that the historicity of human needs and their constant expansion is inextricably tied to living in political communities. His argument has much in common with Herbert Marcuse's point that human needs are nearly always preconditioned by society, and are thus a reflection of what is valued in a given society.[70] As Marcuse argues, this means that the vast majority of needs are historical, and that they are redefined in relation to changing requirements of social production.[71]

Because we share life with others, we frequently find ourselves in need of additional things like safety, security, and intergenerational sustainability—living in political communities can cause us to need specialist medical care, transportation to cover widening work commutes, and the ability to maintain multiple forms of diction and codes of speaking in order to communicate across different social contexts without being misconstrued. Vulnerability to police brutality means an increased need for everything from taillight repairs to psychological support.

Of course, these needs are rarely distributed evenly. That material interdependence renders needs both diverse and changeable certainly complicates any attempt to identify precisely what our needs are.[72] But we should not want to make a priori decisions about what our needs are because doing so would erase the historical and interpersonal nature of their construction.

Needs Against Private Freedom

Aristotle is not a theorist of use and exchange or of moral or ethical values so much as a theorist of needs. Yet political theorists who wish to rinse their hands of *all* types of acquisitive activity in order to elevate the important work of citizenship introduce a troubling interpretive binary. For this reason, Aristotle's descriptions of acquisitive activities are sometimes understood by political theorists as requiring that private needs be kept distinct from public freedom, and as segmenting the *polis* into public and private spheres.[73] As I will show now, this binary framework of needs as private and citizenship as public relies on a substantial misreading of Aristotle. To see what is at stake in moving beyond a binary reading of Aristotle as a theorist of private needs and public deliberation, one need only look at Hanna Pitkin's characterization of a similar oversight in Hannah Arendt's reading of Aristotle.

Pitkin develops a unique perspective on the relationship between material constraints and judgment, membership, and action across her work, and this perspective is critical to her engagement with Aristotelian thinking on needs. Pitkin shows that an Aristotelian perspective on needs haunts modern discourse about public and private spheres, and she does so by way of criticizing Hannah Arendt's interpretations of Aristotle. Pitkin challenges Arendt's argument that private needs be kept separate from public deliberation. "The private sphere," Pitkin explains, "was [according to Arendt] governed by necessity—not just the domination of the master over the family and slaves, but the necessities of life that would rule even the master if he did not have others to provide for him."[74] For both Arendt and Aristotle, Pitkin notes, the activities of acquisition were tied to the affairs of the *oikia* (household), to which the etymological origins of the concept of economics can be traced. For Arendt, Pitkin explains, the household, as a consequence of being consumed by material operations, can be taken to be the space of "private" life.

Noting that 'necessity' for Aristotle and Arendt implies both concrete needs and a general condition of inescapability, Pitkin suggests that Arendt's conceptualization of what is remarkable about the public sphere, by contrast, is its distance from the everyday requirements of resource acquisition and management. As she shows, Arendt's public sphere allows for "self-revelation and the quest for glory," uniqueness and personal expression, distinction, and self-disclosure, whereas the threat of private needs "imposes uniformities."[75] According to Pitkin's interpretation, Arendt thinks that public deliberation allows a sort of self-actualization that is denied in the process of meeting basic needs. Pitkin implicitly characterizes Arendt's argument as follows: economics, or that which serves the needs of the body, must be excluded from deliberation, as deliberation is concerned with that which serves the needs of the mind in our quest for recognition.[76]

Yet despite an alignment in their shared concerns about shared political life and communal self-determination, Pitkin departs sharply from Arendt in her imagination of the content of public discussions and takes Aristotle with her in an effort to blur the boundaries between the private and the public. She does so by identifying shadows of Aristotle's own anxiety about needs in Arendt's argument. Pitkin explains Arendt's reasoning as follows: "if justice were permitted into—let alone made central to—public, political life, she feared it would bring with it the dangerous economic and social concerns, the hungry and passionate poor who would destroy what was to be saved."[77] For these reasons, Pitkin conjectures, "to protect [the public], she felt constrained to sever it...from the economic and social conditions structuring citizens' lives, in which they have something at stake. The public must be valued for itself, not degraded into a mere means to some lesser end."[78] In order to preserve space for public life, Arendt sought to remove all the furnishings of private life from this sphere, so that deliberation might serve purposes beyond resource distribution. Pitkin's own modification to Arendt's argument is in determining the "real value" of the public sphere, which she locates in its potential for prioritizing discussions of material needs. For Pitkin, the unintended consequences of writing about public and private spheres as distinct is to reify their boundaries.[79]

Pitkin consequently argues that Arendt's effort to remove needs from political life to clear space for democratic self-actualization in fact underestimates the critical role of material interdependence in democratic discourse. As Pitkin shows, Arendt's argument about the importance of "the exclusion of everything merely necessary or useful" from political life lends itself to "the exclusion of the exploited by their exploiters, who can afford not to discuss economics, and to devote themselves to 'higher things', because they live off the work of others."[80] As Pitkin notes, Arendt ends up with an amalgamated theory of rational individualism and a social contract to accompany it that is far afield from her original intentions.[81] Though Arendt's writing is in many ways critical of liberalism, Pitkin shows that Arendt's exclusion of the poor from politics results from a liberal imagination of autonomy. Even more damning, Pitkin draws attention to Arendt's discussions of the "terror" of the poor multitudes caught up in the French Revolution and critically characterizes Arendt's position as excluding people living in poverty from politics. Pitkin argues that Arendt saw the poor bursting onto the political scene, driven by their needs and bodies, as detrimental to the cause of unique self-expression.[82]

It is my contention that claims to or about justice are not abstract musings about the best form of society, but arguments about what we need and consequently also about who we are, which is why I find Pitkin to be persuasive. Evaluating Arendt's interpretation of Aristotle, Pitkin shows that while theorists believe public deliberation to be about contestation, freedom, and action, Aristotle importantly describes deliberation as about

justice.[83] Deliberations over justice, Pitkin argues, must include deliberations over needs. As Pitkin writes, "although politics and justice are about
right and wrong, morality and virtue, they are also about economic privilege and social power."[84] She also argues that "wealth is not the point
or purpose of politics, but is certainly a continuing issue in political life,
and justice cannot help but take economic considerations into account."[85]
Pitkin's claim is that deliberation is about our highest values, ideals, or
aspirations, just as much as it is about economic inequalities. This claim
is critical to rooting citizenship in systems of material interdependence,
rather than making deliberation available only to the privileged.[86] Pitkin
therefore argues that needs must be included in deliberation in order for
deliberation to truly be about justice. However, my reading of Aristotle
also indicates that he views deliberation as importantly about *what* we need.

This inseparability of needs from politics that I draw from Pitkin's writing betrays Aristotle's distinction between useful items and the activities
of exchange as a hazardous position. The boundaries between these two
types of acquisitive activities are slippery—what one might consider a
necessary need, another might consider a luxury. Political thought that
draws from Aristotelian categories to distinguish between private accumulation and public deliberation therefore relies on particular biases about
what household consumption should involve. Fortunately, Aristotle's own
thought on this issue was more complicated, and a closer look at Aristotle's
discussions of necessity reveals that the private and public distinction is not
congruous with his vision of economics and politics.

Another possibility for reading Aristotle's discussions of household
management emerges here, and it is one that undoes any clean division
between economics and politics, and thus between acquisition and deliberation in this text. According to this alternative reading, household goods
are not really acquired for private need at all, but rather have use first and
foremost for the political community. As he puts it:

> One kind of acquisitive art, then, is by nature a part of expertise in
> household management, and must either be available or be supplied
> by the latter so as to be available—the art of acquiring those goods, a
> store of which is both necessary for life and useful for the community
> of a city or household. At any rate, it would seem to be these things
> that make up genuine wealth.[87]

This acquisitive art, he tells us, requires that certain items be supplied to
the household or else created therein. These items, he tells us, are "necessary" and "useful," and thus constitute genuine wealth. Yet he is very
specific about who they are necessary to—they are useful not merely, and
perhaps not even primarily, to the members of the private household, but
instead first and foremost for "life" and "for the community of a city."
Needs, in addition to being public to the extent that they are a topic for

deliberation, are also public because they are definitionally shared, and never truly private. This reading indicates that we may have a need for citizenship and its deliberative activities that supersedes even our need for sustenance, and denies the possibility of a clean division between private needs and public concern.

Finding Value in Needs Discourse

Aristotle embeds his discussions of human activities of use and exchange in several paradoxes of human needs. As he reminds us, other people cause our needs to multiply and expand, yet we need other people to meet our needs. We must therefore organize political life to meet our needs, even as we can never fully know what they are. This argument for the important role of needs in political discourse is at the heart of Aristotle's image of civic life in his *Politics*. In arguing that needs are up to citizens to define, Aristotle centers the practices of democratic citizenship, and particularly emphasizes sharing in power and responsibility, as critical to the definition of need. As he places needs in an ambiguous position between acquisitive activities and political freedom, he draws out a paradoxical quality to needs, and a consequent need for political contestation and deliberation to delineate their very boundaries.[88]

Today, we often think of needs as physical and material, succumbing to a faulty mind–body split borne of modern conceptualizations of physicality and materiality. In doing so, we can be reluctant to claim community, companionship, and politics as primary needs. This is why Aristotle's conceptualization of the arts of acquisition is taken as fracturing into needs and desires, where the sustenance we achieve at the household level provides what is necessary for participation in politics, but commerce produces excess. It is certainly true that Aristotle sees anything beyond sustenance, such as the goods acquired through foreign trade, as exceeding these needs and distracting from the ultimate community value in participation in deliberation about the organization of our shared affairs. But Aristotle's discussions of sustenance and necessity force a confrontation with these ambiguities. He also implies that the modern concept of 'use values'—which is today assumed to encapsulate his thinking on physical needs—can always be further specified in political decisions about the quantity and quality of specific goods that are vital for human thriving or that alternatively represent dangerous excess.[89] Meanwhile, deliberations about justice are, for Aristotle, a value of another type altogether, and one that is distinctly not material, suggesting that we might even have something democratically relevant to discuss beyond our needs, and even a psychological need for community and politics.

In the face of these complications, it is no surprise that political-economic analysis has historically focused on the logistics of exchange values in the national and recently global marketplace, assuming the content of use value to be subjective or else confined to the ambiguous realm of 'utility'. Determining what sorts of things are useful and to whom generates a variety of political problems and complicates any attempt to make sweeping claims about uses and needs. Though the splitting of value discourse into 'value' and 'values' seeks to resolve the ambiguities in the concept of need, Aristotle's writing reminds us that the irresolvable tensions of needs nevertheless haunt value discourse.

Despite these conceptual difficulties, needs are a critical focus for political-economic analysis, because the abstractions of modern value discourse can also serve to distract from issues of justice.[90] The categories of use and exchange value emerge from a false start in Aristotle, a theorist who was not writing about value, but about needs, and because these concepts are taken out of the context of Aristotle's political writing they have allowed modern thinkers of value to avoid thinking about value in a way that is more than superficially concerned about politics. These categories obscure the uniting thread in Aristotle's writing about acquisition and household management—which is neither use value nor exchange value, but the ultimate community value in democracy. Being human, for Aristotle, means engaging in dialogue about justice. Through such dialogue, we make judgments about justice in relation to our experiences of pleasure and pain. For Aristotle, like all topics falling under the umbrella of 'justice', choices about resource acquisition and distribution must also be made through deliberation.[91]

If reading Aristotle as a theorist of value decenters contestation over needs, then reading him as a theorist of needs highlights the role of political struggles in the negotiation of our conditions of material interdependence. As Aristotle shows in his discussions of necessity, needs are contentious because any effort to prioritize certain needs has consequences that are distributed unevenly. Contestation over needs is therefore a means of delineating the bounds of citizenship, and this is why Aristotle as a theorist of needs ultimately defers to Aristotle as a would-be citizen of Athens on the problem of their definition. Needs, he argues, must not only be met by the political community, but also defined by it. Theorizing needs in this way, Aristotle casts needs not as problems of negotiating individual preferences, but as a problem of public priorities that are inevitably going to be empowering for some and disempowering for others.

At the same time, Aristotle's thinking about needs allows us to rekindle the political life of value and values. If we assume that any discussion of needs is political, and by 'political' we mean, following Aristotle, that which is not only contentious but also actively involved in a process of constructing citizenship boundaries, then we can think about value as doing similar productive work. The process of producing political exclusions happens even (and especially) when that work is less apparent.

We follow Aristotle's thinking in our modern substitution of needs with the concept of value, which we imagine as infinitely plural. Yet we disregard the critical point that needs, and consequently also values, cannot be private. The result is a conception of needs that can succumb to placation. Marie Antoinette's apocryphal quote, "let them eat cake," is the logical extension of the belief that needs are a matter of private satisfaction rather than public determination. By extension, value discourse also succumbs to a privatizing politics whenever it takes the plurality of values seriously but overlooks the political nature of their construction.

Notes

1 William Frankena, "Value," in P. Edwards, ed., *The Encyclopedia of Philosophy* (New York NY: Macmillan, 1967), and W. J. T. Mitchell, "Value," in Tony Bennett, Lawrence Grossberg, and Meaghan Morris, eds, *New Keywords: A Revised Vocabulary of Culture and Society*, (Malden MA: Blackwell Publishing, 2005).

2 Ibid.

3 Here I follow the *Oxford English Dictionary*'s etymological tracing of the word 'value'. I am also drawing from translations of Aristotle's writing in which the word 'value' seems to be inserted by editors for clarity, where it does not exist in the Greek version.

4 Michel Foucault, "Nietzsche, Genealogy, History," in Donald F. Bouchard, ed., Donald F. Bouchard and Sherry Simon, trans., *Language, Counter-Memory, Practice: Selected Essays and Interviews* (Ithaca NY: Cornell University Press, 1977), 140. I draw my inspiration from Angélica Bernal's destabilization of foundings in favor of embracing political contestation. See Angélica Maria Bernal, *Beyond Origins: Rethinking Founding in a Time of Constitutional Democracy* (Oxford University Press, 2017).

5 Taking insights from Foucault, I also draw from hermeneutic efforts to understand value discourse from within a series of traditions. In particular, I pose Friedrich Nietzsche's question "What really was that which just struck?" when value discourse emerged on the world stage and answer this question by tracing the circumstances and conditions in which value discourse emerged. Friedrich Nietzsche, *On the Genealogy of Morals* and *Ecce Homo* (New York NY: Vintage, 1967). Such an effort is necessarily hermeneutic, as its intended pursuit is to take "the way we experience one another, the way we experience historical traditions" as subjects of study rather than founding assumptions. Hans-Georg Gadamer, *Truth and Method* (New York NY, and London: Continuum, 1989), xx and xxiii. However, I ignore Foucault's proposal to break from linearity in my narrative, and I draw upon genealogical tracings of concepts that do follow a historical chronology, so that we can pinpoint precisely what changed as needs discourse came to be eclipsed by value discourse. See Foucault, "Nietzsche, Genealogy, History," 137.

6 This reading of Aristotle therefore helps draw out the crucial material politics of value that Roman and modern value discourse displaced. Moreover, reading Aristotle as a theorist of value rather than of needs distracts from some of the ways in which political-economic thought has been predicated on exclusions from citizenship. Attention to Aristotle's formulation of needs, by contrast, helps illuminate what is distinctive about the later emergence of value discourse.

7 Examining the dynamic relationship between Aristotle's theory of needs and his theory of participatory citizenship can also foreground the contingency of current patterns of material interdependence.

8 On the definition of *pleonexia* and its sense as an ailment, I draw from Ryan Balot, *Greed and Injustice in Classical Athens* (Princeton University Press, 2001), and Harry Berger, *The Perils of Uglytown: Studies in Structural Misanthropology from Plato to Rembrandt* (New York NY: Fordham University Press, 2015).

9 I show that reading Aristotle as a theorist of needs rather than of value allows us to see how value discourse, as it is deployed in economic and moral thinking, works as a depoliticizing abstraction, and as a means of avoidance of the messy work of thinking politically about needs.

10 On the argument that Aristotle's thinking centers contestation, see Susan Bickford's reading, which conceives of Aristotelian deliberation as centered on a politics of attention rather than friendship. Susan Bickford, "Beyond Friendship: Aristotle on Conflict, Deliberation, and Attention," *The Journal of Politics* 58 no. 2 (1986). See also Adriel M. Trott, "Rancière and Aristotle: Parapolitics, Party Politics, and the Institution of Perpetual Politics," *The Journal of Speculative Philosophy* 26, no. 4 (2012).

11 For commentary on the distinction between needs and values, see Karl Marx, "Economic and Philosophic Manuscripts of 1844," in Robert C. Tucker, ed., *The Marx-Engels Reader 2nd Edition* (New York NY: W.W. Norton & Company, 1978). Marx saw the elusiveness of value as a central feature of all societies. See also Agnes Heller, *The Theory of Need in Marx* (London: Allison & Bushby, 1974), and George Henderson, *Value in Marx: The Persistence of Value in a More-Than-Capitalist World* (Minneapolis MN: University of Minnesota Press, 2013), as well as Jean-Luc Nancy's comment that for Marx, "value is an infinite." Jean-Luc Nancy, *The Truth of Democracy* (New York NY: Fordham University Press, 2010.

12 As Barry Gordon writes: "The nature of Aristotle's contribution to value theory is a topic that has given rise to considerable controversy. Commentators, both old and new, are quite divided on the question of the philosopher's true position on the matter. Passages from his works have been cited in support of widely conflicting approaches to value determination, and some writers have gone so far as to suggest that on this issue he has nothing to offer by way of meaningful analysis." Barry Gordon, *Economic Analysis Before Adam Smith: Hesiod to Lessius* (London: The MacMillan Press, 1975), 53.

13 On metalist theories of value in Aristotle, see Barry Gordon, "Aristotle, Schumpeter, and the Metalist Tradition," *The Quarterly Journal of Economics* 75, no. 4 (1961). M. I. Finley follows Schumpeter's interpretation of the role of use and exchange value in Aristotle's writing. See M. I. Finley, "Aristotle and Economic Analysis," *Past & Present* 47 (1970).

14 Stephen Worland, "Aristotle and the Neoclassical Tradition: The Shifting Ground of Complementarity," *History of Political Economy* 16, no. 1 (1984).

15 Scott Meikle, "Aristotle and the Political Economy of the Polis," *The Journal of Hellenic Studies* 99 (1979).

16 Finley, "Aristotle and Economic Analysis," 5 and 11.

17 Frankena, "Value," and Mitchell, "Value."

18 Mitchell, "Value," 365.

19 This project is further complicated by the fact that the concepts of needs, necessity, and the necessary are contradictory, because they are deployed as a means of considering both what is inevitable and what is required. Hanna Fenichel Pitkin, *The Attack of the Blob: Hannah Arendt's Concept of the Social* (University of Chicago Press, 1998), 190.

20 See, for instance, William Mathie, "Political and Distributive Justice in the Political Science of Aristotle," *The Review of Politics* 49, no. 1 (1987) for a discussion of the tension between needs and freedom, and Jill Frank,

"Democracy and Distinction: Aristotle on Just Desert," *Political Theory* 26, no. 6 (1998) on how questions about needs and distribution are internal to the practice of citizenship.

21 See Hannah Arendt, *The Human Condition* (University of Chicago Press, 1958); Richard Mulgan, "Aristotle and the Value of Political Participation," *Political Theory* 18, no. 2 (1990); and Mary P. Nichols, *Citizens and Statesmen: A Study of Aristotle's Politics* (Lanham MD: Rowman and Littlefield Publishers, 1992).

22 See, for instance, Gordon, "Economic Analysis Before Adam Smith," and Odd Langholm, *Price and Value in the Aristotelian Tradition: A Study in Scholastic Economic Sources* (Oslo, Norway: The Norwegian Research Council for Science and the Humanities, 1979). Indeed, Aristotle's legacy is often claimed by readers of quite different political bents, since his influence on thinkers as diverse as Adam Smith and Karl Marx is considerable. The parallels are certainly uncanny, and it is clear that Aristotle had tremendous influence on these later perspectives—as can be seen, for instance, in how Adam Smith's condemnation of mercantilism seems to resemble Aristotle's own fears about the dangers of trade beyond the *polis*. Gordon, "Economic Analysis Before Adam Smith," 21.

23 Aristotle, *Politics*, trans. Carnes Lord (University of Chicago Press, 2013), 1256b.31–34.

24 Ibid., 1256b.41–1257a.1. For a discussion of how Aristotle divides economic activity between needs and exchanges that exceed those needs, see Patricia Springborg, "Aristotle and the Problem of Needs," *History of Political Thought* 5, no. 3 (1984). For descriptions of later understandings of these categories as denoting a difference between use and exchange value, see Gordon, "Economic Analysis Before Adam Smith," and Langholm, "Price and Value." For a discussion of the ways that luxury erodes our sense of public virtue, see John Sekora, *Luxury: The Concept in Western Thought, Eden to Smollett* (Baltimore MD: The Johns Hopkins University Press, 1977).

25 Louis Baeck, *The Mediterranean Tradition in Economic Thought* (London: Routledge, 1994), 78, 82.

26 Aristotle, *Politics*, 1256a.11–14 and 1257b.31–35, emphasis added.

27 Ibid., 1256a.21.

28 Ibid., 1258a.7–14.

29 Ibid., 1257b.41–42.

30 Ibid., 1256a.8. Aristotle uses the Greek word *trophé*, which Carnes Lord translates as "sustenance," but is generally translated more directly as "nourishment" or "food." As Thornton Lockwood shows, it is quite possible that he had public messes in mind. Thornton Lockwood, "*Politics II*: Political Critique, Political Theorizing, Political Innovation," in Thornton Lockwood and Thanassis Samaras, eds., *Aristotle's Politics: A Critical Guide* (Cambridge University Press, 2015).

31 Aristotle, *Politics*, 1256b.2–8. I am drawing my translation of *chrēmatistikē* from Carnes Lord's translation, in which the term derives, notably, from *chrēmata*, which connotes (material) goods.

32 Ibid. I am using Polanyi's translation of *anagkaion*. This is not, however, to say that Aristotle conceptualizes these two activities as distinct spheres. See Arlene Saxonhouse, "Family, Polity & Unity: Aristotle on Socrates' Community of Wives," *Polity* 15, no. 2 (1982).

33 See, for instance, Daniela Cammack, "Aristotle on the Virtue of the Multitude," *Political Theory* 41, no. 2 (2013).

34 On liberalism, see Peter Schuck, "Liberal Citizenship," in Engin Isin and Bryan Turner, eds., *Handbook of Citizenship Studies* (Thousand Oaks CA: Sage

Publications, 2003). For a critique of liberalism's claim to inclusion, see Judith Shklar, *American Citizenship: The Quest for Inclusion* (Cambridge MA: Harvard University Press, 1998). For republican citizenship, see Richard Dagger, "Republican Citizenship," in Engin Isin and Bryan Turner, eds., *Handbook of Citizenship Studies* (Thousand Oaks CA: Sage Publications, 2003).

35 On the point that only a certain amount of household acquisition is necessary for a good life, see Lockwood, *"Politics II:* Political Critique."

36 Stephen Salkever, "Whose Prayer? The Best Regime of Book 7 and the Lessons of Aristotle's *Politics," Political Theory* 35, no. 1 (2007).

37 Thomas Lindsay, "Was Aristotle Racist, Sexist, and Anti-Democratic? A Review Essay," *The Review of Politics* 56, no. 1 (1994), and Eckart Schütrumpf, "Little to Do with Justice: Aristotle on Distributing Political Power," in Thornton Lockwood and Thanassis Samaras, eds., *Aristotle's Politics: A Critical Guide* (Cambridge University Press, 2015).

38 Ellen Meiksins Wood, *Class Ideology and Ancient Political Theory: Socrates, Plato, and Aristotle in Social Context* (New York NY: Oxford University Press, 1978), 227 and 236.

39 Marguerite Deslauriers, "Political Rule Over Women in *Politics* I," in Thornton Lockwood and Thanassis Samaras, eds., *Aristotle's Politics: A Critical Guide* (Cambridge University Press, 2015), and Thanassis Samaras, "Aristotle and the Question of Citizenship," in Thornton Lockwood and Thanassis Samaras, eds., *Aristotle's Politics: A Critical Guide* (Cambridge University Press, 2015), 130–132.

40 Wayne Ambler, "Aristotle on Nature and Politics: The Case of Slavery," *Political Theory* 15, no. 3 (1987), and Jill Frank, "Citizens, Slaves, and Foreigners: Aristotle on Human Nature," *American Political Science Review* 98, no. 1 (2004).

41 Lindsay, "Was Aristotle Racist."

42 As Frank shows in Frank, "Citizens, Slaves, and Foreigners," the question of who in Aristotle's *Politics* is a slave is fastened to the question of which sorts of activities constitute good citizenship and which sorts do not.

43 See Hannah Arendt, "What is Freedom," in *Between Past and Future* (New York NY: Penguin Classics, 2006), 146–149.

44 Karl Polanyi, "Aristotle Discovers the Economy," in *Trade and Market in the Early Empires: Economies in History and Theory* (New York NY: The Free Press, 1957).

45 Jill Frank, *A Democracy of Distinction: Aristotle and the Work of Politics* (University of Chicago Press, 2005), 39.

46 Patricia Springborg similarly argues that there is an ambivalence in the concept of needs concerning whether needs should be understood as a metaphysical or empirical category. As Springborg explains, both efforts that treat needs as connected to "an essential human nature" and ones that treat them as requiring "specification based on aggregate data analysis, etc." or even as "expressed demands" miss the way that, for Aristotle, needs are first and foremost that "which holds everything [in the city] together." Springborg elaborates that: "Human needs, wants and desires constitute a system in Aristotle, as in Hegel, not because they are themselves systematic, but because they define a realm: that of everyday life, or 'civil society', in which individuals pursue characteristic goals and interests. Needs thus constitute the raw material of justice, by comprising spontaneous and ungoverned aspirations and desires, bound to conflict in a community of scarce resources. At the same time needs describe the motivation and direction of human pursuits as they have been formed within the limits of a specific social system with peculiar historically

developed structures for the production and distribution of goods and services. The heterogeneity and incompatibility of individual needs was what in the eyes of both Aristotle and Hegel (and the contractarians, of course) necessitated the state and its institutions of conciliation, arbitration, and where these fail, government." In fact, she explains, this "conception of civil society as a system of needs" is also present in Plato's writing. She furthermore points out that different ways of translating his discussions of needs, most often in the language of "demands," support modern political projects, but are anachronistic with respect to Aristotle's own ideas about "social exchange" and necessity. Springborg, "Aristotle and the Problem," 393; 393 and 396; 400; and 397–398, respectively.

47 Even a need so prosaic as one for sustenance implicates a particular vision of politics. Aristotle was well aware that Socrates had articulated a need to philosophize, without which he would cease to exist as Socrates—thus rendering martyrdom more necessary than food. Our contemporary analogue might be the hunger strike as a political protest. See Raymond Geuss, *Reality and Its Dreams* (Cambridge MA: Harvard University Press, 2016), 129–130.

48 This is the method of reading Aristotle's categorizations against his focus on activity used in Mary Dietz, "Between Polis and Empire: Aristotle's Politics," *American Political Science Review* 106, no. 2 (2012). For a general account of the centricity of action to Aristotle's thinking, see Salkever, "Finding the Mean."

49 Aristotle, *Politics*, 1252a.26.

50 As Patricia Springborg puts it, "there is, indeed, an analogue for Marx's between 'the realm of necessity' (defined by basic needs) and freedom (freedom from want) to be found in the distinction in Aristotle between a subsistence economy and the requirements of the good life." Springborg, "Aristotle and the Problem," 401.

51 It is important to note here that Aristotle uses the word *trofís*, derived from the word *trophê*. The former is translated as "sustenance," "food," or sometimes "provisions," but this interpretation is based on the verb form, to sustain, maintain, nourish, rear, bring up, or cause to grow or increase. The noun form of sustenance or food therefore has a metaphysical connotation as that which is necessary for an action (growth, nourishment, and upbringing) to happen, rather than any categorical imperative.

52 Aristotle, *Politics*, 1256a 19–31.

53 Here we also arrive at the problem of specificity, wherein needs are abstract, but the means to meeting the needs are particular. See Christopher J. Berry, *The Idea of Luxury: A Conceptual and Historical Investigation* (Cambridge University Press, 1994). Specificity troubles any claim about needs, once we realize that the social and environmental costs of cultivating a caviar supply for the population far exceed the cost of wheat production, and entail different choices about what sorts of trade-offs we are willing to make to achieve a certain threshold of human survival. Choosing the wheat and opting for an economy of food by caloric intake over luxury does not resolve this problem. In an economy based on a minimum threshold of caloric intake from mass wheat production, those with celiac disease would starve, whereas those with slow metabolisms would perhaps be awash in surplus. Berry, *The Idea of Luxury*, and Agnes Heller, *The Theory of Need in Marx* (London: Allison & Bushby, 1974).

54 Aristotle, *Politics*, 1256a.19–31.

55 Ibid., 1256a.31–40.

56 Aristotle's inclusion of brigandage, and his neutrality about different ways of life, is worth pausing on. Presumably, given that all of these figures coexist

in the world, the brigand robs and plunders the resources of the nomads, hunters, fishers, and farmers. So, while Aristotle describes the nomad as able to tame animals "without labor and amid leisure," one can easily assume that the nomad is forced into more work once he encounters the brigand, since he is now preparing dinner for two. To defend against brigandage, the nomads, hunters, fishers, and farmers would need to spend time and resources on other things, such as building walls, weapons, or hiding places, to avoid being victimized.

57 Aristotle, *Politics*, 1253a.20. See also 1252a.1–8.

58 This reading of Aristotle is supported by Adriel Trott's argument for the primacy of community in Aristotle's writing (as well as of *logos* and deliberation as the means to communal self-actualization). Trott argues that Aristotle's casting of community as natural ultimately lends itself to a view of politics as action-oriented, and to a rejection of slavery and the subjugation of women. Adriel Trott, *Aristotle on the Nature of Community* (New York NY: Cambridge University Press, 2014). This reading is also consistent with Jill Scott's argument that for Aristotle, "property and polity constitute one another." Frank, "A Democracy of Distinction," 75.

59 Hanna Pitkin, "Obligation and Consent," *The American Political Science Review* 59, no. 4 (1965).

60 Aristotle, *Politics*, 1253a.20–23.

61 This perspective, at the very least, seems to comport with his comment about the man without a *polis*, as he writes that he "who is in need of nothing through being self-sufficient is no part of a city, and so is either a beast or a god." Ibid., 1253a.27–29.

62 Ibid., 1326b.35–39.

63 Aristotle, *The Nicomachean Ethics*, trans. David Ross (Oxford University Press, 2009), 1113a.

64 Ibid., 1291a.2–4.

65 Susan Bickford identifies a similar tendency in Aristotle's writing about deliberation in *The Nicomachean Ethics*, when she writes that we do not deliberate about matters of fact, such as whether a loaf of bread has been properly baked. Instead, we only deliberate about uncertain things. As she shows, this also means that we often deliberate about whether matters at hand are indeed factual matters, since different tastes and judgments could vary wildly in their estimations of the preparation of this bread. Bickford, "Beyond Friendship," 400.

66 Aristotle, *Politics*, 1257b.10–14.

67 Ibid.

68 In *The Nicomachean Ethics*, Aristotle even argues that we also need friendship, writing that it is "most necessary with a view to living." Aristotle, *The Nicomachean Ethics*, 1115a.

69 Aristotle, *Politics*, 1252b.12–13.

70 Herbert Marcuse, *One-Dimensional Man: Studies in the Ideology of Advanced Industrial Society* (Boston MA: Beacon Press, 1964), 4.

71 Ibid., 241 and 245.

72 To Aristotle's problem of necessity Pitkin therefore adds a contemporary analogue, which is the problem of disassociation—of why we feel like our democratic choices are externalized, such that political problems appear outside of our control, rather than as a product of our collective activity. This dilemma, as Pitkin elegantly summarizes it, is that of "the gap between our enormous, still-increasing powers and our apparent helplessness to avert the various disasters—national, regional, and global—looming on our horizon." She goes on to juxtapose the extent of technological progress, medical innovation,

and social and political advance against the apparently irresolvable threats of nuclear war, climate change, global health and financial crises, and racial and interethnic violence, only to conclude that despite all the supposed progress we have made as a species, "we are ruining our world and seem unable to stop." Pitkin, *The Attack of the Blob*, 190.

73 Judith Swanson, *The Public and the Private in Aristotle's Political Philosophy* (Ithaca NY: Cornell University Press, 1992).

74 Hanna Fenichel Pitkin, "Justice: On Relating Private and Public," *Political Theory* 9, no. 3 (1981), 332.

75 Ibid., 336 and 333.

76 Arendt invites the latter interpretation in her comment that "public life, by contrast, is the quest for secular immortality, the hope of being remembered after one's death so that one's name and fame live on." Ibid., 337.

77 Ibid., 340.

78 Ibid.

79 Ibid.

80 Ibid.

81 Ibid., 337.

82 Ibid., 333–335.

83 Ibid., 338–339.

84 Ibid.

85 Ibid.

86 Applying this logic today, one might even discover needs to be present in much of what we deliberate, even if contemporary claims about our needs are often couched in the presumed neutrality of rights discourse. Current debates about gun control, for instance, can in many ways be boiled down to the competing claims of "we need liberty (understood as our guns) in order to live" and "we need our lives in order to have liberty!" We thus naturalize particular needs in our claims about them, even as we contest, alter, and expand these needs.

87 Aristotle, *Politics*, 1256b.27–31.

88 While this paradox is also present in value discourse, modern political–economic discourses of value typically abandon or ignore this complication.

89 This problem is only complicated by the possibility that the kinds of self-expression Arendt is so excited about meet some sort of psychological need. We then have needs (or desires?) that are physical, material, and embodied, and those that are not.

90 Thus, even as political economists make a habit of invoking common carbohydrates in political–economic discourses—Adam Smith repeatedly mentions corn, whereas Joseph Schumpeter focuses on bread—human needs are ultimately consumed by the price matrix. See Mike Hill and Warren Montag, *The Other Adam Smith* (Stanford University Press, 2015) for discussions of the role of corn in Smith's theory, and see Joseph Schumpeter, "On the Concept of Social Value," *The Quarterly Journal of Economics* 23, no. 2 (1909) for examples of this carb-fixation.

91 Discussions about justice require deliberation, which is based in "judgment about the just and the unjust." Aristotle, *The Nicomachean Ethics*, 1130b.

3 The Just Price or "Just the Price?"

Conceptual History, Community Valuation, and Liberal Sovereignty

This chapter undertakes a conceptual-historical investigation of modern value discourse—of claims to, of, and about value, the history of commercial activities from which they draw, and the imaginations of citizenship they underpin. It analyzes the historical baggage present in contemporary uses of the term 'value' by looking especially to the ways in which the word reveals unresolved discrepancies between liberal individualism ("*my* values") and assertions of shared priority ("*the* value"). We have, I show, inherited this tension in our ambiguous renderings of the concept of "fair market value." The central argument of this chapter is twofold. First, the image of individuals as sovereign, in which economic liberalism is invested, has origins in a despotic form of power. Second, erasure of value's connection to political authority allows the term to be deployed in arguments about economics that implicitly make judgments about particular individuals or groups of people, and in so doing delineate boundaries around political communities while being outwardly framed as detached from such matters.

Drawing from conceptual-historical and *Begriffsgeschichte* studies, I look at the origins of just price discourses in the Roman legal doctrine of *laesio enormis*. I show that these discourses about prices played a key role in the transformation of early linguistic senses of value into the moral and economic positions conjured by the term today. I then look at an impasse in interpretive studies of medieval just price discourses, which sought to provide conceptual grounding for alignments between prices and value. Contemporary readers concerned about problems of fairness in exchange, I argue, tend to position thinkers like Thomas Aquinas as quasi-Marxian and those who interpreted his work with more lenience than him for profit-seeking, such as Leonardus Lessius, as akin to liberal economists. I argue that these anachronistic readings of the original texts articulating the concept of a just price flatten the tensions within these writings—tensions that were present because particular patterns of community valuation were reflected in how people conceived of value. In particular, a critical context of just price discourse was royal control over currency. I discuss how this unacknowledged dimension of just price discourse invests contemporary deployments of the concept of value with a dubious type of authority.

DOI: 10.4324/9781003304302-3

Just price discourse, I show, was grounded in a set of concerns about exchange and theorists of just pricing hoped to find the appropriate and accurate value of market goods. This discourse emerged from a Roman legal doctrine that defined the extent of obligation to others in monetary transactions. However, the extent of that obligation was up to the monarch, and this dimension of just price discourses implicated in the concept of value a particular vision of political authority.

My argument overall is that hidden within modern economic discourses is a means of assessing value that is both personal and biopolitical. The fall of absolutism, I demonstrate, naturally eroded the connection between monarchs and currency, but the assumption that goods are valued according to the worth of the people who transact them rather than their intrinsic qualities or usefulness continued to pervade modern value discourse. In fact, the primary use of the word 'value' through the seventeenth century was to assess the worth of persons rather than goods. To draw out this point, I trace the term 'value' to its use in early modern Britain, as a means of measuring the worth of bodies and declaring one's trustworthiness in court. I argue that doing so uncovers a logic of valuation that remains connected to delineations of status and human worth.

Medieval Prices and the Transformation of Value

The concept of the just price is rooted in the third-century Roman laws of sale, in the specific rules of *laesio enormis*.[1] *Laesio enormis* ('enormous loss') provisions were intended to offset "excessive damage" in market exchange.[2] These provisions gave sellers a route for redressing abuses of bargaining positions in sales and allowed sellers to reclaim sold land if adequate payment was not provided. *Laesio enormis* rules "helped anchor the notion of excessive injury" by setting "a numerical value as a point of reference which established a limit in the aberration to be tolerated."[3] They specifically guaranteed that in sales of land, if the amount paid was less than half the true price, sales could be renegotiated, or else voided.[4] Designed primarily to protect sellers, *laesio enormis* rules, when applied, gave buyers the option of either making up the difference between the actual and initially paid price, or else returning purchased land.[5]

The political significance of these rules is best understood against the backdrop of earlier Roman economic regulations. Classical Roman legal practices divided public from private law and placed far fewer constraints on economic transactions than were placed in later medieval European law.[6] The commonsense assumption in Roman law was that any price agreed to would be the final price—although this came with a thin assumption that prices would always be determined in good faith.[7] A vendor's "ignorance of the true market value of the thing sold" was not considered a case for a reconsideration of the sale, or any modifications therein.[8] G. C. Maniatis reads this classical orientation toward prices as a precursor to *laissez-faire* ideology, writing: "this attitude [toward sales] reflected a free enterprise economic framework, and the liberal spirit, individualist nature, and rigorous enforcement of the Roman law of contracts."[9] *Laesio enormis* provisions, at least initially, did not significantly alter these customs, as they offered a means of challenging only the worst abuses of price-setting norms. Accordingly, many formulations of just price discourses that draw from these earlier forms of *laesio enormis* laws were ultimately grounded in a strictly legalistic understanding of justice—*justum pretium*, the concept of the just price, literally meant "the price by law."[10]

The provisions of *laesio enormis* were first added to Roman law during the crisis of the third century.[11] They were developed at least in part as a response to declines in production, trade, and taxes and spiking inflation, all of which led to major losses for small farmers through "sales of small farmsteads to *potentiores* at ruinous prices."[12] These legal protections were initially quite small, as large landholders still held substantial power.[13] In fact, the doctrine of *laesio enormis* was not fully developed and expanded for several centuries until, under Justinian, legal protections were designed to protect small landholders who sold to powerful neighbors at depressed prices.[14] It is this medieval transformation of *laesio enormis* into the concept of the *justium pretium* that is most useful for understanding value discourse.

Given that the most expansive development of *laesio enormis* laws coincided with the entrenchment and codification of Christianity, it should come as no surprise that theological debates were also infused into the development of these laws during the medieval period.[15] Lawyers involved in arbitrating sales based on Roman and canon law were concerned with the constitution of a "legally enforceable system of sale" and with arbitrating between contracts in accordance with whatever constituted the normal competitive price. Meanwhile, theologians had the distinct goal of constructing "an all-embracing system of human ethics in which the virtue of justice formed the foundation of the good life on earth."[16] These approaches converged, however, in the conceptualization of the just price, which added to legislation about sales an underlying moralism concerning the nature of obligations to others. For theologians, the doctrine of the *justium pretium* was the necessary "result of the penetration of justice into the world of commerce."[17] The implicit assumption was that one must always pay when a good is delivered, and that to renege on such an arrangement was to fail to deliver the good and to deny one's obligation to another person, according to divine law.

In the Byzantine context, *laesio enormis* consequently became an economic tool to ensure that commercial promises were kept, as well as a set of moral guidelines to remedy promises made in bad faith. In particular, to underpay by more than half what the good is worth, from within this heuristic, was also to fail to deliver on one's debt to others. Agreements about goods entailed a contract, enforceable once the first good or payment in a transaction was initially delivered, which put in place a "natural debt."[18]

Such views were pervasive; as John Baldwin notes, "mutual consent to a price was the sign and seal that a sale had been performed."[19] Mutuality was understood as what distinguished contracts from donations, and *laesio enormis* assumed that once a good was delivered the promise made in the sale of that good kicked in, or else the sale was voidable.[20]

It is notable here that this same logic of binding sales was later extended to include the transference of people as property. As I will show later in this chapter, people were also assumed to have a value that could be calculated according to the ways these legal agreements marked adherence to a standard price. Thus, what was created as a specific legal protection for selling land in certain contexts was later taken up in the morally and legally condoned sale not only of a number of moveable goods, but also in the sale of people themselves. These norms about sales are visible in everything from the manumission of slaves to the later practices of settling of marriage contracts and dowries.[21] Similar norms can be identified in modern political-economic rationality. Agreements about the price to be paid in the return of fugitive slaves to their owners, for instance, counted as binding legal agreements.[22] But to see how people were implicated in pricing discourse, one must look more closely at the institutionalization of *laesio enormis* doctrine during the medieval period.

From Laesio Enormis to the Just Price

Thomas Aquinas is cited as one of the early theorists of the 'just price', a concept that arose both from a longstanding tradition of theological debate about morality in commercial exchange and from a specific effort to quell growing concerns about usury. To the extent that buying land without paying the full price up front effectively amounted to receiving a loan from the seller, *laesio enormis* laws were transferrable to a variety of situations in which loans were exploited. As Maniatis explains, "equivalence in exchange implicitly *underpins* the concept of just price, provides the link between just price and excessive injury, and constitutes the bedrock for the relief the law gives when an exchange is heavily one-sided."[23] Scholastic reflections on pricing were also thought to have been sparked by the noticeable rise in urban production and trade; medieval friars were attentive to the spread of commercial life, evidenced by in a prevalence of market metaphors in religious dicta. Moreover, friars' observations of commercial life informed their transformation of the specific laws of *laesio enormis* into the general principle of the just price.[24]

Importantly, Roman and medieval price-setting norms relied primarily on the notion of *quantum res communiter valet* (literally: how much the thing in question is valued by the community), which reflected the "common valuation," or alternatively the "community value."[25] Whereas the more specific requirements of *laesio enormis* guaranteed that a certain community value could be tabulated and the appropriate restitution amount honored whenever prices strayed from this value, *quantum res communiter valet* conjures an image of a general pricing system.[26] But recall that value's root in the Latin *valor* was used to discuss power or strength. The *'valet'* in *quantum res communiter valet* would not have been understood as a way of talking about a good's worth, but about its power or strength. Consequently, *quantum res communiter valet* meant, essentially, "whatever power the community gives a commodity."

Still, the source of information about power or strength in price-setting is ambiguous because the *communiter* in *quantum res communiter valet* is also ambiguous. 'Common' is derived from the Latin *communis, communiter*. This root means, respectively, 'joint', and also 'ordinary' or 'usual'.[27] This language can therefore be used to talk about something that is co-created or else held together by a community, but also to talk about something as being merely typical. If one takes *communiter valet* to mean the common power or strength of a particular good, the just price is simply the average or conventional price. If one takes it to mean "the joint power of a good," or perhaps even "the shared power of a good," then the "community evaluation is put forward as the measure of a commodity's worth."[28] The second image implies that a sort of consensus around a particular price must be reached, whereas the former image of the "common" price could be set by variables outside of community control. In practice, both of these images of *communiter* were folded into theories of the just price, and just prices were consequently conceived of as encompassing both jointly determined and usual prices. The general concept of the just price, in other words, perplexingly included both the "moral limits that should be respected by merchants," and also the variety of other considerations that go into the variability of pricing, such as scarcity, need, use, labor, risks, demand, availability and type of money, and the nature of the sale.[29]

For all of these reasons, the definition of a just price was and is contentious—among medieval theologians as well as modern readers. Some historians of just price discourses implicitly follow the "community power" narrative and cast the just price as an early formulation of quasi-Marxian humanism. Others implicitly follow the "common power" narrative and cast just price discourse as the precursor to economic liberalism, which assumes the market price to be the fairest and most equitable means of distributing material resources.

Most interpretations of just price discourse have settled on the 'market price as just price' interpretation. Raymond de Roover, for instance, explains why just price discourses have been read both ways; however, he ultimately finds the Marxian readings to be less persuasive. De Roover notes that "according to widespread belief" the just price corresponded to a quasi-minimum wage, understood as "a reasonable charge which would enable the producer to live and to support his family."[30] De Roover believes that this position is based on a co-option of just price discourses by contemporary readers hoping to read communitarian principles into just price discourse. As he argues:

> The generally accepted definition of the just price is wrong and rests on misinterpretation of the scholastic position on the matter. According to the majority of the doctors, the just price did not correspond to cost of production...but was simply the current market price, with this important reservation: in cases of collusion or emergency, the public authorities retained the right to interfere and to impose a fair price.[31]

This latter point about public authorities (*communiter valet*) notwithstanding, he argues, the works of thinkers like Thomas Aquinas are more accurately filled with complacent perspectives on existing prices. As he elaborates, this fact alone "destroys with a single blow the thesis of those who try to make Aquinas into a Marxist, and proves beyond doubt that he considered the market price as just."[32] De Roover's account of just price discourse is also congruent with Michel Foucault's interpretation of just price discourse. Arguing that the market has long been seen as the site of veridiction, Foucault explains that throughout the medieval period the market was considered "a site of justice in the sense that the sale price fixed in the market was seen, both by theorists and in practice, as a just price."[33] This vision, he argues, later morphed into modern forms of this same rationale, which reverberate in the language of "good," "normal," and "natural" prices.[34]

Efforts like these, which are sympathetic to the broader goal of mounting evidence against free market dogmatism, and which aim to approach the study of just price discourse with a critical realism, ultimately dispel the notion that there was anything particularly "just" in the just price. They demonstrate that medieval political economists and early Christian political theorists conceptualized the just price not as an abstract ideal of fairness, but rather as a disinterested description of how prices tended to align. Yet this is even as de Roover himself admits that in the various texts theorizing the just price (namely those of Aquinas and his interlocuters) "the passages relating to price are so scattered and seemingly so conflicting that they have given rise to varying interpretations."[35] Such a reading of these texts also downplays the important qualification that public authorities could step in to alter prices in "emergency" circumstances. That the concept of the just price is nevertheless debated today, I argue, is actually a reflection of earlier ambiguities in its theorization. Rather than attempting to provide a "correct" account of what medieval friars truly had in mind, I revisit some articulations of this idea without erasing these internal tensions. Moreover, as I will show, looking more closely at the content of these debates reveals tension, as de Roover rightly describes, between and even within the texts that sought to lay out these ideas.

Rereading Aquinas and Lessius

A closer reading of the texts famous for early articulations of the concept of the just price reveals a certain degree of ambiguity on the part of their authors about which actors were allowed particular actions associated with pricing. However, seeing this quality requires that diverse efforts to delineate between just prices and unjust prices be read alongside one another. Thomas Aquinas's renderings of the concept of the just price are the most famous of all the theological texts on this subject and are assumed to have sparked the debates that were carried out across a number of texts that followed. Of them all, his writing is also considered to do the least to naturalize existing prices. He argues in the *Summa Theologiae* [1485], for instance, that "it is altogether sinful to have recourse in order to sell a thing for more than its just price, because this is to deceive one's neighbor so as to injure him."[36] By writing that the duplicitous act of selling an item for more than its just price as well as having recourse to do so are both sinful, Aquinas condemns economic systems that allow people to take advantage of bargaining positions as well as actual instances of usury. He also writes that defective goods "are of less value" and that "if such like defects be hidden, and the seller does not make them known, the sale will be illicit and fraudulent."[37] In both statements, Aquinas's writing does not merely seek to justify existing prices, but also to prevent exploitation.

Aquinas's views are underpinned, moreover, by a commitment to prices that maintain a certain parity between buyers and sellers. As he writes, "in commutative justice we consider chiefly real equality."[38] However, Aquinas also makes some significant qualifications to this argument. For instance, he adds that "the recompense [for the good] should depend on the usefulness accruing, whereas in buying it should be equal to the thing bought," meaning that the actual quality and use of a good are of some real importance in understanding the good's value according to commutative justice. Aquinas also writes that slight deviations from the correct price are acceptable because "the just price of things is not fixed with mathematical precision, but depends on a kind of estimate, so that slight addition or subtraction would not seem to destroy the equality of justice."[39] These qualifications are significant, because Aquinas is interested in protecting buyers against usury, but he is also seeking to protect sellers. For instance, Aquinas articulates a moral obligation to pay at the just price in any purchase:

> For sometimes it happens that the seller thinks his goods to be specifically of lower value, as when a man sells gold instead of copper, and then if the buyer be aware of this, he buys it unjustly and is bound to restitution.[40]

What is implicit here is that Aquinas's just price represents a significant transformation of the laws of *laesio enormis*—his vision of the just price assumes that there is one true price for every good, and that either a buyer *or* a seller can be at fault if either of them fails to deliver that correct price. Yet he is not clear about who decides this one true price—and as I will argue later in this chapter, in Aquinas's world this is because the monarch, who was considered responsible for prices, was thought to function as the physical presence of God's authority on earth.

Articulating the concept of the just price in the way Aquinas does indicates that the usual price is not always justifiable, because the price is pegged to an abstract notion of what prices must be (i.e., market prices), rather than to the specific interests of small landholders. In practice, this means that the justness of the price is measured according to the relative bargaining power of the people involved in its sale. The result is to increase the role for currency in revealing which prices are just. Aquinas writes that "gold and silver are costly not only on account of the usefulness of the vessels and other like things made from them, but also on account of the excellence and purity of their substance."[41] As he writes, "according to [Aristotle] a thing is reckoned as money if its value can be measured by money."[42] Aquinas's arguments assume an intrinsic value in money beyond its function as a medium of exchange. Because Aquinas believed that the value of gold and silver was absolute, his efforts at conceptualizing prices as just only if they promote equality were undermined by an implicit naturalization of the then-current prices.

It is easy to see why Aquinas's writing was open to multiple contradictory interpretations, and why de Roover and Foucault both detect market dogmatism in his writing. There are tensions within Aquinas's writing, and the fact that he draws from Aristotle's discussions of money does not help him sort out the correct value of goods because, as I showed in Chapter 3, Aristotle was interested not in value but in need.[43] These contradictions account for the variety of interpretations of Aquinas that followed. For example, as Toon van Houdt argues, Leonardus Lessius, who was one of Aquinas's later and more conservative readers, came to have fewer "objections against exploiting information surpluses" on the basis of his own readings of Aristotle. As Van Houdt shows, Lessius's reading of Aquinas in "On Buying and Selling" [1605] actually led him to focus on the needs of the merchant, who Lessius argued should always demand "the current just price."[44] Lessius's interpretation consequently moves further away from Aquinas's efforts to articulate just prices in terms of the relative bargaining power of sellers and buyers, and more directly echoes the legal logic of earlier *laesio enormis* laws.

Nevertheless, Lessius begins his own treatise on just prices by echoing Aquinas. "The just price," he explains, "is held [by Aristotle] to be that price that is determined either by the public authorities in consideration of the common good or by the common estimation of people."[45] In these cases, he argues:

> Goods are defined neither by affection nor by private advantage
> but rather in common. The reason thereof is that private judgment

is fallible and easily perverted by love of gain, whereas a common judgment is less subject to error. Because this rule is the most reliable guideline available, we should observe it. The common estimation, then, is realized by considering all the circumstances mentioned above.[46]

In this passage, Lessius articulates an even more striking interventionist position than Aquinas. He argues that the common estimation of people is superior to private valuations because it is less interested and thus more accurate.

Read on its own, Lessius's discussion of common valuation in this passage appears to offer more of a radical take on pricing than Aquinas's. His arguments about the dangers of private judgment raise the possibility that Lessius was concerned that "the power of the strong [be] limited by the personal dignity of the poor and weak who would be streamrolled in a world based on mere commutative justice."[47] However, Lessius also explains that "the common price depends on the assessment of many people who do not judge perfectly."[48] The influence of Roman and canon law leads Lessius to the assumption that minimal rules would actually lead merchants to be *more* just in their pricing.[49] From this point, Lessius argues that "the [just price] of goods should be derived from the judgment of a knowledgeable merchant who considers the circumstances that affect the value of the good."[50] Here, the estimation of the merchant is considered to be the most expedient way to assess value, and also the most accurate and just. On this basis, Lessius argues that the legal price is actually the best price, because it is not liable to "opportunity." Rather, the legal price is determined by nothing other than whatever price merchants provide.[51] Evident in this argument is a way in which the justness of the price is ultimately a function of the presumed justness of the various actors involved in setting it. The fault lines between Aquinas's and Lessius's positions have less to do with an assumed means of calculating a just price, and more to do with the presumed likelihood of virtuous behavior from merchants, buyers, or public authorities.

Anachronistic readings of the debates between thinkers like Thomas Aquinas and Leonardus Lessius tend to flatten these tensions within their writings—tensions that were present because economic and moral logics of valuation were so often conflated. We have inherited this ambiguity in our contemporary renderings of the concept of "fair market value." Foregrounding this political dimension of value discourses rather than disavowing it enables an acknowledgment of the role of interpersonal estimations in claims about value. As I will show, this dimension to value discourse has been forgotten, and the result is that political economists take the category of value itself as neutral and apolitical.

Sovereign Value and the Biopolitics of Worth

A variety of philosophical positions are evident in the theory and practice of "just" pricing. Some have attributed shifting theoretical disagreements to fluctuations in actually existing prices, caused by an inconsistent money supply and by the interests of monopoly-holding guilds.[52] Following from this effort to put these debates into historical perspective, I suggest that arguments about just pricing would not have seemed contradictory at the time when they were written. The concept of community value, particularly when written in Latin, would have been understood as pertaining to the power or strength of particular goods as a function of the power or strength of their buyers and sellers in the social hierarchy. Though the modern tendency is to assume that the value of a good corresponds in some way either to a good's use or to market conditions, this former understanding of value as power or strength was more transparently grounded in systems of social hierarchy. In fact, that Aquinas and Lessius had inherited a way of thinking about value from the Roman tradition indicates that they might not have seen a contradiction within their own texts or between differing interpretations of the basis for the just price. Medieval estimations of the value of goods did not consider the worth of goods without considering the relative strength and power of the people involved in their exchange, which meant that the worth of goods was most often determined by public authorities. Merchants and buyers alike were necessarily constrained, in other words, by prices that were set at least in part by monarchs.

This semantic difference is critical, because the power of market goods was *not* prone to random fluctuations but to organized ones. Specifically, only the monarch had the power to mint gold and set prices, so the power of a particular good always in some way reflected the strength and will of the sovereign. Examples of how this practice was reflected in common attitudes abound. Take, for instance, the blending of these ideas in medieval poetry. In one of John Gower's 1393 poetic descriptions of an (unspecified) unusual event, he writes about the relationship between money and value as follows: "the mighty king's revenue that day stored no value."[53] Gower is hyperbolically writing about an imagined day when the world as his readers knew it had been upended. Writing that on this remarkable day the king's treasury stored no value, he shows that a situation in which the king's treasury did not reflect the king's power was practically unthinkable.[54] The important implication in Gower's line is that the might of the monarch transfers or corresponds directly to the strength of the currency.[55]

The validity of the market price, measured in its "justness," rested primarily on the strength of the currency—and correspondingly on acceptance of the authority of the person seen as responsible for that strength.[56] The predominant assumption was that the monarch had an ultimate

monopoly on prices and could transform the value of the coins that determined them at any moment. It was commonplace, then, to view the
monarch as the ultimate "regulator and measure of value."[57] The discourse
of *lèse-majesté*, for instance, considered counterfeiting to be treason against
the monarch. Laws pertaining to the weighting of gold were strictly en-
forced, and coin clipping or counterfeiting was treated as a direct injury
to the monarch and punishable by death.[58] The severity of punishments
for this offense reflects the belief that the face and name of the monarch
on coins guaranteed the value of the currency.[59] The presumption that
Aquinas, Lessius, and their contemporaries were operating from, which
they would have considered more fundamental than all other price factors,
was that the ultimate source of value was royal power.

If we look to Lessius again in this light, his text reads quite differently.
For example, as Lessius explains, prices are set in two ways—either by
"the prince," or by "the common estimation of the people." Describing a
situation in which the price is set by the prince, he writes:

> The prince or magistrate fixes the price at which a particular good is
> to be sold by considering all the circumstances on which the estima-
> tion of goods depends, lest the buyers be deceived or forced to give
> in to the sellers' whims. The doctors call this price the legal price,
> as though it were laid down by law. It is obvious that this price is to
> be held just (except maybe for the case in which the price certainly
> came about through bribery, discrimination of the sellers, or gross
> ignorance). Whatever the public authorities decide by virtue of their
> office cannot be called into question by the subjects, which is exactly
> the case with the legal price. Just as in other circumstances it pertains
> to the public authorities to promote the common good; likewise, in
> business, they should prevent fraud and the exploitation of the poor.[60]

It at first appears as though Lessius considers the price set by public authorities to be the just price. Yet he then goes on to juxtapose the legal price
with the just price. The latter, he argues, is chosen by the common estimation of the people—and their collective determination of the fair price
expressed in the market price. As he argues, this route is a better means of
determining price than the decisions of the monarch, because:

> The market price...does not depend on the advantage of one person
> or a few people, but rather on the public estimation, that is to say, on
> the value they would get if they were publicly offered for sale on the
> marketplace with the whole town coming together and responding to
> the auctioneer.[61]

Read one way, Lessius's argument appears to be a precursor to laissez-faire
economic theory because of his obvious preference for sales clearing at the

market price. However, he frames this argument as a means of arguing against the arbitrary imposition of prices by the monarch—the king's understanding of the common good, he explains, cannot measure up to the aggregate knowledge of the whole town.

Just price discourses were developed in a context in which legal justice ultimately reflected royal might rather than the decisions of a sovereign people, and this reality has implications for the political projects of arguments like Lessius's, which sought to establish a case against intervention in the marketplace. Had Lessius seen parliamentary government supersede monarchical rule, we might imagine that he would have had more faith in the ability of the public authorities to set priorities that did not allow the exploitation of the poor.

Reading Aquinas and Lessius, an observant reader can find multiple places in which these texts appear to be ambivalent and oftentimes even contradictory on the appropriate means of determining prices and the role of public authorities therein.[62] However, the uniting thread in these diverse arguments was an assumption about who guaranteed the value of goods—namely the sovereign. This unacknowledged dimension of value discourses persisted in political discourse even as monarchical authority diminished. In particular, the idea that prices are better reflections of the will of the people lived on well beyond medieval and early modern monarchical rule. Indeed, the idea underpinning just price discourse—that value springs from the authority of powerful people—was transferred over along with the rise of both democracy and capitalism in Western Europe. Early British parliamentary discussions about choosing a house speaker advocated, for instance, selecting a "gentleman of great value" and implied that value is something that is embodied by wealthy people more so than by products.[63] As absolutism waned, the assumption that goods had value by authority of the monarch faded into the background, but some of its entailments persisted, such as the idea that goods have a particular value not by virtue of their qualities, but rather in accordance with the power or might of the people involved in their exchange.[64]

Valuing People to Price Goods

There is one more implicit entailment of the assumption of royal authority embedded in just price discourses. This privileging of royal authority necessitates a ready hierarchy of other social actors. This hierarchy can be seen in the ways judgments were frequently made about the worth of goods—positions on the virtue and importance of particular goods reflected attitudes about the morality and status of the people buying them.[65] Necessary goods, for instance, were considered to require special vigilance in adherence to a *just* price, whereas thinkers tended to be more willing to chart the just price of luxury goods to whatever the prices happened to be at the time.[66] Likewise, restrictions on the sale of goods were more readily justifiable if these goods were considered "improper." Examples of goods described in this way included poisons and other dangerous substances, gambling equipment, and weapons (usually when sold to "the infidel"), and "cosmetics and female finery."[67] The idea that the just price was connected with "an objective value which was inherent in the nature of the goods" only extended as far as judgments could be made about *who* required what sorts of things.[68] If respectable citizens needed a basic good, then careful adherence to a principle of justice in pricing was deemed important. However, when transacted items were claimed by people who were deemed a threat to the established distribution of power and authority, access to the goods was restricted or their prices left unfettered.[69]

This political dimension of just price discourse was evident even in its earliest formulations. *Laesio enormis* left explicit room for a person's value to define their relationship to the goods in an exchange. For instance, Grotius reports that, though contracts are typically considered binding, this is not so for all, as "acts of madmen, ideots, and infants [are] invalid."[70] He explains that while the law requires that promises must be honored:

> The Civil Law, for reasons of publick Advantage, nulls many Promises of this Kind also, which the Law of Nature would oblige us to; as that of a Man or Woman already married, who promise some future Match, and several other Promises made by Minors, and Children while under their Parents.[71]

Maniatis identifies a similar dynamic in his argument that:

> Out of concern for potential abuses, the right of restitution was also extended to minors when they sustained great loss in the sale of property; women who were incapable of conducting their own affairs or were not allowed to do so; and persons of full legal age for cause and at the judgment of the praetor or magistrate.[72]

What sort of person one was judged to be was deeply intertwined with expectations about the due price. Though just pricing was written about as if it applied universally, the reality was that "madmen," "ideots," children, and women were exempt from its provisions and any exchanges they engaged in could be considered void. Whereas the monarch guaranteed the value of a transaction, the participation of anyone from these groups was thought to nullify it. Significantly, this logic was echoed many centuries later to justify discriminatory housing policies like redlining, wherein property values depreciated, and loans were considered risky if people of color moved into a neighborhood.[73]

These ways in which value was biopolitical persisted even as monarchical authority waned. The rise of commercial society coincided with extensive debates about how to control population growth, with particular populations in mind.[74] As Michel Foucault argues, the discourse of race struggles played a central role in the production of surplus populations from the seventeenth century onward.[75] In fact, he shows, racialization (not yet 'racism') worked as a means of normalizing uneven power.[76] Foucault further shows that fears of foreigners and deviants infiltrating society led to the state being recast as a necessary protector.[77] However, the logics of biopower contained within value discourse were most fully unleashed just as the overtly political aspects of the concept were concealed.

Liberal Sovereignty in Early Modern Britain

The tendency to think about value as inextricably connected to the power of particular people in the marketplace was extended far beyond the medieval period. Yet even as copious effort was devoted to assessing the worth of humans alongside the goods they transacted, diminishing sovereign authority was also accompanied by the rise of a discourse of value as detached and impersonal—and thus apolitical. This dimension of value discourse persisted throughout the seventeenth century as the practice of giving accounts of one's individual worth became increasingly commonplace.[78] For example, along with the rise of the monetary economy in England and the accompanying social upheaval, the Poor Laws required that decisions be made about how best to rate the value of a person in order to assess eligibility for relief.[79] Likewise, the connections between estimations of values of particular goods and implicit estimations of those who buy them were part of a long history of regulating consumption and display, including everything from sumptuary laws restricting fashion, to the practice of taxing luxury goods.[80] For instance, Alan Hunt shows that sumptuary law ensured the maintenance of class boundaries.[81] Hunt cites Henry Fielding, an English "Justice of the Peace" writing in 1751, to show that these boundaries were reinforced by keeping highly valued goods off the bodies of "the very Dregs of the People" and those who aspire "to a Degree beyond that which belongs to them."[82] Likewise, valuable goods were thought to be inappropriate for those whose quest for mobility would end in either "a State of Starving and Beggary" or in becoming "Thieves, Shapers and Robbers."[83] These lines echo the ways medieval sales were nullified if conducted by less powerful people.

In early modern Britain, as Alexandra Shepard shows, the practice of estimating the actual worth of people became a widespread means of assessing social standing.[84] Appearing before court and attesting to one's worth, she argues, was in fact so pervasive a practice as to be considered almost routine. From 1550 to 1728, in what Shepard writes was arguably the "most litigious age," people were frequently called upon to testify in court and "it became increasingly common to prove the 'worth' of the witness, as represented by the moveable value of their estates."[85] The commonsense assumption was that a person's class constituted the principal means of determining their trustworthiness; if the true measure of one's credibility was their status in the social hierarchy, then the belief was that the worth of one's material possessions accurately reflected, rather than created, that status.[86]

The credibility of a person's court testimony was assessed on the basis of their personal worth—however, there were also norms in place that prevented accruals of material goods from undermining already defined roles in the social hierarchy. Women, for instance, frequently described themselves as having no worth, since couverture laws did not grant them a right to joint ownership of their husbands' property.[87] Meanwhile, women who in fact did own personal property described their worth in terms of the credit limit given to them by their husbands, or otherwise did not answer questions about their worth at all.[88] These answers were expected, but also confirmed these women's position near the bottom of the social hierarchy.[89] Lacking any material stake in the commonwealth," it was believed, "people of no worth could not be trusted to serve its interests."[90] In this way, accounts of one's worth represented and reflected one's standing as a citizen.[91]

Consequently, people would often misrepresent their wealth in order to publicly meet symbolic thresholds that corresponded to the type of person they needed to be.[92] For instance, Shepard's extensive review of legal testimony during this period also shows that a surprisingly high number of people assessed their value as precisely 40 shillings—surprising, at any rate, until Shepard further explains that 40 shillings was the threshold for eligibility to participate in jury duty, the ability to receive poverty relief funds, and even the right to sue.[93] Forty shillings was essentially the equivalent of the modern-day poverty line, and served as the typical annual wage of the domestic servant.[94] Declaring oneself to be worth 40 shillings in court was another way of affirming one's status as an autonomous member of British society.

This culture of value estimations inherited from just price discourse, which in early modern Britain took the form of accounting for one's worth by attesting to material assets in court, served as a means of reifying social hierarchies and reinforcing the boundaries of citizenship. Lorraine Daston's discussion of the rise of life insurance in eighteenth- and nineteenth-century Europe offers another example of the widespread modern practice of valuing people.[95] Daston discusses the insurance trade as part of her effort to track the emergence of probabilistic rationality. As she shows, the life insurance industry rose in eighteenth-century England, and initially took a form that was indistinguishable from gambling; whereas in the nineteenth century gambling and life insurance came to be opposed practices.[96] Her purpose is to track how life insurance premiums ultimately came to be pegged to large-scale assessments of risk, and in accomplishing this aim she shows that life insurance prices were fueled by gambling sensibilities, which meant that prices were aligned with speculative wagers rather than consistent mortality statistics.[97]

Although it is not her project to do so, Daston also demonstrates that early forms of life insurance were actually based in valuations of individual cases, even if premiums were discussed as if they were established on an abstract likelihood of life.[98] Indeed, insurance represented one of many examples of prices and property values being affected by the contingent valuation placed on certain lives.[99] General insurance practices at this time, as Daston shows, were always specific, whether to a particular length of time, such as a merchant's time on a certain voyage, or to a particular practice, since one could buy insurance against cuckoldry, lying, or losing the lottery.[100] With life insurance, one could even insure the life of a stranger, such as a prince or bishop.[101] In many cases, prices were justified on the basis of their cohesion with the just price, even if they actually reflected a speculative recklessness.[102] Importantly, as life insurance was differentiated from gambling during the nineteenth century, this connection to individual valuation was sublimated rather than eliminated—for instance, precautions were increasingly taken to insure only "healthy" lives.[103]

Meanwhile, explicitly rating people as material goods continued to be a pervasive practice—so much so that between 1527 and 1660 the term 'value' even took on a definition as "the estimated worth of a marriage arranged by a lord for an infant ward or heir, and payable by the heir to the lord, should the heir later refuse to enter into the marriage."[104] 'Value' was understood as the amount of money due to an injured party if an arranged marriage did not come to fruition.[105] The person being exchanged (most often the woman to be married) guaranteed the value and also became the conduit of it.

This way of thinking about value as an apolitical estimation of the worth of a person was also at the forefront of the development of much of modern English law.[106] In William Blackstone's reflections on the legal complications that arose from differences between moveable goods and fixed property, for instance, he pauses for some time to analyze the rules of marriage afforded by the tenure of knightship. He finds that the Statute of Merton guaranteed the value of marriage such that payment was due for "the price or value of his marriage, if he refused such wife as his lord and guardian had bartered for, and impofed upon him; or twice that value, if he married another woman." Indeed, he found the right of guardians to arrange marriages for their wards to be binding:

> If the infants refufed, they forfeited the value of the marriage, *valorem maritagii*, to their guardian...and if the infants married themfelves without the guardian's confent, they forfeited double the value, duplicem *valorem maritagii*.[107]

These lines demonstrate an easy slippage between assessing one's worth in terms of one's possessions and actually treating people as possessions. Moreover, all of these practices reflected the attitude that one's value, measured in status, determined whether people could themselves be constituted as a form of moveable good.[108] Yet what is most striking here is the transparency of these practices. Today's free market enthusiasts, by contrast, are adamant that value is neutral and depersonalized. The types of subjugation that were a central part of value's history are forgotten or disavowed by those who imagine exchange to take place on level terrain.

As I show in Chapter 4, there is an enduring and significant biopolitical undercurrent to value discourse, and this is evident if one looks to one of the most brutal instances of transfiguring humans into moveable goods—namely chattel slavery and its long aftermath. However, I first discuss liberalism's roots in modern political economy and how these roots obscure value's biopolitical dimensions. As liberal political economists sought to distance themselves from their 'political' modifier, they also fled from discussions of value's political expressions.[109] Key to this effort was a move to distinguish between moral and economic discourses of value, and various efforts to parse the relationship between value's material and aspirational expressions began to serve as a distraction from the biopolitics of valuation.

Revisiting Classical Political Economy

Political-economic theory has historically had a controversial relationship with efforts to understand what is valuable, to whom, and why—mostly due to the uneasy way in which the political aspect of political economy has been sidelined in favor of the economic. The Industrial Revolution and the birth of liberal political economy are widely acknowledged as markers of the construction of the idea of "market value," but political economists of this period were not entirely in agreement (with one another, and with themselves) about whether value exists in the world without its "market" prefix. Consequently, the claims about value often involved conceptual slippage. To take one example of this sort of fogginess around understandings of value: Adam Smith's "invisible hand" was rooted in the visible mercantilism of his time and the justifications for resource extraction that went along with it, and he believed gold and silver to be naturally and intrinsically "valuable," even as he hesitated to naturalize markets.[110]

However, absent the fusion of religious dicta and price-setting practices that animated just price discourse, moral and economic discourses of value began to drift apart. A separation of value discourse into separate moral and economic strands, even if the lines between these two strands were still blurred in practice, was a key feature of many accounts of value by classical political economists. In particular, classical political economy was paradigmatically concerned with understanding exchange value and the labor that went into it—a problem economists struggled with because there is no actual relationship. For instance, in *The Wealth of Nations*, Smith attempts to sort out this trouble with different logics of value, by providing a schema for understanding prices that can bring these two logics together.

If prices and values sometimes seem misaligned, he initially explains, this is because:

> The word VALUE has two different meanings. It sometimes expresses the utility of some particular object, and others the power of purchasing other goods which the possession of that object conveys.[111]

Smith is differentiating, famously (if not originally), between use and exchange value, and showing that they do not often align. "Nothing is more useful than water," he insists, "but it will purchase scarce any thing," whereas "a diamond, on the contrary, has scarce any value in use; but a very great quantity of other goods may frequently be had in exchange for it."[112] Smith's ensuing analysis of this problem ultimately draws together insights from Locke's labor theory of value, Ricardo's understanding of scarcity, and Hume's concept of utility in a Frankensteinian discussion of the origins of prices.[113]

Smith's discussions of utility, which are often bracketed in his discussion of prices and developed most thoroughly in his *Theory of Moral Sentiments*, are integral to understanding his theory of prices. There are many generous ways to read these passages. For instance, as Emma Rothschild argues, Smith's use of the metaphor of the invisible hand shows that he was critical of luxury consumption. She notes that he uses this image ironically, and often to make a point about human vanity and selfishness.[114] In Smith's *Theory of Moral Sentiments*, he uses the invisible hand image in connection with what Rothschild calls "unpleasant rich proprietors," who Smith says advance the interests of society despite their best intentions. As Rothschild notes, Smith thought that they did so as an inadvertent and unanticipated outcome of "their own vain and insatiable desires" and "their natural selfishness and rapacity."[115] As Rothschild elaborates, Smith believed that these proprietors were "quite undignified," even if the outcome was acceptable or even beneficial.[116]

Yet Smith's discussions of utility also contain significant political baggage—they reveal that any account of value is also an account of the people involved in an exchange.[117] Consider, for instance, his remark that people often "ruin themselves by laying out money on trinkets of frivolous utility."[118] At first glance, this comment appears to simply explain why diamonds might be priced more highly than water. However, the effect, he tells us, is that we "walk about loaded with a multitude of baubles, in weight and in value not inferior to an ordinary Jew's box."[119] The (very thinly) veiled anti-Semitism is notable not only because it betrays Smith's prejudices, but also because of the ways it slips an estimation of people into his judgment of the worth of objects.[120]

Given the way that the famous proponent of the "invisible hand" slipped valuations of people into his theory of economic value, it is evident that the political hierarchies of just price discourse continue to haunt efforts to neutrally determine value. Specifically, the splintering of value discourse into moral and economic registers represented a secular way of picking up the work of just price discourse without acknowledging its political (and often biopolitical) origins. Though Smith was far from the only classical political economist engaged in this project, his splitting of moral and economic logics of value comes through in the difference between his discussions of utility and pricing, and more broadly, in his messy attempts to grapple with the complex relationship between economics and morality.

This uneasy splitting of value in two persisted in modern political–economic discourse well beyond its early theorization. For example, the years leading up to and immediately following the formal adoption of the gold standard in the U.S. were marked by a resurgence of concerns about value that demonstrated many of the anxieties inherited from just price discourse. Discussions about value unfolded across many major American newspapers and print publications during these years.[121] On July 9, 1891, for instance, the *Washington Post* published a commentary on a tax assessment, in which a distinction was drawn between "true value" (what a thing is reasonably and fairly worth) and "market value" ("what persons generally...would be willing to pay for it").[122] In 1891, the American Economic Association was formed, and its first project was an attempt to sort out the complex relationship between value, utility, and cost.[123] In 1898, the *Wall Street Journal* apologetically limned a discussion of the value of agricultural exports to a "discussion of value as prices," and followed that piece up a few months later with the quip that "we think it will surprise Wall Street and all persons familiar with the English language...that 'face value' in the revenue act means 'market value'."[124] In the years immediately following the adoption of the gold standard, a significant uptick in articles describing value in broader registers also gave voice to such concerns as "life's intrinsic value." These were published, coincidentally, at the same time as an extensive series of "studies in value" were produced, which detailed the assets and worth of companies.[125] All these attempts to measure and understand value were the result of conflicts about the basis for value, since the naturalized authority of the monarch or class hierarchy could no longer be value's explicit linchpin. However, value's splintering into distinct moral and economic registers only amounted to a way of concealing the political decisions at the heart of any calculation of value.

Re-Politicizing Value

It has thus far been the central claim of this book that the language of value mediates a relationship of politics—that the language of value and values is used in conversations about both commerce and justice to make decisions about how market transactions should be enacted, and about who rightly sets these norms. Ambiguity concerning who rightly holds power allowed hierarchical power to be cemented into how people conceived of value during debates about just prices. Though early theorists of the just price likely had a very different world in view than the one that is typically projected upon their texts, the slippery nature of their positions on the question of what constitutes a just price and who rightly decides reflects historical contestation over claims to value, and hence claims to power. That the word 'value' at its root is open to alternative claims about groups that might wield power, or other imaginations of such a power distribution—namely as democratic—does little to assuage the ways it has been involved in political projects that have reinforced hierarchies. Indeed, early modern political–economic discourse retained this political strand of value discourse and also mobilized value discourse as a means of exercising biopower.

Today, we more often think of value as negotiated in market transactions than as something that depends upon the relative status of the people involved in market exchange. This means that the disagreements between just prices and power also remain unresolved and live on in present-day uses of the concept of value. For instance, despite an extensive history of rating and assessing people in order to reify class status and hierarchy, proponents of free markets imagine economic exchange as based in horizontal power relations rather than in hierarchical ones. That we have inherited both biopolitical discourses of value and their corresponding disavowals is in many ways traceable to efforts to depersonalize value in classical political economy.

A historical analysis of the concept of value demonstrates semasiological origins of our present-day senses of value in the imperial culture of Ancient Rome. These origins positioned the power associated with value in its wielders rather than in collective judgments. The traveling of the juridical use of the language of value into medieval discourse about the relationship between prices and morality retained an attachment to individual power in debates that attempted to navigate problems of divine judgment and the common good. Where the legal tradition of *quantum res communiter valet* had its greatest impact was in the way its indeterminacy cleared ground for those with the most power to push prices, and in the medieval European context those with the most power were the monarchs. The image of the consumer-citizen as sovereign is therefore dependent on an image of sovereignty that is originally based in actual monarchical power.

As the attachment of the concept to monarchical power later dissolved, the concept of value retained a connection to a deeply personal form of valuation, as it came to be mobilized in judgments about individual market actors. It is no wonder, then, that value and values have posed such a problem for political theory. While the pervasive assumption among contemporary market enthusiasts is that any person can achieve their desired social status through an expansion of their material wealth, this view is underpinned by longstanding practices of determining the value of those very goods by looking to the social standing of the people who held them.

In this way, the political struggles at the heart of economism are never fully foreclosed, because judgments about value are never made in the abstract—they are always made about particular people, and they always delineate a relationship between politics and the material world.

It is to the more recent stakes of these implicit judgments about political community and agency within value discourse that I will turn next. As I will show, the language of value continues to operate as a mode of assessing the relative value of persons. Moreover, users of modern value discourse continue to participate in the political (and frequently biopolitical) projects that the concept inherits from its Latin origins and uses in just price discourse. However, the fracturing of modern discourses of value into economic and moral theory conceals these political roots behind a guise of distanced neutrality.

Notes

1 John W. Baldwin, "The Medieval Theories of the Just Price: Romanists, Canonists, and Theologians in the Twelfth and Thirteenth Centuries," *Transactions of the American Philosophical Society*, New Series 49, no. 4 (1959), 16, and G. C. Maniatis, "Operationalization of the Concept of Just Price in the Byzantine Legal, Economic and Political System," *Byzantion* 71, no. 1 (2001), 141.

2 Maniatis, "Operationalization of the Concept," 134.

3 Ibid., 143.

4 Baldwin, "The Medieval Theories," 18.

5 Maniatis, "Operationalization of the Concept," 134.

6 Baldwin, "The Medieval Theories," 19. Baldwin describes *laesio enormis* as curtailing the unchecked bargaining freedom that was the norm before these laws were implemented.

7 Ibid., 17.

8 Baldwin, "The Medieval Theories," 16.

9 Maniatis, "Operationalization of the Concept," 132.

10 Ibid., 133.

11 CJ.4.44.2 and 8, specifically.

12 Maniatis, "Operationalization of the Concept," 136.

13 Ibid., 140.

14 Ibid., 143, and Baldwin, "The Medieval Theories," 19. These protections were later abolished during the French Revolution when inflation caused prices and value to diverge sharply such that demands for rescission would have become too common. Hermann Marcuse, "Unbalanced Transactions Under Common and Civil Law," *Columbia Law Review* 43, no. 7 (1943), 1072.

15 Of course, theology was treated as the highest science throughout the Middle Ages, and theologians were the prominent economists and legal experts. Michael Allen Gillespie, *The Theological Origins of Modernity* (University of Chicago Press, 2009).

16 Baldwin, "The Medieval Theories," 12.

17 Ibid., 8.

18 Hugo Grotius, *The Rights of War and Peace, Book II* (Indianapolis IN: Liberty Fund, 2005), 699–700; 717.

19 Baldwin, "The Medieval Theories," 19.
20 Melius de Villiers, "The Roman Contract According to Labeo," *The Yale Law Journal* 35, no. 3 (1926), 292–293.
21 Baldwin, "The Medieval Theories," 20.
22 De Villiers, "The Roman Contract," 294.
23 Maniatis, "Operationalization of the Concept," 145.
24 Odd Langholm, *The Merchant in the Confessional: Trade and Price in the Pre-Reformation Penitential Handbooks* (Leiden NL: Brill, 2002), 4. See also Eric MacGilvray, *The Invention of Market Freedom* (Cambridge University Press, 2011). In practice, this transformation resulted in uneven applications and enforcement of transactional norms, even as just pricing principles became more commonplace in commercial law.
25 Dean Mathiowetz, *Appeals to Interest: Language, Contestation, and the Shaping of Political Agency* (University Park PA: The Pennsylvania State University Press, 2011), 41.
26 Ibid., 146.
27 Langholm, *The Merchant*, 246.
28 Barry Gordon, *Economic Analysis Before Adam Smith: Hesiod to Lessius* (London: Macmillan, 1975), 132.
29 Toon van Houdt, "Just Pricing and Profit Making in Late Scholastic Economic Thought," *Supplementa Humnnistica Lovaniens* 16 (2000), 399; Langholm, *The Merchant*, 236; and Van Houdt, "Just Pricing," 403, respectively.
30 Raymond de Roover, "The Concept of the Just Price: Theory and Economic Policy," *The Journal of Economic History* 18, no. 4 (1958), 418.
31 Ibid., 421.
32 Ibid., 422.
33 Michel Foucault, *The Birth of Biopolitics: Lectures at the College de France, 1978–1979* (New York NY: Palgrave, 2008), 30.
34 Foucault, *The Birth of Biopolitics*, 31. It should also be noted that de Roover's reading comports with the overwhelming number of examples of friars describing the just price as the conventional price, and across significant linguistic and theological divides. Langholm, *The Merchant*, 246.
35 De Roover, "The Concept of the Just Price," 421.
36 Thomas Aquinas, *Summa Theologiae* (1485), 2018.
37 Ibid., 2021–2022.
38 Ibid., 2020.
39 Ibid., 2019.
40 Ibid., 2021.
41 Ibid., 2021.
42 Ibid., 2028.
43 Van Houdt also reads Aquinas's discussions as deeply contradictory, although he draws from modern political-economic concepts as a way of explaining away why Aquinas might have been willing to entertain the importance of selling goods at typical prices. Toon van Houdt, "Tradition and Renewal in Late Scholastic Economic Thought: The Case of Leonardus Lessius," *Journal of Medieval and Early Modern Studies* 28, no. 1 (1998), 410. On Lessius's use of modern political-economic concepts, van Houdt writes, for instance, about the problem of "information availability" as one reason why prices may have been incorrectly predicted.
44 Ibid., 412 and 410.
45 Leonardus Lessius, "On Buying and Selling," Wim Decock, trans. (2007), 466.
46 Ibid., 467.

47 Wim Decock, "Introduction," *Journal of Markets & Morality* 10, no. 2 (2007), 461.

48 Lessius, "On Buying and Selling," 468.

49 Ibid., 445. The just price was not technically codified in Roman law; rather, it was the benchmark for the calculation of the amount owed in the case of fraud or imperfect information. Langholm, *The Merchant*, 234. One significant aim was to prevent monopolies, which were more clearly defined in Roman Law, 242. See also Kenneth S. Cahn, "The Roman and Frankish Roots of the Just Price of Medieval Canon Law," in William M. Bowsky, ed., *Studies in Medieval and Renaissance History Volume VI* (Lincoln NE: University of Nebraska Press, 1969).

50 Lessius, "On Buying and Selling," 471.

51 Ibid.

52 De Roover, "The Concept of the Just Price," 430–431.

53 The line rendered in Modern English above comes from the line: "the mihti kings retenue/that dai may stoned of no value." John Gower, *The English Works of John Gower*, G.C. Macaulay, Vol. 1 (Early English Text Society, 1900), 222. This text is one of the *Oxford English Dictionary*'s examples of the use of the word 'value' as a way of invoking 'power' or 'might'.

54 A modern reading might assume that the line merely describes a fluctuation in currency strength and calculable with or without a monarch. However, it is more likely that this line would be interpreted by Gower's contemporaries as describing an event in which value is impossible to perceive without a monarch to back it.

55 This is a similar point to the one Michel Foucault makes when he shows that the power to punish restores royal sovereignty by casting crimes as personal injuries against the monarch, and by granting him the power to seek restitution through the elaborate rituals and spectacles associated with punishment. See Michel Foucault, *Discipline and Punish: The Birth of the Prison* (New York NY: Vintage Books, 1991), 48.

56 This tradition in many ways lives on in present-day placements of the face and name of political patriarchs on coins and bills.

57 Ibid., 151.

58 See Pierre Vilar, *A History of Gold and Money 1450–1920* (New York NY: Verso, 1991) on minting gold; Cahn, "The Roman and Frankish Roots"; and Paul Strohm, *England's Empty Throne: Usurpation and the Language of Legitimation 1399–1422* (New Haven CT: Yale University Press, 1998), 133; 143–144.

59 Ibid., 149. These punishments did not prevent counterfeiting from becoming an increasingly pervasive practice. See, for instance, Constantine George Caffentzis, *Clipped Coins, Abused Words, and Civil Government: John Locke's Philosophy of Money* (Brooklyn NY: Autonomedia, 1989).

60 Lessius, "On Buying and Selling," 466–467.

61 Ibid., 502.

62 Andreas Blank tracks a similar tension in the work of prominent Spanish just price theorists. Andrea Blank, "Value, Justice, and Presumption in the Late Scholastic Controversy over Price Regulation," *Journal of the History of Ideas* 80, no. 2 (2019).

63 "Debates in 1679: Addendum – March (8th–13th)," in Anchitell Grey, ed., *Grey's Debates of the House of Commons: Volume 6* (London: T. Becket and P. A. De Hondt, 1769), 409–439. *British History Online*, accessed November 1, 2017, http://www.british-history.ac.uk/greys-debates/vol6/pp409-439.

64 Mariana Mazzucato elaborates this point with several examples of how the language of value is used to legitimize these actions. Mariana Mazzucato,

The Value of Everything: Making and Taking in the Global Economy (New York NY: PublicAffairs, 2018), 8. As she writes, "the way the word 'value' is used in modern economics has made it easier for value-extracting activities to masquerade as value-creating activities." Ibid., xviii. By this, she means that any act of "value creation" involves an implicit claim about who creates value (most often someone with a vested interest). Ibid., 7 and 12.

65 One's status in the social hierarchy determined the price of goods in a practice reminiscent of *weregild*, wherein one's status in the social hierarchy determined one's price in blood money.

66 Langholm, *The Merchant*, 241.

67 Ibid., 238. Here it is also important to note that Roman prices were stable for many years, and the noticeable fluctuations occurred when public officials intervened to change the price of goods like weapons. See Peter Temin, *The Roman Market Economy* (Princeton University Press, 2013).

68 Baldwin, "The Medieval Theories," 14.

69 Concerns about extravagant spending and sumptuary laws were not new to this period. See, for instance, Odd Langholm, *Economics in the Medieval Schools: Wealth, Exchange, Value, Money, and Usury According to the Paris Theological Tradition 1200–1305* (Leiden NL: Brill, 1992) on the role of consumption in Aristotle's work, and see James N. Davidson, *Courtesans and Fishcakes: The Consuming Passions of Classical Athens* (Hammersmith, London: Harper Collins Publishers, 1997) for a discussion of the consumption habits of classical Athens which likely inspired these concerns.

70 Grotius, *The Rights of War*, 715.

71 Ibid.

72 Maniatis, "Operationalization of the Concept," 133.

73 Richard Rothstein, *The Color of Law: A Forgotten History of How Our Government Segregated America* (New York NY: Liveright, 2017).

74 See Frederick G Whelan, "Population and Ideology in the Enlightenment," *History of Political Thought* 12, no. 1 (1991). There is indeed a wide and varied debate on the extent to which capitalism, since its onset, has depended on the extraction of value from surplus populations. In just one example of this sort of argument, see Robert Brenner's argument that capitalism's growth in England depended on the destruction of serfdom, but also on the "the short-circuiting of the emerging predominance of small peasant property." Robert Brenner, "Agrarian Class Structure and Economic Development in Pre-Industrial Europe," in T. H. Aston and C. H. E. Philpin, eds., *The Brenner Debate: Agrarian Class Structure and Economic Development in Pre-Industrial Europe* (Cambridge University Press, 1985), 30. Certainly, the upheavals that have accompanied industrialization, such as transitions from peasantry to factory work, have relied on force, and capitalism has played an integral role, historically, in the construction of large-scale agricultural slavery, and in particular racialized slavery. For examples of force, see Michael Perelman, *The Invention of Capitalism: Classical Political Economy and the Secret History of Primitive Accumulation* (Durham NC: Duke University Press Books, 2000); for discussions of large-scale agricultural slavery, see Werner Sombart and Philip Siegelman, *Luxury and Capitalism* (Ann Arbor MI: University of Michigan Press, 1967), 142–144; for discussions of racialized slavery, see Eric Williams, *Capitalism and Slavery* (Chapel Hill NC: University of North Carolina Press, 1994).

75 Michel Foucault, *Society Must Be Defended: Lectures at the Collège de France 1975–1976* (New York NY: Picador, 2003), 76.

76 Foucault, *Society Must Be Defended*, 65–66; 61.

77 Ibid., 69; 81.

78 In fact, the *Oxford English Dictionary* shows that the primary use of the word 'value' through the seventeenth century was to assess individual worth.

79 Andrew Appleby, *Famine in Tudor and Stuart England* (Stanford University Press, 1978); E. Lipson, *The Economic History of England Volume 2: The Age of Mercantilism* (London: A & C Black, 1934); D. M. Palliser, *The Age of Elizabeth: England Under the Later Tudors 1547–1603* (Essex UK: Longman Group, 1983); Paul Slack, *Poverty and Policy in Tudor and Stuart England* (Essex UK: Longman Group UK, 1988); R. H. Tawney, *The Agrarian Problem in the Sixteenth Century* (New York NY: Burt Franklin, 1912); Ellen Meiksins Wood, *The Origin of Capitalism: A Longer View* (Brooklyn NY: Verso, 2002); J. R. Wordie, "Deflationary Factors in the Tudor Price Rise," *Past & Present* no. 154 (1997). These practices were accompanied by the explosion of statistical techniques for accounting for populations, and, alongside them, the emergence of the idea of "population" altogether. Catherine Gallagher, *The Body Economic: Life, Death, and Sensation in Political Economy and the Victorian Novel* (Princeton University Press, 2005), and Mary Poovey, *A History of the Modern Fact: Problems of Knowledge in the Sciences of Wealth and Society* (University of Chicago Press, 1998).

80 On sumptuary laws, see Susan Mosher Stuard, *Gilding the Market: Luxury and Fashion in Fourteenth-Century Italy* (Philadelphia PA: University of Pennsylvania Press, 2006), and on taxation, see Christopher J. Berry, *The Idea of Luxury: A Conceptual and Historical Investigation* (Cambridge University Press, 1994), 206–211.

81 Alan Hunt, *Governance of the Consuming Passions: A History of Sumptuary Law* (New York NY: St. Martin's Press, 1996), 72.

82 Ibid., 83.

83 Ibid.

84 Alexandra Shepard, *Accounting for Oneself: Worth, Status, and the Social Order in Early Modern England* (Oxford University Press, 2015), 26.

85 Ibid., 11.

86 Ibid., 1–2; 35–36. Toward the middle of the sixteenth to the early seventeenth century, these accounts began increasingly to include stock as well as property, credit, loans, and investments. The pervasion of the practice can be seen in the ways in which its justification seeped into broader discourse, such as in Hobbes's comment, "for let a man (as most men do,) rate themselves at the highest Value they can; yet their true Value is no more than is esteemed by others." Thomas Hobbes, *Leviathan*, ed. Richard Tusk (Cambridge, 1991), 63, as quoted by Shepard, *Accounting for Oneself*, 2. This statement relays the pervasive logic of valueat the time—Hobbes's line is about the importance of social esteem, but he wrote this line during a period in which the value of people was frequently estimated by others in court, and as a means of sharply criticizing that practice.

87 Shepard, *Accounting for Oneself*, 53.

88 Ibid., 58–59.

89 Still others said that they did not know their worth. These answers were deliberately misleading given that women, who were responsible for household affairs, were more likely to accurately estimate household worth than their husbands could. Ibid., 118–119. Because one's account of personal possessions and assets determined whether one could be considered a reliable person, this practice served the function of reinforcing unequal social positions.

90 Ibid., 134.

91 Ibid., 100.

92 Ibid., 112.

93 Ibid., 76, 97–98.

94 Ibid., 99.

95 Lorraine Daston, *Classical Probability in the Enlightenment* (Princeton University Press, 1988).

96 Ibid., 163–165.

97 Ibid., 165, 170, 172–173.

98 Ibid., 8, 114–116, 137.

99 Ibid., 114.

100 Ibid, 164.

101 Ibid., 166.

102 Ibid., 172.

103 Ibid., 180.

104 Ibid.

105 *Middle English Dictionary*, "Value," and *Oxford English Dictionary*, "Value."

106 This practice even represented the main use of the word 'value' in written texts through the end of the seventeenth century. Ibid.

107 Books 1, 2, 5, 24, and 25 in *Blackstone's Commentaries on the Laws of England*, The Avalon Project at Yale Law School Lillian Goldman Law Library, accessed November 1, 2017, http://avalon.law.yale.edu/subject_menus/blackstone.asp, and *Oxford English Dictionary*, "Value."

108 A 1590 document even stated that the value of one's marriage was commonly associated with the value of one's land. H. Swinburne, *A Briefe Treatise of Testaments and Last Willes iii* (London UK: John Windet, 1590).

109 On the separation of economics and politics and the eclipse of politics with economics in liberalism, see Ute Tellmann, *Life and Money: The Genealogy of the Liberal Economy and the Displacement of Politics* (New York NY: Columbia University press, 2018).

110 Mike Hill and Warren Montag, *The Other Adam Smith* (Stanford University Press, 2015). David Ricardo, on the other hand, rejected the notion that the value of any commodity is intrinsic, and historicized the process by which commodities, even those that operate as standards by which the worth of other commodities are judged (such as gold), come to initially have value on the market. For Ricardo and later for Marx, the value of goods is a function of labor inputs rather than a product of their inherent worth. Gold is consequently thought to have value because of the labor required for extraction, rather than because of any inherent worth. For Marx, use value is determined by labor inputs, and when placed on the market, goods become commodities that are priced by what people are willing to pay for them, which means that the appearance that a commodity's value is directly related to its utility is deemed "fetishism."

111 Adam Smith, *An Inquiry into the Nature and Causes of the Wealth of Nations* (New York NY: Oxford University Press, 1993).

112 Ibid., 34–35. With corn he encounters a complication; however, it is one that Ricardo's understanding of scarcity and rents resolves. "The average or ordinary price" Smith explains, is "regulated...by the value of silver, by the richness or barrenness of the mines which supply the market with that metal." Ibid., 41.

113 As Duncan Foley argues, Smith abruptly switches between an exchangeable labor theory of value (based on how much work individuals are willing to put into obtaining an item) and an additive one (which accounts for scarcity, rents, stock, and wages). Duncan K. Foley, *Notes on the Theoretical Foundations of Political Economy* (1999).

114 Emma Rothschild, *Economic Sentiments: Adam Smith, Condorcet, and the Enlightenment* (Cambridge MA: Harvard University Press, 2001), 116.

115 Ibid., 117.

116 Ibid., 123.

117 Smith has been critiqued for his presentation of people different from him from a number of perspectives—though most in discussions of his thoughts on imperial expansion. Some are more forgiving—Marc William Palen, for instance, argues that Smith's ambiguity on the problem of empire, as an advocate of both devolution of the British empire and imperial federation, left his arguments open to being used differently depending on one's political agenda. E. A. Benians and Dermot Ryan, meanwhile, argue that Smith in fact had his own unified agenda, which incorporated both of these concerns into a critique of imperialism as it was practiced, couched within a broader defense of global expansion as a means to prosperity. In either case, the possibility remains that Smith's purported anti-colonial goals may have been grounded in racialized assumptions which undermine them. Elias Khalil's point that his broader concerns about extensions of sympathy provide a "mush ground" for the question of the boundaries of civil society, against which those to whom sympathy is due, can be easily construed to include only those who he imagines as equal in personhood. See Marc William Palen, "Adam Smith as Advocate of Empire," *The History Journal* 1, no. 57 (2014); E. A. Benians, "Adam Smith's Project of an Empire," *The Cambridge Historical Journal* 1 no. 3 (1925); Dermot Ryan, " 'The Beauty of That Arrangement': Adam Smith Imagines Empire," *Studies in Romanticism* 48 no. 1 (2009); and Elias Khalil, "What Determines the Boundary of Civil Society? Hume, Smith, and the Justification of European Exploitation of Non-Europeans," *Theoria: A Journal of Social and Political Theory* 60, no. 134 (2013). Perhaps most significantly, the ways classical thinkers like Smith elided thinking about the ways people are themselves subjected to logics of valuation were ultimately the basis for Marx's critique of political economy.

118 Adam Smith, *The Theory of Moral Sentiments* (Cambridge University Press, 2002), IV.i.6.

119 Ibid.

120 Treatments of utility theory are varied and complicated. Jeremy Bentham, for instance, developed a theory of utility to avoid the problem of accounting for why people erroneously value the things they do. In the opening lines of his *Principles of Morals and Legislation*, for instance, he describes the principle of utility as recognizing the subjection of questions or right and wrong to pleasure and pain. See Jeremy Bentham, *An Introduction to the Principles of Morals and Legislation* (Kitchener: Batoche Books, 1781).

4 What's the Matter with Value?

Anna Julia Cooper's Political-Economic Thought

Claims about value are always political; yet how and for whom they are political has consequences for our understanding of value's entanglements with inequality. That value discourse has historically been involved in biopolitical projects should certainly inspire skepticism about modern attempts to provide neutral accounts of value. In fact, modern political–economic discourse's treatment of value as neutral conceals the ways both moral and economic discourses of value have historically been gendered and racialized. Drawing from the insights of Anna Julia Cooper's political-economic writings, I argue in this chapter that value and values, markets and morals, and the constellation of issues entangled in modern discourses of valuation continue to be involved in maintaining hierarchies by producing and measuring the relative value of persons—as they have the effect of devaluing Black women's lives. I explore the tensions between economics and moral sentiments as Cooper depicts them in her discussion of the concepts of worth and material. Cooper demonstrates the concept of matter to rely upon an equivocation between material goods and the common good, and this point is critical for understanding how political priorities mesh with systems of material interdependence.

Cooper lays out how matter and mattering are deeply tied up in the afterlife and legacy of slavery, both in white supremacist economic structures and logics, and in the various forms of resistance that are a critical part of anti-racist material history. Her examinations of historical devaluations of Black life, including of the particular kinds of devaluation confronting Black women, offer potent tools with which to begin thinking about value and values in ways we need in order to make sense of their relationship with racial exploitation. Wrestling with the relationship between political economy and Black devaluation, Cooper considers the problems of human 'worth' and 'material' as ways of measuring value, and ultimately uses her discussion of these concepts to provide critical insight into the ways competing systems of value in economic and moral discourses reflect similar disregard for Black lives and livelihoods. Cooper reverses discourses that conceive of value as abstract and ahistorical through a parodic treatment of the concepts of worth and material as they are deployed in commonsense economic discourse and in the work of

DOI: 10.4324/9781003304302-4

John Locke and Adam Smith. In so doing, she shows that although economic and moral reasoning often appear at odds, they are often politically congruous. She also argues for bringing together these two approaches, grounded in Black lived experiences, for a radical shift in how value is conceived, measured, and nurtured.

Reading Cooper for insights on value discourse is uncommon. Cooper is frequently hailed as the originator of Black feminism, and the first to articulate a clear program of what intersectional feminism requires.[1] There is also a significant political-economic strand in her writing, and it is this perspective that is key to understanding her perspective on value discourse.[2] Yet her political-economic thought has not been sufficiently analyzed or treated as a crucial contribution to political theory, even though it resonates with a variety of efforts at rethinking racialized citizenship.

Engaging Cooper's work shows that we have not really begun to think about value as an important grounding for contemporary political theoretical analysis. Specifically, Cooper shows that while arguments about value often move in apparently seamless ways between economic or material and moral or ethical logics, there are fundamental tensions between them. She furthermore shows that each of these two logics seem to promise unambiguous tools for navigating complex dilemmas, but in fact that both are politically derived, dependent, and mediated. Indeed, Cooper shows that these competing accounts of valuation actually function in a mutually reinforcing way in their devaluation of Black lives and livelihoods. Reframing value discourses in the way that she does shows our mismanagement of value to be a problem of politics. This political dimension of value, she shows, is most evident in cases where the people or issues in question are *undervalued* or seen as lacking value. However, Cooper's conclusions about the utility of value discourses are ultimately ambivalent. She finds moral and economic logics of value to be irredeemably shortsighted, but nevertheless engages them as political tools critical for her advocacy for investment in Black labor and education.

To build these points, I analyze Cooper's effort to expose racial and gendered dimensions of material inequalities, contestation, and experiences of precarity and exclusion—in short, her effort to think value politically. I turn first to an exploration of the tensions and surprising congruities between economics and moral sentiments as Cooper depicts them in her discussion of the concept of worth. I then turn to her exploration of the concept of material in the discursive work of classical political economy, through which she shows value discourses to reflect a dilemma with respect to linkages between material goods and arguments about the common good. I next show that the slippage Cooper sees between materialism and moralism is critical to understanding her casting of a labor theory of value as historical in order to show its connection to both structural and personal instances of racism and discrimination.

Anna Julia Cooper: Writing for Intersectional Liberation

Lauded as one of the key figures in the development of the intersectional politics of Black identity, Anna Julia Cooper (1858–1964) was a key critical voice of the late nineteenth and early twentieth centuries.[3] She is considered to be one of the key progenitors of Black feminism in her championing of intersectionality and Black education, and in interdisciplinary work that spans an array of topics. Born a slave in North Carolina (and the child of her slaver), Cooper began school shortly after the passing of the Thirteenth Amendment.[4] She earned Bachelor's and Master's degrees from Oberlin College and went on to spend 43 years as an educator and professor. She played a pivotal role in the conceptualization and implementation of liberal arts curricula at Washington DC's famous M Street School, all the while advancing the cause of Black education and the scholarship of radical pedagogy.[5] Cooper earned her Ph.D. in history at the age of 67 from the University of Paris-Sorbonne, the fourth African American woman to do so.[6] Her dissertation was a study of the Haitian Revolution that rivaled the more often recognized historical work of C. L. R. James and W. E. B. Du Bois.[7] Cooper was also a prolific activist, and one of the founders of the Pan-African Congress.

Despite this distinctive background and work, Cooper has been confined to relative obscurity within political theory. As Vivian May laments, Cooper's scholarship on the Haitian revolution and transatlantic revolutionary consciousness was overshadowed by Aimé Cesaire's and C. L. R. James's writings on the subject and her activism by the more well-known work of Charlotte Perkins Gilman, W.E.B. Du Bois, and Marcus Garvey. Her intersectional feminist philosophy was likewise eclipsed by the works of earlier and later thinkers like Mary Wollstonecraft and Simone de Beauvoir.[8]

The mark of Cooper's personal struggles within and against dominant norms and expectations of Black womanhood can nevertheless be seen in her writings, which are highly interdisciplinary.[9] She articulates a vision of Black liberation that transcends the confines of dominant discourses, and her biographers describe work that flows across disciplinary lines.[10] Cooper's writing has also been characterized as devoted to a project of intersectional feminism which "refus[es] to be contained by parameters of knowing that she did not help to create and that were not made with her in mind," even those of philosophical inquiry itself.[11]

Across her work, Cooper holds fast to ideals like equality, freedom, emancipation, and solidarity while also highlighting incomplete attempts at their realization. Her perspective on the racial fault lines of liberation movements especially informs her writing about political economy. Despite the ways in which questions of democracy, freedom, autonomy, community, and identity are central to her thinking, her work has flown under the radar in most political-theoretical treatments of these problems.

There are two notable readings of Cooper that display the utility of revisiting her writing from the perspective of political theories of identity and democracy. Penny Weiss positions Cooper alongside a number of other marginalized women political theorists in a discussion of the way the concept of "voice" plays a central role in Cooper's thinking about emancipation. As Weiss writes, one persistent theme in Cooper's writing is an amplification of the "voices of the silent" and an exploration of the "means by which they are silenced, the consequences of silencing, and finally the means for regaining voice."[12] Jane Anna Gordon, meanwhile, draws Cooper into conversation with Jean-Jacques Rousseau on questions of legitimate governance and interdependence. Gordon especially shows how Cooper extended Rousseau's concerns about economic inequality into a discussion of "the consistent refusal of many mainly white persons to recognize the contributions of the freed slaves to society and to acknowledge their reliance on the freed slaves and their labor."[13] Clear especially from Gordon's work is the usefulness of Cooper's political thought for conceptualizing the relationship between political economy and emancipation.

Though fewer researchers have remarked on Cooper's political-economic writings, there is a growing consensus that value features centrally in her conceptual schema.[14] These connections are not incidental. Though Cooper argues "without qualification" that "there are no greater returns than investing in the development of people," Gordon explains, the historical context in which she was writing rendered women always measured by "relative" value and Black Americans as a source of value that had been "forcefully extracted."[15] On this basis, Lewis Gordon situates Cooper's work in relation to Marxist theories of alienation, and shows how Cooper generates an "efficiency theory of value" in which value can be measured in terms of the relationship of inputs to outputs.[16] Cooper uses this analysis to demonstrate a significant racial disparity between investment and production.

Seeing this contribution to political-economic thought in Cooper's writing may be disorienting for those who wish to read her as wholeheartedly rejecting dominant economic discourses for their racial prejudices, rather than as a political economist in her own right.[17] However, a careful analysis of Cooper's pointed responses to classical political economists offers insight into how value discourses delineate the bounds of political community. Cooper's writing consequently offers provocative material for thinking value politically, rather than reducing the problem of value and values to one of algorithms, econometrics, or morality. Moreover, she makes visible the ways in which value discourses and American racial injustices are contingently yet inextricably bound.

Cooper's Intersectional Economics

Cooper's reflections on political economy rest within her broader perspective on the intersectional politics of Black identity, from which she brings discussions of economics to bear on ethical concerns about equality and freedom for all people. For instance, she often adopts sweeping moral positions, like when she writes that, "we owe it to humanity...to enlarge and enrich, so far as in us lies, the opportunity and grasp of every soul we can emancipate," only to point out the systemic failures in the realization of such ideals.[18] However, she also shows that movements that claim to do the same, like her contemporaries in first-wave feminism, have exclusions that prevent them from making good on their vision. In a biting criticism of the movement to support women in the workplace, for example, she exposes the limitations of these efforts:

> Recently I listened to one who went into pious agonies at the thought of the future mothers of Americans having to stand all day at shop counters...I am always glad to hear of the establishment of reading rooms and social entertainments to brighten the lot of any women who are toiling for bread—whether they are white women or black women. But how many have ever given a thought to the pinched and down-trodden colored women bending over wash-tubs and ironing boards...with children to feed and house rent to pay, wood to buy, soap and starch to furnish—lugging home weekly great baskets of clothes for families who pay them for a month's laundrying barely enough to purchase a substantial pair of shoes![19]

The women for whom emancipation is proposed, she is adamant, are not those most in need of advocacy. While the spotlight has typically been on improvement in working conditions for white women, she shows, the economic inequality between them and Black women suggests that a truly emancipatory movement ought to put more effort into aligning its advocacy with its stated priorities. Moreover, the efforts of Black women, she shows, underpin the claims not only of feminist movements, but also of the economy more broadly.

Efforts to show how market systems contribute to racialized and gender-based oppression appear across Cooper's work.[20] These efforts are visible in Cooper's extensive discussions of colonialism and even in her analyses of misrepresentations of Black vernacular speech practices and their relationship with accumulation.[21] For instance, as May points out, Cooper's 1925 dissertation on the political action of Haitian slaves exposes the ways in which "the abusive *practices* of expansionist capitalist empires dependent on slave and colonial labor" play an integral role in the ideological construction of French ideals of republican rights and citizenship.[22] As May explains, Cooper:

> suggests that the French were not really capable of transforming their economy or following through on the full implications of Enlightenment ideals on their own because they were too deeply invested, literally and metaphorically in...an exploitative economy.[23]

The profit motive of the colonists, Cooper shows, is to blame for the shortsightedness of these debates in France.[24] Throughout this text, she repeatedly describes the slave trade as "lucrative," "prosperous," and as resulting in "material gains" even as she condemns the practice in the strongest terms.[25]

But Cooper is best known for her *A Voice from the South*, in which she presents the problems of racial justice and gender equality as intertwined. Though this text is divided rather deceptively into two parts—beginning with a series of essays on gender politics followed by a series of essays on segregation and racial injustice—the intertwined way she writes on both issues makes it clear that, for Cooper, these are not distinct problems. Instead, her writing on both race and gender presents an intersectional vision of autonomy and freedom. Her discussions of the political economy of race therefore speak to a range of ways in which value is linked with identity and political boundaries, and to its critical role in the realization of projects of intersectional liberation both past and present.[26]

In this text, Cooper's efforts to improve the situation of Black women are underpinned by a specific set of claims about the racial politics of the post-bellum South. These claims display the limitations of emancipation at the end of the nineteenth century as well as the pernicious political-economic systems that entrench power and privilege, and that contribute to multiple dimensions of social stratification. Though her purposes were ultimately to promote the higher education of Black women at the end of the nineteenth century and to expand opportunities for their growth and self-development, she also takes a range of canonical philosophers to task for their racialized blind spots along the way.[27] In fact, Cooper develops some of her most pointed arguments about American racism in her critiques of classical political-economic thought. As she shows, the intersections of gendered and racialized oppression display the limitations of emancipation at the end of the nineteenth century, as well as the pernicious political-economic discourses that entrench power and privilege.

What Are We Worth?

Cooper's provocative essay on political economy "What Are We Worth?," in her *A Voice from the South*, carries out an analysis of how value discourse intersects with modern racism. In this piece, she demonstrates the price system to be a flawed metric of accounting for the value of human life; despite this, Cooper is also adamant that we should not give moral concerns any more weight than economic metrics. As she shows, these two logics which are so often treated as distinct are actually compatible in their shared complicity in the devaluation of Black life. Yet their complementarity in this political project, she shows, does not mean that tensions between them can or should be ignored.[28]

Cooper's accomplishment is not to resolve the complexity of this rela-tionship between economic or moral logics of accounting, but rather to show how these discourses are each deployed in ways that reinforce racial injustices.[29] In order to draw out this point, Cooper begins with the ques-tion: "Were Africa and the Africans to sink to-morrow, how much poorer would the world be?"[30] She poses this question in response to a statement by Henry Ward Beecher that "if African people were to vanish, the world would lose nothing of value."[31] Beecher was a prominent abolitionist, and Cooper deliberately misreads him to mirror some of the ways this line was taken out of context and mobilized by Jim Crow. However, in posing the question with feigned seriousness, Cooper tacks back and forth between treating this question as an economic one and as a moral one, only to re-veal that these are not discrete projects.

She commences her discussion as if certain that such accounts of the worth of Black life must be done in economic terms. She asks:

> How much owest thou? What have you produced, what consumed? What is your real value in the world's economy? What do you give to the world over and above what you have cost? What would be missed had you never lived? What are you worth? What of actual value would go down with you if you were sunk into the ocean or buried by an earthquake to-morrow? Show up your cash account and your balance sheet. In the final reckoning do you belong on the debit or the credit side of the account?[32]

This set of questions, she argues, allows such an assessment to be made "ac-cording to a fair and square, an impartial and practical reckoning," and it is "by this standard that society estimates individuals: and by this standard finally and inevitably the world will measure and judge nations and races."[33] The inevitability evoked in her argument, that value "will" be measured in this way, is for her an indication that a pragmatic politics must follow suit. It is less the case that human material *ought* to be measured in terms of its productivity, she shows, but rather that there is no real alternative.

On the basis of this satirically proposed cost-benefit analysis, Cooper provides the conventional answer to these questions, describing how "oth-ers see us."[34] From this perspective, she argues, Black people have made few contributions: "a little less gold and ivory, a little less coffee, a con-siderable ripple, perhaps, where the Atlantic and Indian Oceans would come together—that is all; not a poem, not an invention, not a piece of art would be missed from the world."[35] This is not a "flattering" image, she grants, but she nonetheless suggests that it is an accurate one simply because the "standard" by which races are measured is generally in terms of production and consumption, "value in the world's economy," cash ac-counts, and balance sheets, even if all of these metrics have roots in global trade, including the slave trade.[36]

Cooper's response is to turn to the domain of moral thinking about human worth only to show this approach to be equally unflattering; however, her way into this discussion is to first feign an attempt at offering a moral accounting of value as a substitute for these balance sheets. "With them," she argues, "it is simply a question of dollars and cents"—and by "them" she means those who share Beecher's view that African cultures have produced little value.[37] Cooper then adds that "the highest gifts are not measured in dollars and cents."[38] She underscores this point by playfully suggesting that value can be measured in courage, that debts to the world can be paid in songs and sculptures, and that value can be added even in the contribution of "sweet fragrances" to the world.[39] In fact, she argues, value cannot be reducible to dollars and cents because treating value as economic denies the moral worth of personhood. Everyone, she writes, "can at the very least give themselves," and the worth of a person can be measured in infinitudes.[40] After all, she argues:

> The world will always want *men*. The worth of one is infinite. To this value all other values are merely relative. Our money, our schools our governments, our free institutions, our systems of religion and forms of creeds are all first and last to be judged by this standard: what sort of men and women do they grow? How are men and women being shaped and molded by this system of training, under this or that form of government, by this or that standard of moral action?[41]

Here it is apparent that for Cooper, economic value just represents one set of values, which errs whenever it strays from valuing human life above all else. Value calculated in market terms is therefore inadequate for rigorously measuring value unless it is guided first and foremost by moral thinking.

Cooper carries this same logic into the household and here too she initially reaffirms moral logic, as she finds that economic calculations cannot fully justify the important work that is carried out in the household. No animal is as weak at birth as a human baby, she tells us. Such creatures are "unsentimentally and honestly...worth just as much as a leak is worth to a ship."[42] But a newborn baby's mother, she says, "would not sell him, she will tell you, for his weight in gold."[43] This despite the obvious fact that raising a child is "a heavy investment" and one "which requires a large outlay of money on long time and large risk, no end of labor, skill, pains."[44] As she writes:

> The world knows well what an outlay of time and money and labor must be made before he is worth even his weight in ashes...what an expenditure of toil and care, of heart power and brain power, what planning, what working, what feeding, what enriching, what sowing and sinking of values before one can tell whether the harvest is worth the output. Yet, how gladly does the mother pour out her strength

and vitality, her energy, her life that the little bankrupt may store up capital for its own use.[45]

She is quite clear in these lines (unless one ignores her life's work advocating for children and mistakenly reads the text as a diatribe against children) that the problem of economic quantification versus morality is a false one, because sentiment supersedes any assessment of value, especially when valuations concern human life.

Yet because sentiment is bound up in human hierarchies, Cooper also shows the problem to be more complex than that of a binary choice between prioritizing economic and moral calculations of value, as she proceeds to show that moralistic accounts are equally inadequate. She moves into this discussion by conceding that the endeavor of measuring worth economically is not easily dismissed, and in fact may be worthwhile. "It may not be unprofitable then for us to address ourselves to the task of casting up our account and carefully overhauling our books," she writes, and here she ultimately waffles on her prior condemnation of economistic logic.[46] She notes that "it may be well to remember at the outset that the operation is purely a mathematical one and leaves no room for sentiment."[47] Though this point that sentiment is left out initially appears as unambiguously critical of economism, Cooper actually uses it to build an argument against moral logics of valuation.

Cooper's language shifts a bit here in order to show that moral judgments are ultimately made on the basis of arbitrary feeling rather than careful logic. Sentiment, she argues, deploying the concept interchangeably with "prejudice," is not counted in such an economic rendering. But more importantly, her argument continues, it should not be counted.[48] After all, she points out, racism too is a sentiment (just as homophobia and misogyny are values), and there are:

> sections of this country in which the very name of the Negro, even in homeopathic doses, stirs up such a storm of feeling that men fairly grow wild and are unfit to discuss the simplest principles of life and conduct where the colored man is concerned.[49]

As she explains, "sentiment, whether adverse or favorable, is ephemeral. Ever shifting and unreliable, it can never be counted in estimating values," and therefore, "just as impervious to reason is the man who is dominated by the sentiment of race and prejudice."[50] The implication here is that such a man would never follow a levelheaded economic assessment of value, but if he were to do so, Black people would be better served. Indeed, Cooper later says so directly, in the description of this man's judgment as "warped" which she contrasts with judgment that is "just and true."[51] She argues that "waves of sentiment or prejudice" that are enfolded in moral visions actually blur otherwise "intensely practical" economic assessments.[52]

Cooper thus arrives at something of a stalemate, and she moves forward from here by again feigning a full-fledged return to economism. "Sentiment and cant, then, both being ruled out," she proceeds, "let us try to study our subject as the world finally reckons it—not certain crevices and crannies of the earth, but the cool, practical, business-like world."[53] Circling back to a modified version of her original question, she asks:

> What are we worth? not in Georgia or in Massachusetts; not to our brothers and sisters and cousins and aunts, every one of whom would unhesitatingly declare us worth a great gold-lump; nor to the exasperated neighbor over the way who would be just as ready, perhaps, to write us down a most unmitigated nuisance. But what do we represent to the world? What is our market value. Are we a positive and additive quantity or a negative factor in the world's elements. What have we cost and what do we come to?[54]

Here, she is adamant that individual prejudices, whether overly generous as in the example of our relatives, or miserly as in the example of the exasperated neighbor, must be avoided. In Cooper's rejection of perspectives limited by geography ("not in Georgia or in Massachusetts") in favor of posing the question of value on a world scale, she also proposes a way of valuing human life that is not bound by these limitations.

However, this effort, her work shows, is troubled by the inadequacy of the universalizing logics of economic and moral discourses of value. Having discarded and then once again taken up economic and moral systems of valuation, Cooper is sometimes characterized as contradictory. For instance, Carolyn Cusick accurately describes Cooper as "refusing to accommodate white norms of worthiness and white views of black worthlessness" but also criticizes her "practical attempt to calculate the worth of a person and a people" as being "not quite as simple as Cooper seems to make it out to be."[55] The implication is that Cooper's own adherence to the categories of investment, production, consumption, and worth might limit her thinking to economistic concerns, rather than allow her to extend her discussions of value beyond the confines of the marketplace.

Yet as Thomas Meagher shows, part of Cooper's issue is the lack of rigor, or the uneven application in economic metrices. For instance, he points out that Cooper shows racial statistics to be diligently collected when crime rates are calculated, but totally absent in the calculations involved in the production of cotton. Meagher concludes that Cooper's point is to show that for Black people, "it is their crimes that merit racial demarcation, not their contributions."[56] The result, he shows, is that Black people are viewed "as infantile and dependent on white guardianship," whereas an "unsentimental assessment" actually shows that "the relationship is the inverse: whites have erected a world in which they are licensed to be infantile by way of a parasitic dependence on oppressed blacks."[57]

Indeed, as Cooper's next set of points demonstrates, the problem is not in her writing, but in the racialized world she is reflecting upon, and the way racism infects both economic and moral discourses of value.

Taking the same insight about the perils of moral sentiment into discussions of life insurance and gentrification, Cooper again affirms an economistic metric. Here, she finds something redeeming and perhaps even genuinely impartial in the price system, as she contrasts sentiment with "business," implying the two to be mutually exclusive.[58] She argues that:

> It is no use to go into hysterics and explode in Ciceronian philippics against life insurance companies for refusing to insure or charging a higher premium for colored policies. With them it is simply a question of dollars and cents. What are you worth? What are your chances, and what does it cost to take your risks in the aggregate?[59]

Whether or not insurance premiums are racialized, she argues, it is not the price system at fault—but is instead the racist sentiments that caused Black life to be valued less highly in the first place. It is, perversely, the higher risk of death that makes Black life more expensive to insure, and thus determines their value to insurance companies. Cooper is demonstrating here that economic measurements are rendered only after decisions of sentiment or prejudice have already been made.

Racist values, then, can beget economic value. Elsewhere, in a detailed linguistic exposition of the relationship between different dialects of English, Cooper blurs the color lines between Black and white vernaculars. However, she points out that there are economic interests behind representations of Black vernacular in ways that deny this history, and that even construct impossible formulations.[60] Focusing on the *Amos 'n' Andy* show, she argues that the characterization of African American Vernacular English, as depicted in popular media, relies on purposefully incorrect renderings of Southern vernacular because there is an economic demand for these racialized productions.[61] Incorrect formulations of Black vernacular are pervasive, she shows, simply because they have entertainment value and are therefore lucrative—racist representations of Black speech turn greater profits than accurate ones.[62]

Cooper's argument helps us to see how both the material and aspirational dimensions of value are mobilized to devalue Black people, and especially Black women. Rather than simply replace moral sentiment with impartial economic calculations, Cooper suggests, we ought to recognize that both logics of valuation entail judgments about the worth of other people. Dismantling white supremacy and misogyny would thus shift the economics. Moreover, the failings of both economic and moral means of assessment show them to be imbricated with one another. The point that morality and markets are deeply interconnected is not original to Cooper—even classical liberals and Marxists agree on this dimension of value discourse. Cooper's contribution is to show their relationship to the politics of race and gender. Though the questions of "what is our market value?" and "what do we represent to the world?" together guide her discussion, Cooper shows the questions to be in tension with each other on a conceptual level, but complementary in their actual effects for Black life. In this way, economism and moralism are each treated by Cooper as stemming from the same problem of value—a problem that is neither economic nor moral but political. However, seeing this dimension to Cooper's handling of the tension between moral and economic thought requires that she be read directly alongside that to which she is responding. Looking to Cooper's use of satire in her responses to the canon of classical political economy unmasks the ways in which economism and moralism both fall victim to racist values.

Values that Matter

Having cracked open the question of human worth, Cooper next pivots into a discussion of the concept of material, demonstrating the centrality of racialized labor and ownership practices to our understandings of workmanship, utility, and history. Her own work on these concepts reveals narratives about progress and growth to depend on exploitative racialized systems of labor. Cooper's efforts thereby challenge liberal imaginations of humans as autonomous agents who interact with a material world, treating humans as instead a critical part of the material world.

She builds these points by engaging political–economic discourses focused on workmanship and utility in order to expose a relationship between histories of racial discrimination and theories of value. In doing so, she ultimately reframes the issue by articulating a labor theory of value that is more attuned to the question of *whose* labor is put into *whose* material. From Cooper's vantage point, classical political economy exemplifies a style of conducting presumably neutral studies of value from the perspective of very particular values. Cooper's own treatment of the relationship between economic and moral discourses of value cuts right to the core assumptions of classical political-economic thought—assumptions that she demonstrates to be deeply gendered and racialized.

Cooper never explicitly names particular political economists as interlocutors. Seeing this dynamic in her writing therefore requires attention to what Vivian May describes as Cooper's "interdisciplinary method and complex rhetorical strategies," which allow her to simultaneously echo and critique dominant discourses.[63] These strategies are a key part of Cooper's effort to emphasize "the prejudice and false universals within the very democratic premises she invokes in order to be heard."[64] The playful reversals Cooper uses rely especially upon rhetorical strategies of "using parody and irony to vary her analytic voice," frequently "miming the voice of the oppressor," and, constructing "an intersubjective, dialogic relationship with her audience, an active pedagogical and methodological space of encounter."[65] Cooper, for example, often:

> deploys rhetorical techniques commonly found in slave narratives (such as dissemblance or textual withholding) and tones in order to create textual and political space for her critiques and assertions. For instance, she often combines a seemingly conciliatory voice with a bitingly sarcastic one.[66]

In doing so, she "simultaneously shifts "the terms regarding whose knowledge 'counts' and what should constitute an adequate means of proof."[67] As May argues, Cooper uses these approaches to show "how discursive and material forms of power work hand in hand to maintain inequality... and Cooper accentuates how multiplicity, difference, and reflexive forms of accountability are necessary for a more dialogic form of freedom to emerge."[68] For instance, Cooper frequently sets up a series of dichotomies only to later blur them, a move that she does by "employing such rhetorical strategies as repetition, anaphora, and anthypophora" in order to "redefine and redeploy" words.[69]

These strategies all come into play in Cooper's discussions of the political-economic concepts of workmanship and material.[70] Her response to John Locke's exposition of these two concepts is particularly extensive— though his influence is evident only in the language she uses to discuss these concepts, as she never mentions him by name. At first, Cooper echoes many of Locke's considerations—that any theory of property rests upon moral foundations, that property ought to be used rather than be something that can lay fallow, that people should be able to enjoy the products of their labor, and especially, that resources are to be held in common.[71] She is concerned, like Locke, about the future, and because of this concern she is adamant that labor is necessary before anything can be of use, and that material should not be wasted.[72]

However, the definition of material becomes the central problem for Cooper, as she replaces Locke's abstract discussion of workmanship with a set of claims that are explicitly about the materiality of people. In Locke's imagination, the world is full of resources, and people turn them into useable goods.[73] For Cooper, people are the primary resource. She explains that, though "it would seem sometimes that it is labor that creates all value," it is imperative that we "see if there is a parallel rise of value in the material of which men are made."[74] In this line, she identifies a slippage in economic uses of the concept of material, and then puts people firmly at the center of her own understanding of Locke's theory of value, thus opening up questions about the various means of improving upon human material.

Cooper is not the only thinker to point out the hidden values, or relationships of dependency, in Locke's theory of value.[75] However, unlike other feminist readings of Locke, Cooper poses this problem as primarily a racialized one. In an echo of Locke's own questions about workmanship of the earth's resources, she asks, "what sort of workmanship are we putting on our raw material. What are we doing for education?"[76] This intentional slippage leads to an extended discussion of Black participation in higher education. Though she grants that raw numbers were low, she shows that they were quite high considering the numerous obstacles to educational access that Black students face. Black participation numbers reflect, she writes, "an attempt, to say the least, to do the best we can with our material."[77] She also makes the point more firmly in the statement that:

> Labor must be the solid foundation stone—the *sine qua non* of our material value; and the only effective preparation for success in this, as it seems to me, lies in the establishment of industrial and technical schools for teaching our colored youth trades.[78]

In order for Locke's labor theory of property to work, she demonstrates, we must treat humans as the primary resource to be cultivated. This argument is made in implicit contrast to Locke's, whose argument treats humans as ahistorical and autonomous agents who turn acorns into plantations with willpower alone. Moreover, such an assumption, she shows, necessitates investment in Black education.

In a similarly motivated description of the dramatic disparity between white and Black District of Columbia residents in nutrition and mortality, Cooper concludes that the relative suffering of Black people "unquestionably represents a most wanton and flagrant *waste* of valuable material."[79] As labor is the foundation or "the *sine qua non* of our material value,' she argues, it must be used to maximize the potential of Black livelihood.[80] Here she builds on Locke's argument by extending it to include humans as a type of material upon which other people work, rather than treating people as the products of God's workmanship. She argues, for instance, that "the individual is responsible…not for what he has not, but for what he has; and the vital part for us after all depends on the use we make of our material." There are, she finds, "no flaws in this first element of value, *material*."[81] Cooper takes Locke's central tenets at face value. Her issue is not with his concepts of material and workmanship, but with the limitations of the imagination of equality embedded within his utopic and ahistorical state of nature.[82]

Cooper consequently validates measurements of human worth on the basis of material property; however, the affirmation comes with an important complication. This response to Locke can be seen most acutely in Cooper's inversion of what James Tully characterizes as Locke's discussion of appropriation.[83] "In estimating the value of our material," she argues, "[it is] plain that we must look into the deeds of our estates."[84] In an example of inheritance gone awry, she pointedly describes landed property as leaving one "chained."[85] She notes the peculiar ways in which the

English "system of entail by which a lot of land was fixed to a family and its posterity forever" renders "an heir coming into an estate…often poorer than if he had no inheritance" and writes that land that simply cannot be developed is doomed to "barrenness and squalidness," not to mention "poverty and degradation."[86] Yet again, Cooper is affirming Locke's own critique of hereditary property.

However, Cooper also finds fault with Locke's rosy imagination of a world in which natural resources could be free for anyone's appropriation. The problem she sees, evident in her careful deployment of the image of being left "chained" to land, is that Black Americans have, like land, *also* been constituted as property, and human development is thus assessed in the same way as the land he describes.[87] This is a dynamic she locates both historically, and in Locke's own theoretical formulations. Having referenced the former status of Black Americans as property, she inverts Locke's argument about workmanship in order to show how his logic slides seamlessly from a discussion of agricultural growth to one of humans as property.

Unsurprisingly, Cooper makes a similar analytic move to expose the blind spots in Adam Smith's discussions of utility. Smith's efforts to reconcile his moral philosophy, and his opposition to mercantilism, with his effort to provide empirical foundations for a scientific account of consumption, were very much informed by Locke's labor theory of value. Moreover, his notorious efforts to sweep the political nature of value under the rug in his infamous defense of the price system make him a perfect target for Cooper.[88]

Drawing from Hume, Smith defines utility in *Theory of Moral Sentiments* as the "fitness of any system or machine to produce the end for which it was intended." He then applies this logic in an extended complaint about the purchase of luxury watches:

> A watch… that falls behind above two minutes in a day, is despised by one curious in watches…the sole use of watches however, is to tell us what o'clock it is, and to hinder us from breaking any engagement, or suffering any other inconveniency by our ignorance in that particular point.[89]

Watches, he is telling us, are designed to tell time. Utility, the efficacy of an object to propel you toward some end that you value, is therefore something he would reasonably expect to be derived from the ability of a watch to meet that purpose—to tell time well. However, in his critique of "frivolous" consumption, he admits to a problem: the people who buy expensive watches are not necessarily any more prone to arrive on time! As he continues:

> But the person so nice with regard to this machine, will not always be found either more scrupulously punctual than other men, or more anxiously concerned upon any other account, to know precisely what time of day it is. What interests him is not so much the attainment of

this piece of knowledge, as the perfection of the machine which serves to attain it.[90]

At first glance there does not appear to be an obvious racial oversight in such a statement. However, Cooper's response is to echo Smith's discussion of the watch, but to make explicit the judgments hidden in his own use of this image.

Rather than use the image of the watch to try to pin down a universal way of estimating value, Cooper makes it clear that present in any such discussion are the lives of the people who are inadvertently assessed. She writes:

> *Men* are not very unlike watches. We might estimate first the cost of material—is it gold or silver or alloy, solid or plated, jewelled or sham paste. Settle the relative value of your raw material, and next you want to calculate how much this value has been enhanced by labor...then the utility and beauty of the product and its adaptability to the end and purpose of its manufacture.[91]

This satirical treatment raises questions that Smith only alludes to, and that demonstrate the complications to finding a common, let alone a neutral, means of assessing human value—whether it be worth, material, utility, or something else entirely. Cooper presents a litany of questions that mock all possible accounts of the watch's utility, ranging from "does it meet a want" to "does it keep good time?"[92] Here, she references Smith's discussion, but also identifies a direct connection between claims about consumption habits and judgments about people.[93] Utility, Cooper shows, is much more political than Smith's analysis of the watch suggests, and this becomes apparent as soon as we realize that political–economic discourse also has a nasty habit of assessing people as if we too are objects.[94]

Cooper shows Smith's abstract discussions about utility (as a measure of value) to be implicitly based in political judgments. This dimension of her argument comes through most clearly in a pointed critique of extravagant spending that in many ways echoes Smith's own commitment to prudence and parsimony.[95] Cooper argues, for instance, that "the love of lavish expenditure and costly display" comes from a "laxness of morals."[96] She concludes that "a man living on his earnings should eschew luxuries, if he wishes to produce wealth" because "luxuries deteriorate manhood, they impoverish and destroy the most precious commodity we can offer the world."[97] Though Smith's own discussion of luxurious consumption follows Bernard Mandeville in treating ambition and display as necessary evils that propel positive societal effects, Smith is nevertheless wary of the dangers of extravagant expenditure.[98] On this point, his and Cooper's arguments share some common ground.

However, Cooper shows that a more vital concern than consumption is distribution. To illustrate this point, Cooper provides an imagined scenario in which a Black man is asked to respond to a question about his productivity: "What do you give—are you adding something each year to the world's stored up capital?"[99] In her scenario, the man replies:

> I give back *all*. I am even now living on the prospects of next year's income. I give my labor at accommodation rates, and forthwith reconvert my wages into the general circulation. Funds, somehow, don't seem to stick to me. I have no talents, or smaller coins either, hid in a napkin.[100]

As Cooper shows, there are serious limitations to a logic of economism in which this man's labor is not commensurate with the value he gets in returns—one that puts him in such a position of deprivation, strain, and sacrifice for the benefit of (white) society at large. Like Smith's watch, the value of this material is carefully measured; however, in his case it is measured by others in a way that is entirely inaccurate. There is an explanation for this error. "They tell us" Cooper explains, "that the waste of material is greater in making colored men and women than in the case of others."[101] The implication in her use of the pronoun "they" is that racists refuse to acknowledge the productivity of Black labor.

Cooper's project is therefore twofold. She challenges economic discourses that think in terms of supply and demand and "absolute and inherent value."[102] Yet in asking with feigned naïveté, "have I a margin on the side of consumption for surplus production?" she ultimately does not take issue with the concepts deployed by political–economic discourse so much as with their application.[103] "It is only they who produce more than they consume," she argues, "that the world owes, or even acknowledges as having any practical value."[104] If we must look to the price system for guidance, she therefore suggests, let us at least do so rigorously. If such a project were done in good faith, she shows, Black people would be considered incredibly valuable because they produce more than they consume. This is a fundamental point of distinction that she holds on to, even as she troubles a strictly cost-benefit analysis of value.

Cooper's ambivalence about the logic of bank accounts and balance sheets is also evident in her political arguments for active investment in Black labor. Cooper does not find investment in Black labor to be an entirely satisfying solution to the problems she identifies, but she nevertheless sees it as an essential stopgap measure for the ongoing waste of Black material that she sees. As she writes:

> Our labor interests lie at the foundation of our material prosperity. The growth of the colored man in this country must for a long time yet be estimated on his value and productiveness as a laborer.[105]

Though on the surface these lines affirm her earlier points about workmanship, particularly in her argument that labor is "the foundation" of prosperity, her point that this must be done for "a long time yet" casts this effort as an important ameliorative measure rather than as an intrinsic good. This perspective is also evident in her comment that:

> With most of us, however, the material, such as it is, has already been delivered. The working of it up is also well under way...now can the world use it? Is there a demand for it, does it perform the functions for which it was made, and is its usefulness greater than the costs of its production? Does it pay expenses and have anything left over...the world in putting these crucial questions to men and women, or to races and nations, classifies them under two heads—as consumers or producers.[106]

Cooper has serious misgivings about how the world classifies humans in such reductive roles as "consumers or producers." However, her comment that the material has "already been delivered" references slavery and signals that we are stuck with these limited ways of thinking about people.

Unlike in Smith's image of the watch, no careful considerations of the function or purpose of this material can remedy this situation. Smith's writings about the various considerations that go into utility estimations, in fact, are willfully ignorant of this problem because they contain their own prejudices. Smith's discussions of utility were deeply classist—he attributed the greatest dangers of luxury to the potential that rich men might spend money on servants, thus leaving capital immobile in "unproductive hands."[107] It is no coincidence that Smith's image of the servant as "unproductive" is echoed in Cooper's example of the poor Black man who is not recognized for his contributions and hence is not reimbursed for his extensive labor. As Cooper points out, any delineation of value also draws a line, and most often, a "color line."[108] Whenever Black productivity is inaccurately estimated and under-rewarded, she shows, no abstract theory of the origins of prices can remedy this situation—as such theories are built on racial exclusions.

Cooper and the Historicity of Matter

This evidence of racial exclusion is the critical point of departure from which Cooper's own labor theory of value emerges. Like Marx's, her theory is concerned with the historicity of present relations of production. Her own effort, however, is a focused exposition of the various ways racial prejudice is tangled with the incentive structures and ideological practices of capitalist production, such that people are assessed a value that has little to do with their potential. This dimension to her argument becomes evident in her efforts to put her understanding of the labor theory of value in historical context.

Labor plays a complicated role for Cooper, coming into her analysis as both the means and the ends of value production. This perspective is evident in her comment that "the fundamental item" is "the question of material" and in her subsequent discussion of "the refining and enhancement of that material through labor.[109] In other words, humans are both the original material *and* the laborers who enhance that material. However, unlike Locke and Smith, Cooper does not imagine material as ever existing in a "pure" state prior to the labor conducted on it. As she puts it, we "all concede that no individual character receives its raw material newly created and independent of the rock from whence it was hewn."[110] She elaborates:

> The materials that go to make the man, the probabilities of his character and activities, the conditions and circumstances of his growth, and his quantum of resistance and mastery are the resultant of forces which have been accumulating and gathering momentum for generations.[111]

The cultivation of human material, she shows, is a multi-generational process. When discussing human worth, she argues, we cannot simply account for the worth of original material and then add the costs of production that go into it, simply because the production process is part of the story of the original worth of the material.

Instead, she explains, we must think historically. She writes: "rightly to estimate our material, then, it is necessary to go back of the twenty or thirty years during which we have been in possession, and find out the nature of the soil in which it has been forming and growing."[112] Because we do not all start out with the same amount of value bestowed to our raw material, she argues, we must assess our property but also its "history."[113] In this statement she shows that we need to account for histories of resource distribution as an integral part of thinking about the value of any particular form of human material. She is aware that this is not the dominant image of human potential. As she insists:

> Happier were it for him if he could begin life with nothing—an isolated but free man with no capital but his possibilities, with no past and no pedigree. And so it often is with men. These bodies of ours often come to us mortgaged to their full value by the extravagance, self-indulgence, sensuality of some ancestor.[114]

Though she admits that the image of material free of history, as in Locke's utopic state of nature, is compelling, the unfortunate reality of ancestry for human material makes this vision faulty. This is why she insists, as Marx does, that any measure of human worth that effectively accounts for history therefore cannot allow an image of a rational, solitary individual, upon which economism depends, that has any grounding.

Cooper's alternative is a historically grounded theory of value that positions racial prejudices rather than exchange at the center. Regarding Black people, she shows, value measurements have been conducted incorrectly.[115]

Describing "raw material," she claims that "certainly the original timber as it came from the African forests was good enough...whatever may be said of its beauty, then, the black side of the stream with us is pretty pure, and has no cause to blush for its honesty and integrity."[116] However, she argues, this soon changed with the advent of chattel slavery, as "the infusions of white blood that have come in many instances to the black race in this country," she glibly puts it in an inversion of anti-miscegenation talk, "are not the best that race afforded."[117] Obviously, "not the best" here is significantly toned down from what she truly has in mind, particularly since she is writing in the immediate aftermath of slavery, an institution in which rape and sexual violence conducted by white men against Black women was systematized. Here it is worth noting that Cooper's father was a slaveowner and her mother a slave, so it might very well be Cooper's father's "self-indulgence" she has in mind when she writes that ancestry delivers our bodies already fully mortgaged. She continues from this point with the comment that "if anything further is needed to account for racial irregularities—the warping and shrinking, the knotting and cracking of the sturdy old timber, the two hundred and fifty years of training here are quite sufficient to explain all."[118] "There is no doubt," she continues, "that the past two hundred and fifty years of working up the material we now inherit has depreciated rather than enhanced its value."[119] As she shows, the erosion of Black material through multi-generational experiences of chattel slavery is more than enough to account for present racial disparities.

Notably, those who put the most work into human material are Black women. Returning to Cooper's story of the newborn child who is worth, "unsentimentally and honestly," very little, Cooper importantly notes that it is the "infatuated mother" who values her child, and that this valuation is not merely sentimental—it is based in actual labor and toil.[120] She remarks:

> How anxiously does she hang over the lumpish little organism to catch the first awakening of a soul. And when the chubby little hands begin to swing consciously before the snapping eyes, and the great toe is caught and tugged towards the open mouth, when the little pink fists for the first time linger caressingly on her cheek and breast, and when the wide open eyes say distinctly "I know you, I love you,"—how she strains him to her bosom as her whole soul goes out to this newly found intelligence.[121]

Cooper describes the emotional and physical labor the mother undertakes in order to keep this child alive, but also, and perhaps more importantly, to help him store up capital. She elaborates:

> It is labor, development, training, careful, patient, painful, diligent toil took that must span the gulf between this vegetating life germ (now worth nothing but toil and care and trouble, and living purely

at the expense of another)...it is a heavy investment, requires a large
outlay of money on long time and large risk, no end of labor, skill,
pains.[122]

In other words, when Cooper discusses the ways we invest in other people, she is thinking of that investment as material, and as built upon the
invisible labor of women. For Cooper, historical disparities are evident
not only in the racialized investments made in human material, but also
in the gendered distribution of labor involved in working on said material. As she argues, it is Black women's labor that most consistently goes
unacknowledged.

The exclusion of Black women from efforts to correct these disparities
is a broader concern that animates Cooper's writing. For instance, in the
opening pages of the book, she details an array of problems that affect
women around the world differently according to race, class, and national
origin before turning to the feminist issues that she sees as quintessentially
American.[123] She then decries the unequal footing of women in society as
tantamount to the lack of progress in society as a whole, while critiquing
the double standards of feminist movements and the unequal application of
Christian virtues and moral codes. She ultimately argues that no issue is more
vital to the modern American polity than the liberation of Black women
from invisible experiences of discrimination.[124] In this way, Cooper's
own approach to the labor theory of value is less concerned with articulating universal foundations of political economy, and more focused on
exposing the ways Black Americans, and particularly Black women, have
been systemically undervalued.

From this perspective, some of Cooper's seemingly contradictory arguments can be understood as appearing to be contradictory only if they are
read with ahistorical assumptions, and without attention to inequality as
it is structured. Her arguments, moreover, engage rather than discard racialized discourses of value, with the distinct goal of improving the lives of
Black women. Warning that value is something often "acknowledged" and
showing that for Black people it in fact most often goes unacknowledged,
she also takes political economy's implicit project of identifying sources of
intrinsic value very seriously.[125] For instance, Cooper discusses how limited ways of conceptualizing economic growth have resulted in a devaluation of "[Black] creativity, and potential productivity."[126] For Cooper,
the limitations of narrowly construed economic growth are also in their
undervaluing of the accomplishments of Black women. Giving examples of
famous artists, she describes the work of Phillis Wheatley, and of Edmonia
Lewis, "the colored sculptress," and places them in the same company as
"the Shakespeares and Miltons, the Newtons, Galileos and Darwins" in
order to demonstrate the extent of their hidden contributions.[127]

Cooper's writing makes it abundantly clear that the standard means
of account are limited in their ability to capture the most important

dimensions of the human experience. Yet taking up these terms of debate, she shows us, is vital to any project of effectively revaluing Black life in the present. She therefore argues for economic investment in Black people and advocates labor unionization.[128] Cooper aims to revalue the contributions of Black people while simultaneously rejecting discourses that seek to quantify production—a double move evident in her argument that work and wealth must be generated before intellectual capacities can be vindicated.

Navigating the Valences of Value

Even though her essay is titled "What Are We Worth?" Cooper ultimately plays with the connections between racial equality and liberal narratives about progress, growth, and development more than she engages in a genuine project of accounting for the value of humans on the market through economistic means. Yet she is also critical of alternatives to economism and sees moral discourses of value as being just as driven by prejudice. In her response to canonical political-economic thought, she brings her argument full circle. Like the subjects she is describing, she is merely working with the material (in this case, a history of political-economic thought) that she has been given. However, absent the influence of such discourses, she shows, value would and should be considered in very different terms. Cooper's seemingly contradictory statements can therefore be read as responding to political–economic discourses *about* value from within a particular and pre-existing political economy *of* value.

Cooper's intervention shows the ways both discourses of value as they come together in the context of United States politics are complicit in racialized valuation. Yet even as values feed a culture of racialized discrimination, Cooper shows, revaluing Black life requires engagement with rather than disavowal of existing discourses of valuation. In this way, Cooper's perspective on political–economic discourse is ultimately ambivalent. She shows classical political-economic thought to have been actively involved in a patterned devaluation of Black women. As she demonstrates, this devaluation is not based in incidental neglect, but in structural exclusion. Her overall project is therefore to demonstrate the pervasion of racialized exploitation in political–economic discourse, identifiable even in the key concepts and language produced by the classical canon. However, Cooper herself does not cast aside these concepts. Instead, she actually treats their inheritance as an opportunity for reversing their pernicious effects—as she shows, some of the core assumptions of political-economic thought also present useful tools for intervening in and challenging contemporary racial disparities.

As Cooper exposes both economic and moral systems of valuation as failing to resolve systems of exploitation and oppression, her work anticipates a variety of uncomfortable convergences between these discourses and racial discrimination in the form of workfare, insurance premiums, redlining, and mortgage predation. She demonstrates the naïveté of seeking to prioritize one logic, such as in the argument that markets be treated as impartial, or conversely, in claims that capitalism simply be replaced by humanistic concerns. Cooper's account of these things reveals that value is always political rather than abstract. In showing both logics to be inadequate in valuing Black life, she demonstrates the limitations of providing technical solutions—whether moral or economic—to political problems. As she shows, political contestation precedes, or always expresses itself through economic or moral logics. Any decision about what is expedient, right, or just is therefore always a judgment about who is appropriately involved in such a decision.

Notes

1 LaRese Hubbard, "When and Where I Enter: Anna Julia Cooper, Afrocentric Theory, and Africana Studies," *Journal of Black Studies* 40, no. 2 (2009); "Anna Julia Cooper and Africana Womanism: Some Early Conceptual Contributions," *Black Women, Gender, + Families* 2, no. 4 (2010); and Shirley Moody-Turner and James Stewart, "Gendering Africana Studies: Insights from Anna Julia Cooper," *African American Review* 43, no. 1 (2009).

2 Saidiya Hartman, *Lose Your Mother: A Journey Along the Atlantic Slave Route* (New York NY: Farrar, Straus and Giroux, 2008).

3 Kathryn Belle (formerly Kathryn T. Gines), "Anna Julia Cooper," *Stanford Encyclopedia of Philosophy* (2015); "Black Feminism and Intersectional Analyses: A Defense of Intersectionality," *Philosophy Today* 55 (2011); and "Race Women, Race Men and Early Expressions of Proto-Intersectionality, 1830s–1930s," in Namita Goswami, Maeve M. O'Donovan, and Lisa Yount, eds, *Why Race and Gender Still Matter: An Intersectional Approach* (London UK: Pickering & Chatto (Publishers), 2014).

4 Lewis Gordon, "Anna Julia Cooper and the Problem of Value," in Lewis Gordon, ed., *An Introduction to Africana Philosophy* (Cambridge University Press, 2008), 69–73.

5 Leona C. Gabel, *From Slavery to the Sorbonne and Beyond: The Life and Writings of Anna J. Cooper* (Smith College Studies in History, 1982), and V. Thandi Sulé, "Intellectual Activism: The Praxis of Dr. Anna Julia Cooper as a Blueprint for Equity-Based Pedagogy," *Feminist Teacher* 23, no. 3 (2013).

6 Penny A. Weiss, *Canon Fodder: Historical Women Political Thinkers* (University Park PA: Pennsylvania State University Press, 2009).

7 Cooper's dissertation also explicitly challenged the racism of one of her own advisers. See Vivian May, *Anna Julia Cooper: Visionary Black Feminist* (New York NY: Routledge, 2007), and Charles Lemert, "Anna Julia Cooper: The Colored Woman's Office," in *The Voice of Anna Julia Cooper* (Lanham MD: Rowman and Littlefield Publishers, 1998).

8 May, *Anna Julia Cooper*, 2–3.

9 Cooper is also a controversial figure. Though she has been, as Shirley Moody-Turner describes it, "mythologized" or "valorized by some as the founding mother of black feminist thought," she has also been "dismissed for her ostensibly Victorian values and Christian moral code," and ironically, given the presumed propriety of these positions, even severely criticized for sexual deviance. Karen Baker-Fletcher, *A Singing Something: Womanist Reflections*

on Anna Julia Cooper (New York NY: The Crossroad Publishing Company, 1994), and Shirley Moody-Turner, "A Voice Beyond the South: Resituating the Locus of Cultural Representation in the Later Writings of Anna Julia Cooper," *African American Review* 43 (2009).

10 Baker-Fletcher, *A Singing Something*, and Janice W. Fernheimer, "Arguing from Difference: Cooper, Emerson, Guizot, and a More Harmonious America," in Kristin Waters and Carol B. Conaway, eds, *Black Women's Intellectual Traditions: Speaking Their Minds* (Burlington VT: University of Vermont Press, 2007); Kathy L. Glass, "Tending to the Roots: Anna Julia Cooper's Sociopolitical Thought and Activism," *Meridians* 6, no. 1 (2005). See also Vivian May, "Writing the Self into Being: Anna Julia Cooper's Textual Politics," *African American Review* 43, no. 1 (2009). As May writes, "moving from theology to economics to law to literature to history to education, Cooper refuses to be bound by discipline. Moreover, by bringing together analyses of the economy with literary, historical, legal, and theological discussions, Cooper teases out modes of thinking she not only finds troubling (such as objectivism, the use of false universals, or rigid binarisms) but also finds to be patterned or systemic across various discourses usually not engaged together. Tonally and syntactically, Cooper buttresses her analyses of the multifaceted and multidimensional nature of the self, of oppression, and of liberation politics." Ibid., 24.

11 Vivian May, "Thinking from the Margins, Acting at the Intersections: Anna Julia Cooper's A Voice from the South," *Hypatia* 19, no. 2 (2004), 75–76; Thomas Meagher, "Black Issues in Philosophy: On Teaching Anna Julia Cooper's 'What Are We Worth' in Introductory Courses," *American Philosophical Association*, May 30, 2018.

12 Weiss, *Canon Fodder*, 84.

13 Jane Anna Gordon, "Unmasking the *Big Bluff* of Legitimate Governance and So-Called Independence: Creolizing Rousseau through the Reflections of Anna Julia Cooper," *Critical Philosophy of Race* 6, no. 1 (2018), 11.

14 Fernheimer, "Arguing from Difference"; Gordon, "Unmasking the *Big Bluff*"; Gordon, "Anna Julia Cooper and the Problem of Value"; May, *Anna Julia Cooper*. Gordon describes this role of materialism in Cooper's writing most comprehensively. As Gordon explains, Cooper "disdained the complete obsession with monetary gain and profit that instrumentalized relations among human beings." At the same time, Cooper was unwilling to discount economic value entirely because, as Gordon writes, "Her political thinking was anchored by a paramount concern with how a community of *very* recently freed slaves could transform themselves into democratic citizens in a country that refused to recognize their massive contributions to the development of the nation as the result of their labor." Gordon, "Unmasking the *Big Bluff*," 26. Italics are Gordon's emphasis.

15 Ibid., 12, 15, and 19.

16 Gordon, "Anna Julia Cooper and the Problem of Value," 71–72.

17 May, "Writing the Self into Being."

18 Anna Julia Cooper, *A Voice from the South* (New York NY: Oxford University Press, 2008), 258.

19 Ibid., 254.

20 Cooper frequently and notably makes these points about the relationship between capitalism and racist valuations through direct accounts of personal experiences, a move that reminds readers that, as Elizabeth Alexander puts it, "she lives and moves within a physical body with sensations and needs." Elizabeth Alexander, "'We Must Be About Our Father's Business': Anna

Julia Cooper and the In-Corporation of the Nineteenth-Century African American Woman Intellectual," *Signs* 20, no. 2 (1995), 345. Brittney C. Cooper therefore describes Cooper's work as immersed in a "narrative of embodied discourse" in which Black women writers "demand the inclusion of their bodies...by placing them in the texts they write and speak." This effort fits in with a broader mode of feminist self-narration, and serves another purpose in this text, which is to challenge readers to think about the way we rate the value of people, whether by assessing the value of physical bodies or of particular subjectivities. Brittney C. Cooper, *Beyond Respectability: The Intellectual Thought of Race Women* (Champaign IL: University of Illinois Press, 2017), 39, 3.

21 Anna Julia Cooper, *Slavery and the French and Haitian Revolutionists* (Lanham MD: Rowman & Littlefield Publishers, 2006); Anna Julia Cooper, *The Voice of Anna Julia Cooper*, ed. Charles Lemert and Esme Bhan (Lanham MD: Rowman & Littlefield Publishers, 1998); and Gordon, "Unmasking the *Big Bluff.*"

22 Vivian May, "'It is Never a Question of the Slaves': Anna Julia Cooper's Challenge to History's Silences in Her 1925 Sorbonne Thesis," *Callaloo* 31, no. 3 (2008), 904.

23 Ibid., 914.

24 Ibid., 911. Cooper's Sorbonne thesis begins by describing the "shortsighted politics" of slavery that originated out of an avoidance of manual work, but were later expanded by Iberians due to the profitability of adding slaves to the mix of goods bought and sold along the African coasts. This trade, she shows, led to the growth and prominence of cities like Lisbon even before European encounters with the Americas. As Cooper demonstrates, after contact with the Americas, and once expanded to the colonies, an entire infrastructure was created around "this evil institution" that supplied "not only the needs of France but those of half of Europe." Cooper, *Slavery and the French*, 31.

25 Cooper, *Slavery and the French*, 32 and 43.

26 Ibid., 60.

27 Baker-Fletcher, *A Singing Something*.

28 Cooper is not the first to point out that market value is not the only kind of value. However, her way of handling the distinction employs a manner of thinking about race and discourses of value that enables us to make sense of how they operate today.

29 Such a two-pronged critique is quite common to Cooper's approach as part of her effort to point to "biases embedded in ostensibly impartial knowledge practices." See Vivian May, "Anna Julia Cooper's Philosophy of Resistance," *Philosophia Africana* 12, no. 1 (2009), 41.

30 Cooper, "A Voice from the South," 228.

31 Meagher, "Black Issues in Philosophy."

32 Cooper, "A Voice from the South," 228–229.

33 Ibid., 229.

34 Ibid., 228.

35 Ibid.

36 Ibid., 228–229. See also Cooper, *Slavery and the French*.

37 Ibid., 249.

38 Ibid., 273.

39 Ibid., 278–279 and 275–276.

40 Ibid., 281-282.

41 Ibid., emphasis in original.

42 Ibid., 242.

43 Ibid.

44 Ibid., 244.

45 Ibid., 242–243.

46 Ibid., 229.

47 Ibid.

48 Ibid., 231.

49 Ibid., 232.

50 Ibid., 230.

51 Ibid., 232.

52 Ibid., 228.

53 Ibid., 232.

54 Ibid.

55 Carolyn Cusick, "Anna Julia Cooper, Worth, and Public Intellectuals," *Philosophia Africana* 12, no. 1 (2009), 34–35.

56 Meagher, "Black Issues in Philosophy."

57 Ibid.

58 Cooper, "A Voice from the South," 242.

59 Ibid., 249.

60 It should be noted here that Cooper understands linguistic theory and research well enough to make this critique by identifying a linguistic impossibility. This representation, she explains, is obviously inaccurate because "the actual mechanics of speech regarding the pronunciation of consonants and vowels does not lend itself to the combination of a labial mute followed by a dental ('m' "d')." As quoted from "Negro's Dialect" by Moody-Turner, "A Voice Beyond the South," 60–62.

61 Cooper, *The Voice of Anna Julia Cooper*, 230. As she writes, these depictions assume that "a black man is not true black unless he says "am dat.'" However, she shows: "Much of the literary dialect such as 'dis am,' 'he am,' 'him am,' 'ob dis' and 'am dat' which our industrious press turns out by the scoop in its willingness to pander to popular taste for unsophisticated and 'colorful' native speech, would fall flat if held up thus to nature's mirror." Ibid., 241.

62 They, as she puts it, "amuse a nation of millionaires." Cooper, *The Voice of Anna Julia Cooper*, 246.

63 May, "Thinking from the Margins."

64 Ibid., 75, 77.

65 Ibid., 76-77.

66 Ibid., 21.

67 May, "Writing the Self into Being," 23.

68 May, "Thinking from the Margins," 75.

69 Fernheimer, "Arguing from Difference," 292 and 303.

70 In her own discussion of mattering, Cooper anticipates how the language of mattering highlights the political qualities of value—a point I will return to when I discuss the Black Lives Matter movement in Chapter 6.

71 Locke puts the latter point as follows: "The Earth, and all that is therein, is given to Men for the Support and Comfort of their being. And though all the Fruits it naturally produces, and Beasts it feeds, belong to Mankind in common, as they are produced by the spontaneous hand of Nature; and no body has originally a private Dominion, exclusive of the rest of Mankind." However, as he continues, "being given for the use of Men, there must of necessity be a means to appropriate them some way or other before they can be of any use." John Locke, *Two Treatises of Government* (Cambridge University Press, 1960), 286.

72 Cooper, "A Voice from the South," 236. On the note about future anxiety, see Emily Nacol, *An Age of Risk: Politics and Economy in Early Modern Britain* (Princeton University Press, 2016).

73 Constantine George Caffentzis, *Clipped Coins, Abused Words, and Civil Government: John Locke's Philosophy of Money* (Brooklyn NY: Autonomedia, 1989).

74 Cooper, "A Voice from the South," 240–241. She even comments that the "second item of value" after material is typically assumed to be labor, but that labor is actually "the most important item."

75 Nancy J. Hirschmann and Kirstie M. McClure, eds., *Feminist Interpretations of John Locke* (University Park PA: The Pennsylvania State University Press, 2007).

76 Cooper, "A Voice from the South," 245.

77 Ibid., 246.

78 Ibid., 261.

79 Ibid., 249, emphasis in original.

80 Ibid.

81 Ibid., 240, emphasis in original.

82 On the point about the ahistorical quality to this image, see Vanita Seth, *Europe's Indians: Producing Racial Difference, 1500–1900* (Durham NC: Duke University Press, 2010).

83 James Tully, *A Discourse on Property: John Locke and his Adversaries* (Cambridge University Press, 1980).

84 Cooper, "A Voice from the South," 238.

85 Ibid., 236.

86 Ibid.

87 This argument in many ways anticipates later intersections of critical race studies and critical legal studies, such as in Patricia Williams, "On Being the Object of Property," *Signs* 14, no.1 (1988).

88 For critical discussions of Smith's theory of the price system, see Mike Hill and Warren Montag, *The Other Adam Smith* (Stanford University Press, 2015); Emma Rothschild, "Adam Smith and Conservative Economics," *The Economic History Review* 45, no. 1 (1992); and David Winch, *Adam Smith's Politics: An Essay in Historiographic Revision* (Cambridge University Press 1978).

89 Adam Smith, *The Theory of Moral Sentiments* (Cambridge University Press, 2002), IV.i.1–3.

90 Ibid.

91 Cooper, "A Voice from the South," 233, emphasis added.

92 Ibid., 233–234.

93 Ibid., 234.

94 This argument resonates with her broader project of critiquing objectivism in its myriad forms, from her response to Comte's positivism to her arguments against early forms of standardized testing, and her arguments for the importance of subjectivism in both education and politics. See Stephanie Y. Evans, *Black Women in the Ivory Tower, 1850–1954: An Intellectual History* (Gainesville FL: University Press of Florida, 2007), 128, and May, "Thinking from the Margins."

95 Ibid. The reference to the connection between consumption, growth, and Smith's trouble with time is not made in passing. Cooper also talks of value "wasted" through circumstance, and of letting human worth "grow" in a variety of gardening metaphors. Ibid., 258. This is a striking response to Malthusian discourses about the limits to growth—which were themselves deeply connected to anxieties about the value of particular populations. On Malthus, see Catherine Gallagher, "The Body Versus the Social Body in the Works of Thomas Malthus and Henry Mayhew," *Representations* no. 14 (1986). In this way, Cooper's thinking has also been characterized as Aristotelian both in its emphasis on humans as always "evolving, perfecting, and

maturing" and because of her focus on the importance of shifting value discourses from "having to doing." Carol Wayne White, "One and All: Anna Julia Cooper's Romantic Feminist Vision," *Philosophia Africana* 12, no. 1 (2009), 97, and Cusick, "Anna Julia Cooper," 35. As Wayne White further notes, Cooper's use of naturalistic imagery underscores her belief in the inherent value of all people. Carol Wayne White, "Anna Julia Cooper: Radical Relationality and the Ethics of Interdependence," in Melvin L. Rogers and Jack Turner, eds., *African American Political Thought* (University of Chicago Press, 2021).

96 Cooper, "A Voice from the South," 240.

97 Ibid., 240, 273.

98 On the point about Mandeville, see Istvan Hont and Michael Ignatieff, "Needs and Justice in the Wealth of Nations," in Istvan Hont and Michael Ignatieff, eds., *Wealth and Virtue: The Shaping of Political Economy in the Scottish Enlightenment* (New York NY: Cambridge University Press, 1983). On Smith's own reservations, see Dean Mathiowetz, "Feeling Luxury: Invidious Political Pleasures and the Sense of Touch," *Theory & Event* 13, no. 4 (2010).

99 Cooper, "A Voice from the South," 272.

100 Ibid., emphasis in original.

101 Ibid., 247.

102 Ibid., 36–37, 58, and 65.

103 Ibid., 265–266.

104 Ibid., 265.

105 Ibid., 257.

106 Ibid., 263–264.

107 Mathiowetz, "Feeling Luxury," 12.

108 Cooper, "A Voice from the South," 269.

109 Ibid., 234. Cooper, according to Cusick, "does something very interesting and important in valuing labor. She uses the term 'labor' in two ways: first, as the general working of raw material, and second as the more specific term for a job that is manual. Making use of this double entendre, Cooper demands a revaluation of manual labor in spite of its connections to slavery." Cusick, "Anna Julia Cooper," 33.

110 Cooper, "A Voice from the South," 234.

111 Ibid., 235. It is certainly no accident that this line bears an unmistakable resemblance to Marx's's discussion of the objectification of the worker and the process of estrangement in his *Economic and Philosophic Manuscripts of 1844*. Karl Marx, "Economic and Philosophic Manuscripts of 1844," in Robert C. Tucker, ed., *The Marx-Engels Reader 2nd Edition* (W.W. Norton & Company, 1978), 72.

112 Cooper, "A Voice from the South," 236.

113 Ibid., 238.

114 Ibid., 236–237.

115 Lewis Gordon reads Cooper's discussion as "an efficiency theory of human worth," in which we measure people's achievements against their potential with adjustments made for their differential situations and constraints. He suggests that this is the basis for some of her feminist arguments, which point out that women have more work to do than men, since they produce children, and must therefore be assessed with that disparity in mind. Gordon, "Anna Julia Cooper," 72. Many of Cooper's comments comport with this conclusion. For instance, her suggestion that "a man is to be praised primarily not for having inherited fine tools and faultless materials but for making the most of the stuff he has, and doing his best in spite of disadvantages

and poor material" employs this efficiency theory of value quite directly. Cooper, "A Voice from the South," 240. However, Cooper's point also goes beyond this effort, as she is focused on determining the exact means and outcomes of measuring human worth on an individual level, but perhaps even more so on displaying the idiosyncrasies involved in even thinking in such terms. As she shows, the ship of value has already sailed, and these judgments had already been made long ago.

116 Cooper, A Voice from the South," 238.
117 Ibid.
118 Ibid., 239.
119 Ibid., 239–240.
120 Ibid., 242.
121 Ibid., 243.
122 Ibid., 244.
123 Ibid., 12.
124 Ibid., 14, 21, 27, 33, and 91.
125 Ibid., 285.
126 White, "One and All," 96 and 88. On the importance of art, Cooper writes that "there are other hungerings in man besides the eternal all-subduing hungering of his despotic stomach." Cooper, "A Voice from the South," 257.
127 Cooper, "A Voice from the South," 274–276.
128 Ibid., 251–252 and 256–257. Echoing Aristotle's discussions of leisure and freedom, she comments that "work must first create wealth, and wealth leisure, before the untrammeled intellect of the Negro, or any other race, can truly vindicate its capacities." Ibid., 261.

5 Michael Warner and the Values of Public Sexual Culture

Understanding value as political is crucial for understanding queer and trans experiences of marginalization. For queer and trans people, an absence of valuation is felt in disproportionate challenges in housing and healthcare access, heightened vulnerability to mental illness, and higher risks of violence and suicide. The AIDS epidemic represented a devaluation of queer life on a massive scale. Even the experience of shame is an internalization of societal devaluation of queer forms of life. All these examples show that there are pervasive market forces and moral priorities invested in devaluing queer life and livelihoods.[1]

My perspective in this chapter builds upon Chapter 4's argument that political devaluation is a key feature of oppression. Specifically, I extend my argument that the modern splitting of value discourse into moral and economic logics has meant that the presumed neutral language of market mechanisms hides political projects of valuing some lives over others. Yet I also develop my argument that the politics of value contains resources for realizing equality for oppressed communities. While in Chapter 4 I followed Cooper's efforts to draw moral and economic discourses of value together, in this chapter I pry them apart to see what each discourse separately offers as a democratic political tool.

Throughout this book I have argued that although value is typically understood either in economic terms, or as moral or ethical, we need to think about value foremost, and even primarily, as political. In this chapter, I discuss the tension in value discourses between material and aspirational life and address the ways this tension enables political thinkers to mobilize the language of value and values to define a body politic. My ultimate argument is that the language of value and values enables very different representations of human relationships to the material world, with implications for the ways we understand and structure culture around such things as desire, identity, and economic distribution. In this chapter, I show that these representations are present in debates about queer politics, and I show that they pertain to how we imagine and normalize particular boundaries around the essential activities of politics. I argue that looking at queer devaluation is important for thinking about how the politics of value work, and the particular ways the language of

DOI: 10.4324/9781003304302-5

value and values can be used for both anti-democratic and democratic political projects.

To make this argument, I look at how the relationships between different valences of value play out in the terrain of queer activism. I do so by looking at Michael Warner's discussions of the importance of revaluing queer life in his writing on late twentieth-century New York City zoning policy in his *The Trouble with Normal: Sex, Politics, and the Ethics of Queer Life* [1999]. In this text, Warner argues that queer communities should refocus activism away from gay marriage to claiming and transforming public space and promoting cultures of sex positivity. I show that his argument also relies on a contradictory imagination of politics as based both in ongoing contestation over economic resources and in a practice of aspirational thinking about alternative ways economic resources could be produced and distributed. Warner, I show, writes about the oppressive politics of normalization and homogeneity. While doing so, he implicitly draws from value discourse. At times he adheres to a strict understanding of value as material, and at other times he treats it as aspirational. This equivocation leads Warner to make a claim about politics that both opens up possibilities for transforming sexual culture in the United States and challenges activists to think carefully about which queer communities should be prioritized.

Warner's effort resonates with a number of broader efforts in the late twentieth century to focus queer activism on access to things such as healthcare, jobs, and housing over legal equality in the military and in marriage.[2] Several scholars and activists have advanced arguments about the ways seeking equality in institutions like marriage can be both a distraction from and a detriment to the cause of queer liberation. Like Warner, these critics of the fight for marriage equality argue that successes in achieving formal legal equality can conceal ongoing and deeper types of marginalization. The concern here is that mainstream activism has consistently ignored the issues of most importance to marginalized members of LGBTQIA+ communities, such as employment, access to health and legal resources, violence, and trans coalitional support and empowerment.[3]

At the same time, there are numerous issues with the uncomplicated idealization of queer spaces, cultures, and communities to which Warner defaults. Some have argued that Warner's argument is incomplete even by his own standards—that advocacy for marriage effectively resists normalization by centering the politics of gay love.[4] Other scholars have pointed out that an uncritical championing of queer cultures conceals the fact that queer communities are treated as "by default white."[5] Although queer and trans people have been marginalized by society at large, a growing literature has shown that people of color and their experiences have been consistently devalued within queer communities and scholarship.[6] Others have even argued that the very idealization of the queer erotic rests upon uneasy material histories of colonialism and racial fetishism.[7] The potential of Warner's queer theory, then, depends upon its ability to challenge what Kai Green calls "heteronormative valuations of knowledge production"[8] without re-entrenching other hierarchies such as race and gender.

I show that Warner's successes in reframing queer activism around issues of substantive justice, as well as his failures in intersectionality, can both be understood in relation to the complications presented by different discourses of value. My argument in what follows has three parts. First, I outline Michael Warner's theorizing on the politics of gay marriage and public sexual culture and its relevance to present-day queer activism. Next, I argue that his writing surfaces the tensions within the value discourses that I have drawn out. Finally, I show that the tension in his writing between different discourses of value has at stake how queerness is defined, including which people, experiences, and activities are prioritized.

Warner and the Trouble with Normalization

Michael Warner, a Yale University professor of English literature and a queer theorist, is best known for his writings on the politics of sexual shame and gay marriage. In his *The Trouble with Normal: Sex, Politics, and the Ethics of Queer Life* [1999], Warner outlines a radical critique of the movement for gay marriage, arguing that attaining access to this exclusive institution abandons the politics of sexual freedom in favor of a politics of normalization.[9] Validating an intrinsically exclusive institution, he argues, comes at the expense of actual queerness, and also enacts further discrimination against the most marginalized people in queer communities. Warner thus frames the majority of the book as an argument against the agenda of attaining rights to marriage, while offering a blueprint for how to value queer life and livelihoods without homogenizing identity.

In the wake of the United States Supreme Court ruling in favor of the right to marry for same-gender couples in its landmark 2015 decision *Obergefell vs. Hodges*, Warner's argument against investment in the same-gender marriage fight is now outdated. Yet his broader points about the ways fights for rights and inclusion can still contribute to normalization and shame should not be forgotten. Warner wrote at the turn of the twenty-first century to urge an alternative agenda for gay and lesbian advocacy—namely one that avoided the homogenizing tendency he saw in the fight for same-sex marriage. Some of the relevant issues Warner identifies along the way, such as sexual health and safety, continue to be significant challenges for gay communities. Other ongoing struggles that he does not necessarily anticipate, such as activism to create trans- and nonbinary-inclusive norms as well as efforts to address issues like bisexual erasure and asexual infantilization, all have at stake achieving success in fights for legal protections in schools, workplaces, and other public places without incidentally contributing to a politics of homogenization, normativity, and shame. Because Warner theorizes how legal victories can have all these unintended and troubling consequences, his writing continues to offer an important warning that these efforts must heed.

Much of Warner's argument about homonormativity, however, is directed at the specific institution of marriage.[10] Like many critics of gay marriage, Warner sees marriage as a fundamentally straight way of existing, and fears that success in the gay marriage fight could enforce conformity to straight cultural norms. This is why he argues that attaining access to marriage abandons a queer politics of sexual freedom in favor of a politics of exclusion and normalization.[11] In its implicit morality of sexual privacy, he shows, the institution of marriage excludes many queer people, accepting only those who find themselves in same-sex, monogamous, committed relationships.[12]

Warner's main issue is with the ethics of normalization, represented by the institution of marriage. Drawing from a significant literature on the politics of sexual shame, Warner argues that the fight for marriage equality perpetuates rather than resolves the problem of shame.[13] Marriage, Warner shows, is a public activity, and it is one that requires conformity to a particular understanding of what counts publicly as private.[14] As he writes, "marrying makes your desire private, names its object, locates it in an already formed partnership."[15] The institution of marriage contributes to what he describes as the "shaming effects of isolation" because it shuns the diversity of forms of desire and intimacy in favor of one particular form.[16] This is why Warner frames his discussion as a challenge to the problem of sexual norms, and their accompanying "politics of sexual shame."[17] But arguments for gay marriage, he claims, either attempt to release only those who marry from shame and stigma, or else deny that the institution of marriage is connected to shame and stigma at all.[18] Doing so, he shows, the mass media and elite members of the queer community who focus their advocacy on gay marriage enact what he describes as "an implicit devaluation of sexuality."[19] By contrast, Warner demonstrates that in queer circles sex is understood to be diverse, and deviations from straight norms are celebrated rather than erased.[20]

Warner importantly also critiques the history of economic exchange behind the institution of marriage.[21] Marriage, after all, has historically been a way of transferring and consolidating property. That property, as I showed in Chapter 3, has historically been not only possessions but also persons, as property rights over women were consolidated via arranged marriages and dowry payments. Warner reminds readers that the field of struggle over marriage equality is still marred by these exclusions. As he shows, the existence of various legal privileges that come with being married, including, for instance, tax incentives, medical decision-making, insurance, inheritance, wrongful death actions, and hospital visitation, are only accessible to those who get married.[22] Warner notes that marriage equality advocates argue that this is precisely the reason to organize around gay marriage; to which he responds that not all queer people find themselves in long-term, monogamous relationships, and so remain excluded from social benefits that all persons should have.[23] He does not offer a vision of other ways that such privileges and rights could be extended or attached to people who couple or form intimacies differently, simply because he sees rights and privileges as necessarily exclusive.

Warner's critique of the fight for gay marriage thus focuses both on its implicit moral values of normalization, understood as the idea that there should be a narrow set of ways that people reproduce themselves and their society, and marriage's material values in exclusive property rights. To explore the dynamic role of these discourses of value in his writing, one must first situate these arguments within Warner's intended political project. Fitting with his critique of marriage, much of Warner's book is targeted at the contemporaneous gay establishment, led by organizations such as the Human Rights Campaign, and by pundits and activists like Andrew Sullivan and Evan Wolfson. The book is written as a manifesto for a sex-positive culture in defiance of the dominant heteronormative, marriage-sanctified, state culture of sex in America.

But in the final substantive chapter of this text, Warner outlines an alternative vision for queer advocacy, in an extended discussion of New York City's zoning politics and policy. In this chapter, Warner's response to national-level queer activists is to argue that queer communities should fight against the "devaluation of sexuality" by valorizing queer cultures. This alternative means deprioritizing marriage equality efforts and instead prioritizing some of the most important frontiers in queer advocacy, such as sexual health and safety, community-building, and visibility. Reading Warner's political vision as articulated in this chapter, I show that rather than defer exclusively to value's economic or moral expressions, he keeps the tension between the different senses of value very much alive in his discussion of the role of value and values in urban zoning politics.

New York City Zoning and Queer Activism

Warner decries 1990s zoning policies inaugurated by then–Mayor Rudy Giuliani that shuttered gay establishments in neighborhoods like the West Village. As Warner recounts, Giuliani had declared that he would "clean up" New York City, using the AIDS crisis in particular as a pretext for these policies. Warner's response focuses on "the effects of Mayor Rudy Giuliani's new zoning law limiting 'adult establishments,'" a law that Warner writes "has already allowed the city to padlock dozens of stores and clubs, including a gay bookstore."[24] Looking to the way that Warner presents his account of these changes, however, brings into view the diverse ways value discourses appear in his writing.

Right away in Warner's response to Giuliani's efforts, discourses of value and values can be seen to play an important role in urban zoning laws. Discussing the fallout of these policies on NYC's gay strip on Christopher

Street, Warner notes a transformation in the production and circulation of economic value. Where once a visitor could find a variety of what Warner called "gay merchandise," including sex toys and sex literature proudly displayed in window fronts, Warner describes the "surreal scene" caused by their replacement with a vacant wasteland. He writes that this change was the result of a new law intended to crack down on "adult establishments."[25]

> Along Christopher Street, you can tell immediately that something is wrong. In Harmony Video, for years one of the principal porn stores in New York's most legendary gay strip, they now display $3.95 videos of football games, John Wayne movies, and music videos by the fundamentalist pop singer Amy Grant.[26]

As a reader, one is immediately drawn from the questions of rights and equality that Warner had tackled throughout most of the book in his discussions of the gay marriage debate, and into the world of shops, sales, and merchandise. This transition marks a shift from moral values to the production and circulation of economic value. Yet he also demonstrates a subtle shift in priorities via his mention of football games and John Wayne movies—merchandise that connotes a very different grouping of priorities.

Positioning the recent changes as part of a Giuliani's targeted crackdowns on urban access for queer people, Warner draws readers' attention to other, similar scenes in New York of queer stores having to sell their merchandise undercover, changing ownership, or else closing down entirely.[27] Of course, Warner does not limit his concern to this one street, or even to New York City. Instead, he uses the specific politics of this street to add texture to the politics of devaluation that he sees playing out in a variety of spaces—local, national, and even global. Though his examples are drawn from 1990s New York City, he shows similar developments to be happening across the country and around the world. He writes, "the effects of the zoning law are [also] felt" across town, at a sex toy store opened by two lesbian entrepreneurs from Seattle. Telling this story, he explains:

> Clare Cavanaugh, one of the owners, told me that they are watching court rulings with a wary eye. (Sex toys are among the gray areas of the law.) In Seattle, their store has a large glass display window, lending queer visibility to the street and the neighborhood. In New York, the display windows stay empty, with nothing but discreetly drawn curtains.... In Seattle, the store features a large selection of lesbian porn. In New York, the owners feel too unsafe to stock any.[28]

The drawing of the curtains affirms Giuliani's view that what is for sale should be hidden. Warner shows that these measures are taken by queer shop owners as a response to violence, as he also laments the closing of gay bars across Manhattan following police raids. The few locales that remain, he writes, are so conservative that patrons describe them as being "in a gay bar trying to act straight."[29] From these examples, Warner concludes that "all over New York, in fact, a pall hangs over the public life of queers."[30] Warner, in other words, sees Giuliani's removal of queer merchandise as an essential part of a broader effort at queer erasure.

Warner laments the destruction of Christopher Street by these zoning laws, yet he argues that Christopher Street's importance goes beyond the economic value of goods formerly bought and sold in its shops. The importance of these places for him is also in the value produced for queer communities by enabling particular cultural practices, and especially as a mecca for cruising. The presence of these former shops, he explains, meant that queer people could flock to the strip to eat and drink un-harassed and to seek sex or companionship along the waterfront.[31] Even those not interested in cruising, he argues, could window shop, wander the waterfront, and simply be themselves without the fear of harassment. The stores, in other words, contributed to the creation of a public space, as they provided safety and community in addition to merchandise.

While it follows logically that Warner would have simply opposed Giuliani's moralism around driving out the gay culture of the West Village, Warner argues counterintuitively that the changes were the result of the "aggressive demand of market capital," not just homophobia.[32] This demand, he writes, was met in several waves: first in real estate development, then in tourism, then in an increased police presence, and finally in Mayor Giuliani's zoning laws.[33] In fact, he explains, these laws were justified (if inaccurately) by Giuliani as the unfortunate fallout of the "low" and "falling property values" that living next door to a property associated with sex created, and this is why Giuliani saw the laws as a contribution to general "decency" and to improving the "quality of life" in New York City.[34] These zoning laws, Warner shows, are particularly insidious because they were carried out not only in the name of urban revitalization and economic growth (i.e., value), but also in an explicit rejection of the *values* of self-expression and diversity in favor of the values of "decency."[35] As Warner's writing reveals, Giuliani drew upon economic and moral rationales for this policy—citing both property values and decency (oftentimes framed in terms of "cleanliness") as reasons for shutting stores.

Giuliani apparently saw these two logics as completely complementary. As Warner argues, these logics came together quite neatly in marginalizing queer people and sex positivity, even when they were deployed by queer activists. Warner shows national-level gay rights organizations to similarly combine a moral justification (normalization or assimilation) with an exclusionary means of distributing economic value. Implicating gay rights activists in Giuliani's agenda, he writes:

> The current conditions in New York vividly illustrate what happens when national and international forces push the expansion of the

market at the expense of public space and public autonomy, while at the same time lesbian and gay organizations decide that privacy and normalization are their goals.[36]

The culmination of these two forces is no accident to Warner. Indeed, he indicates that other members of the queer community have accepted a set of values that are not homophobic per se, but that are nevertheless exclusionary to queer people and queer lives through their material consequences. Revealing the queer community to be deeply divided in its values, he writes that "the erosion of public sexual culture, including its nonnormative intimacies is too often cheered by lesbian and gay advocates" who, he writes, "embrace a politics of privatization that offers them both property value and an affirmation of identity in a language of respectability and mainstream acceptance."[37] This is why Christopher Street has been altered beyond recognition, he argues—it is because these changes were met with complacency and oftentimes enthusiasm from members of the gay community who saw no reason to "romanticize" or "be nostalgic" about the West Village.[38]

Warner's argument is twofold. First, he claims that national gay rights organizations have focused on accruing the wrong value (property rights sanctioned by marriage) and the wrong values (normalization), while ignoring the way market forces have devalued Christopher Street's material culture. Second, his argument is also that the market forces that drive urban renewal, and in this case, the devaluation of queer merchandise, are especially dangerous when they are guided by moralizing discourses that devalue already marginalized people. By drawing out this argument, he exposes equivocations between different sets of values, but also between dominant standards of value, sterilized in the image of "market value," and the diverse cultural values of the queer community. Warner's response is to follow a similar formulation and settle on the importance of Christopher Street's queer strip by arguing that its economic benefits (its value) should be aligned with queer cultural priorities (values). Replacing erotica with pop videos in the name of what Giuliani called "decency," Warner explains, is also a rejection of the values of diverse self-expression and community; and these values of diverse self-expression and community, he argues, rely on the visibility of queer culture in everything from pride parades to lesbian bookstores.

Warner's Divergent Values

This chapter about New York City nightlife contains a key shift in Warner's argument, as he develops a case for an alternative set of values to unite queer communities. Warner's alternative values in community-building, visibility, and diversity put the life of Christopher Street and the space of commercial culture into relationship with each other. The importance of

Christopher Street, for Warner, is not just in the economic value produced and circulating in its sex shops and bookstores, but also in the cultural value produced by the flocking of the queer community to the strip to eat and drink, and to the waterfront to cruise.[39] This presence of economic value is why he argues that this privatization and relocation of queer real estate to Chelsea entails a "real loss" for queer communities.[40] As he writes: "one problem with this view [that relocation is not a loss] is that Chelsea has no noncommercial public space to match the old piers at the end of Christopher."[41] Just as economic and moral values are together mobilized to devalue the queer cultures created on Christopher Street, Warner shows, the value and values of sex-positive queer cultures go hand in hand. Activism against the privatization of Christopher Street, he argues, is also activism in favor of a culture in which sex is treated as something to celebrate, rather than to hide behind the closed doors of marriage. As he shows, these same doors form a barrier between the isolation of the closet and its "uncertainty and fear," and the pleasure of being part of a visible community.[42]

These points about safety and community are essential to Warner's argument for alternative values. As he shows, Giuliani's laws are also accompanied by public health campaigns that inhibit safer sex measures, enact policing of cruising spaces, and constrain access to public space by placing heavy restrictions on adult businesses.[43] Despite the claim to be promoting public health and safety, he argues, AIDS activism is actually "endangered by a new politics of privatization."[44] The politics of privatization, he writes, "share the desire to make sex less noticeable in the course of everyday urban life and more difficult to find for those who want sexual materials."[45] The concerning result of these policies, for Warner, is that "sex has gone undercover. The consequence seems to have been the nearly perfect obliteration of a visible culture of safer sex."[46] As Warner writes, "peep shows, masturbation, and porn consumption are, above all, safe. Porn stores are among the leading vendors of condoms and lube."[47] Politics that prevent the "circulation and accessibility of sexual knowledge," he shows, also contribute to the marginalization of queer lives and culture.[48]

His alternative *values* are, in other words, underpinned by *value* for the queer community because of the way they facilitate safety. Indeed, even the merchandise sold in Christopher Street's stores, Warner adds, has value beyond helping generate sexual pleasure and a livelihood for shopkeepers— these stores and venues also provide the education and materials necessary to enjoy sex safely. As he writes,

[T]he availability of explicit sexual materials, theaters, and clubs… is how we have learned to find one another, to construct a sense of a shared world, to carve out spaces of our own in a homophobic world, and since 1983, to cultivate a collective ethos of safer sex.[49]

With these new zoning changes in place, Warner writes,

> [T]hose who want sexual materials or men who want to meet other men will have to travel to small, inaccessible, little-trafficked, badly lit areas, mostly on the waterfront, where heterosexual porn users will also be relocated, where risk of violence will consequently be higher and the sense of a collective world more tenuous.[50]

These changes, he notes, go against the advisement of experts who work in AIDS prevention.[51]

Warner also argues that a public sexual culture has value that goes beyond sexual safety. Valuing public cultures of sex, he shows, would restore, rather than threaten, meaningful privacy and intimacy, by facilitating a diverse array of relationships and forms of self-expression.[52] Through public sex, he explains, people are able to learn not only "the elaborated codes of a subculture...but also simply the improvisational nature of unpredicted situations" and "the pleasure of belonging to a sexual world."[53] Warner further argues that despite the persistence of "the naïve belief that sex is simply an inborn instinct," in reality, "most gay men and lesbians know that the sex they have was not innate nor entirely of their own making, but *learned*—learned by participating."[54] Elaborating upon this point, he notes that "a public sexual culture...changes the nature of sex, much as a public intellectual culture changes the nature of thought."[55] By this, he means that desires are not privately experienced and then perhaps publicly expressed, but rather are constantly shaped through shared cultural production.

As Warner shows, albeit more incidentally than intentionally, real flows of economic resources (value) are necessary for moral visions (values) to be fully understood, let alone actualized. Realizing the benefits of a public sexual culture, by which he means not only waterfront hookups, but also the visibility of sexuality in queer bookstores, gay bars, free condoms, etc., is nearly impossible without actual traces of sex and sexuality in public spaces. But even as he proposes a realignment of values within the queer community, Warner shows that any vision of moral values must be enacted through a claim to economic value. He asks: "will our position be justified on First Amendment, civil liberties grounds or on more substantive grounds about the benefits of public sexual culture"?[56] Here, he contrasts the values of free speech and civil liberties with the value of Christopher Street's material culture. To the extent that a public sexual culture is a material culture, he is juxtaposing abstract rights and ideals with concrete productions of economic value.

This point about the material culture of Christopher Street is essential to Warner's argument, since it hinges on the claim that queer shops make transformations of American sexual culture both tangible and imaginable. The loss of queer values, Warner argues, cannot be remedied without keeping the sex shops in business. As he glibly puts it, "the trannies are not going to hang out at Banana Republic."[57] His use of a derogatory term and easy stereotyping of trans culture are a problematic element that I will address later, but his broader attempt to point out that the priority issues for some of the most vulnerable populations in queer communities require an open sexual culture is an important one. The point of his argument that trans people will not hang out at Banana Republic is that if Christopher Street's shops do not exist, they will have nowhere else to go. In this way, Warner shows moral and economic discourses of value to be inextricably connected to processes of dividing and bounding the public. Doing so, Warner makes a compelling case that the moral benefits of public sexual culture exceed the moral benefits of marriage, and that some of the ways they do this are by protecting the lives of those vulnerable to AIDS, those whose lives and relationships do not fit the instituted confines of marriage, and the most precariously positioned members of queer communities.

Sorting Warner's Values

To the extent that his writing tends to the question of the relationship between economic value and moral values and so focuses on the political exclusions that have affected queer people, Warner wrestles with the political dimensions of value. However, hidden within his argument is a productive tension between value and values that I argue a democratic politics needs to retain. While Warner sees both moral and economic value(s) as directed against queer culture, he also holds out space for a set of values that prioritize queer lives, and an organization of value that reflects this priority. Warner's argument demonstrates that alternative values can be hard to imagine, let alone realize, without material transformation. For instance, he notes that moral principles have been hard to marshal in the face of an incentive structure that perpetuates a politics of sexual shame, division, and alienation.[58] His Marxian influences show through on this point. At the same time, he is unwilling to let go of the aspirational perspective on values as something that we can decide, because to do so would be to assume that he and likeminded citizens cannot imagine ways of life that do not cohere with present material conditions. That there is now a significant industry around cultivating and catering to gay consumers, despite Warner's evidence that market capital at one point drove gays out of the West Village, is in fact a testament to the ways that shifting valuation of particular communities drives, rather than just follows, particular demands.

Warner's writing thus foregrounds a complex dialectical relationship between value and values. This dialectical relationship is visible in the language Warner uses to criticize Giuliani's bill. Giuliani's language about rezoning Christopher Street to improve the "quality of life" posits the elimination of queer businesses as an act of moral decency. But Warner also exposes some contradictions in Giuliani's use of moral discourse. As Warner shows, this language of "quality" is an ideological construction that actually devalues queer life. He writes:

> There is a circularity in this rhetoric, since it serves to reinforce the disrepute of adult businesses and therefore helps to bring about the depression of property value that it appears to lament.[59]

By this, Warner means that Giuliani's moralizing about the "indecency" of queer culture signals developers and city service providers to avoid queer neighborhoods. In the same way that redlining Black communities has historically relied on newspapers and property owners inflaming racialized fears, Warner shows that Giuliani's moral vision fulfills its own economic prophecy.

As Warner further argues, Giuliani's language of "quality" conceals disagreement on what it would mean to improve the quality of life.[60] As he writes:

> The assumption of unanimity behind the phrase "quality of life" produces its own kind of shame…the rhetoric of "quality of life" tries to isolate porn from political culture by pretending that there are no differences *of value or opinion* in it, that it therefore does not belong in the public sphere of critical exchange and opinion formation.[61]

The implication in Warner's use of the word "opinion" as complementary or at least adjacent to value in this sentence implies that he believes that values are not necessarily self-evident, that they are always up for debate, and thus also contingent.

This perspective importantly drives Warner's case for an alternative set of values to unite the queer movement. These values come through in his argument that "there is very little sense in this country that a public culture of sex might be something to value, something whose accessibility is to be protected."[62] To address this issue, Warner calls for a "principled defense of a public culture of sex." [63] As he argues, "the fact that public sex is not the statistical norm ought to have nothing to do with its *value or its morality.*"[64] Or, as he also puts it, "a public sexual culture is not just a civil liberty…but a good thing." [65] This language of moral value as a principle or good to protect implies that moral values can be adopted even at the exclusion of economic value. The implication in this language is that one can hold a principle or belief about the virtue of a lifestyle regardless of whether it is profitable to do so. A variety of people who might never need or enjoy Christopher Street's nightlife should work to preserve it simply because it is the right thing to do.

On the one hand, Warner's writing reveals that a certain amount of economic activity is necessary for us to even know what sorts of values we might hold. We need the nightlife of Christopher Street, he argues, in order to understand its role in community-building. On the other hand, he is unwilling to let go of the view that values are something we can decide to prioritize, even if such priorities go against compelling economic incentives—in this case, the property values associated with marriage—and even if we lack the experience of living out such values. His writing therefore shows the dangers of existing sexual repression, and in this way it is a diagnostic or even materialist project. Yet it still articulates an alternative vision for queer activism and is thus an imaginative or aspirational one.

Consequently, Warner implicitly challenges conventional understandings of value. For instance, liberalism treats value as a matter of free choice absent any monetary incentivization, and thus sweeps away its material side. By ignoring the ways that desire is created and cultivated liberalism obscures the ways that values are often manifestations of conflicts over resources. Yet reducing valuation to materiality alone denies an important role of aspirations in political life. Warner shows that the relationship between value and values goes both ways—that material culture and ideas are inextricably connected, yet conceiving of them as separate allows us to hold out a space for human agency and responsibility in material life.

This perspective on agency and responsibility comes through in Warner's implicit points about prioritization. He makes these points by reserving space for a discussion of urban zoning policy in a book that is otherwise focused on the landscape of queer activism around same-gender marriage at a national scale. In doing so, he demonstrates an alternative set of prioritizations that queer communities might enact. In point of fact, Warner could not have seriously meant that queers across the country would be better served if national gay rights organizations refocused their energy toward conserving one New York City block. One must therefore assume that he wanted gay rights organizations to do some imaginative work to think about what the set of priorities in safety, visibility, diversity, and community that he articulates in this chapter would look like, scaled up to the level of the whole country, or at the very least in their own neighborhoods and communities.

However, despite Warner's insights, his writing is often vague about the implicit "we" of his own discussions. In fact, Warner's persuasive account of the need for public sexual culture collides with certain shortcomings in the intersectionality of his approach.[66] In Warner's text, it is unclear who he even thinks he is speaking for. For instance, he frequently shifts back and forth between describing his agenda as one that should unite all queer people and specifying its particular relevance to white gay communities. Here are the problems with Warner's ambiguity on this question, which his use of the slur "trannies" and his presumption that trans people avoid Banana Republic brings to the surface. Warner claims to be in favor of diversity, but then he immediately writes off the possibility that people with the same sexual or gender identities might have widely different motivations. Passing has historically been, and continues to be, a vital way whereby some trans people can maintain safety in public space, as well as perform authentic identities. Moreover, many trans people may very well have wished to go to Banana Republic, and for a variety of reasons. By ignoring this fact, Warner implicitly prioritizes a particular vision of queer community, even as he attempts to juxtapose this community against a singular heterosexual community. Likewise, many asexuals, the groups represented by the "A" in the LGBTQIA+ acronym, would likely find his aesthetic of public sexual culture to be deeply exclusionary.

Similarly, Warner's argument against marriage on the basis that it confers a special value on its members is overstated—even as he argues for economic investment in the queer communities of the West Village, he dismisses the tangible material benefits of marriage. This is a striking choice, because Warner initially shows the importance of the economic dimensions of queer life for vulnerable populations; yet this importance seems to slip away when he thinks the wrong values are in place. This is also too cavalier a rejection of marriage benefits like spousal health insurance, which would have been vital resources for many people suffering from AIDS. Indeed, although he could not necessarily have known this at the time, plenty of analysis has since shown that poor and of-color queer people benefit more strongly, proportionally speaking, than do wealthy and/or white queer people from marriage.[67]

Recasting Value as Political

Warner settles on the importance of Christopher Street's subculture by arguing that this neighborhood's economic benefits (its value) should be aligned with queer political priorities (values). This he contrasts with the argument that inclusion in the institution of marriage, and all the material benefits it confers (its value), should be the primary focus of queer political priorities (values). Warner makes a convincing case that the economic benefits of public sexual culture exceed the economic benefits of marriage, in so far as they support the lives of those vulnerable to AIDS, those whose ways of life do not fit into the institution of marriage, and in general, the most vulnerable members of the queer community. In fact, it is not only his imagined trans community who can benefit from the alternative values he is articulating, or even necessarily queers writ large—a public sexual culture like the one he is proposing would be an enormous step forward for transcending broader cultures of sexual violence. As the #MeToo movement has more recently sought to show, an avoidance of sexual culture in public discourse, and thus also a refusal to think seriously about how to define consent, invites all sorts of abuse.[68]

At the same time, Warner's explicit exclusion of trans people who shop at Banana Republic, and his implicit exclusion of other segments of LGBTQIA+ communities—and whether or not he would have been aware of the term, asexual communities in particular—cut against his broader goal of advocating a more inclusive queer politics. In some ways, Warner recognizes that his value claims are by definition exclusive. He is quite comfortable excluding relatively privileged queers who want to get married in favor of supporting the types of lives that are only livable within a public sexual culture. In this way, Warner identifies and challenges important exclusions in contemporaneous queer activism. Yet his own omissions also cut deeper than he realizes, because they preclude the possibility of a real diversity of values—and Warner thus enacts his own politics of normalization around the subculture of a particular moment in New York City, even as he frames his argument as one that goes against any politics of normalization.[69] He succumbs to a slippage between value and values that inadvertently reifies his particular set of values—an unsatisfying conclusion for an argument that contains such a promising case for ways to transcend the violence of American sexual repression.

At the same time, Warner's argument not only reveals the political dimensions of value—it also offers a complex perspective on how a politics of devaluation works. There is also a slippage in his argument between a discussion of economic and moral value, and each of their corresponding objective (price, norms) and subjective (utility, ethics) expressions. At a shop on Christopher Street, the value of the goods in transaction is obvious, but the utility, morality, and ethical content of them are not—and showing us their utility and moral and ethical value is precisely why Warner draws out the relationship between a public sexual culture and economic production. Looking to his writing, one can see how arguments about value betray the extent to which we imagine what people want to be mediated through the market. Finding the tensions of value discourse in Warner's work is also a reminder that even from within the confines of an argument made on the basis of one iteration of this problem—either through value *or* values, or some a slippage between the two—decisions about how we frame our political positions have important consequences for how we navigate the relationship between material and aspirational life.

Warner's argument in many ways exemplifies all the political dimensions of value that I have tried to draw out in previous chapters. In Chapter 2, I showed that the ways we imagine our needs is a critical part of how we define a body politic. Arguing that we need a public sexual culture, Warner engages in a type of political claim-making that avoids fast distinctions between economic and moral value and instead centers the political qualities of value, as he articulates a set of needs in safety, community, and visibility. In Chapter 3, I showed that the value of particular bodies is usually present in any abstract assessment of worth. Value, as Warner sees it, is biopolitical, because it both invokes relationships between individual and political bodies, and shapes and produces them through narratives of shame and the dangers of AIDS. In Chapter 4, I showed that moral and economic logics can work together to devalue the lives of the most marginalized. Like Cooper, Warner shows that how we position our arguments in relation to tensions in value discourse is a critical part of how we imagine our relationships to the material world and to one another.

Reading Warner's text, one can also see both moral and economic value at work in the "quality of life" zoning and urban renewal policies and the ways in which either means of presenting a description of what we value is implicitly also a way of naming *who* we value. Valuating public sexual cultures would also mean a revaluation of queer lives. In Warner's explicit argument for the value of public sex, he does not pretend to care about the politics of "decency," but instead makes a positive case for a culture of sex positivity over one of repression. In this way, his value claims engage directly in a politics of contestation. As his writing shows, claims to value offer a democratic resource precisely because they foreground an ambiguous relationship between material and aspirational life.

Ultimately, the troubling equivocation between value and values that Cooper draws our attention toward is very much present in Warner's writing. But, as Warner shows, we should not want to escape this tension between the different valences of value, because the tension reminds us that our political positions are not always as entrenched and immutable as we think they are. Whenever we make an argument on the basis of a particular distribution of value, we could reasonably be making it instead on the basis of values, or vice versa. In either case, we have a significant choice to make about how we frame our relationship to the material world. The tension between value and values raises the important reminder that we can and should think outside our own economic interests—indeed, outside our own perspectives on these interests—and that it is always more possible to do so than it seems. In conclusion, Warner's work helpfully surfaces the tension between value and values, even as he fails to transcend or escape it. He shows that any decision we make about how to mobilize around a set of economic resources, moral principles, or some combination of the two is always going to favor a particular set of lives and ways of living. The tension between the concepts of value and values is therefore vital for democratic practice. It enables us to define the people and activities of politics, whether the activities be in fighting for an expansion of rights or creating a public sexual culture. At the same time, the tension reminds us that any such delineations of political communities and activities are contingent.

Coda: The Supreme Court's Value Slippages

These slippages between different valances of value continue to be politically salient, and not even the highest court in the United States manages to avoid succumbing to this slippage. In June 2018, the United States

Supreme Court made a determination of the value of queer life in the widely anticipated *Masterpiece Cakeshop, Ltd. V. Colorado Civil Rights Commission*. In this case, free speech and religious freedom were weighed against equal protection in order to determine whether a Christian bakery owner, Jack Phillips, was obligated to make a wedding cake for a gay couple. The court issued a narrow ruling in favor of Masterpiece Cakeshop, much to the dismay of LGBTQIA+ rights advocates.

The text of the ruling included some peculiar statements about the values at stake. Citing *Obergefell v. Hodges*, Justice Kennedy delivered the Court's opinion. "Our society," he wrote, "has come to the recognition that gay persons and gay couples cannot be treated as social outcasts or as inferior in *dignity and worth*." Moreover, he argued, though "religious and philosophical objections are protected, it is a general rule that such objections do not allow *business owners* and other actors in *the economy* and in society to deny protected persons equal access to *goods and services*."[70] Much is at stake in these opening arguments. First, the value of gay people, measured in "dignity and worth," is affirmed against any forces that would seek to deny it. Second, the juxtaposition of the dignity and worth of gay people with "religious and philosophical objections" indicates that the values of equal protection and dignity can come into conflict with religious values. Third, two types of value are affirmed—both "dignity" and "worth." Yet while "dignity" is a moral value, "worth" is not so easy to pin down. Whereas "worth" might be presumed to describe something intrinsic about the importance of human life and dignity regardless of sexual orientation, another type of "worth" is introduced via the stakes for "business owners" and "the economy" in the following lines—namely their investment in "goods and services."[71]

The inclusion of words like 'worth' in these lines suggests that the values of religion and philosophy can come into conflict with the value produced by the market.[72] After all, Kennedy continues in his explanation of the decision by writing that a critical mass of "purveyors of goods and services who object to gay marriages for moral or religious grounds" would "impose a serious stigma on gay persons."[73] If the decision were merely one of the moral values in conflict—the value of religious freedom, and the value of equal protection—then the court claims it would have ruled in favor of the gay couple. However, the decision was complicated by the roles of economic value in the form of goods and services, and the court was all too eager to avoid the politics of economic regulation. That equal protection is measured in this case in terms of dignity, but also, ambiguously, "worth"—which could mean either economic or moral worth—indicates an ambiguity in the Court's priorities. Of course, had Kennedy read Warner, he would have realized that ruling on economic transactions implicitly favors particular moral values anyway, and that his concerns about economic value had eclipsed his stated moral priorities.

Notes

1. As Sima Shakhsari argues, there is an "economy of queer death," and it positions queer and trans subjects "between biopolitics and necropolitics." Reading Shakhsari, I glean that queer subjects are either produced and managed and consequently assigned a particular value in the global economy, or else treated as dispensable, and thus as without value. Sima Shakhsari, "Killing Me Softly with Your Rights: Queer Death and the Politics of Rightful Killing," in Jin Haritaworn, Adi Kuntsman, and Silvia Posocco, eds., *Queer Necropolitics* (Abingdon UK: Routledge, 2015), 95.

2. Morgan Bassichis et al. term advocacy for the former goods, and thus for economic justice, "deep transformation," in contrast with calls for formal legal inclusion, which they call a "trickle-down brand of equality." Morgan Bassichis, Alexander Lee, and Dean Spade, "Building an Abolitionist Trans and Queer Movement with Everything We've Got," in Eric Stanley and Nat Smith, eds., *Captive Genders: Trans Embodiment and the Prison Industrial Complex* (Chico CA: AK Press, 2015), 16. For another critique of formal legal equality, see Wendy Brown and Janet Halley, eds., *Left Legalism/Left Critique* (Durham NC: Duke University Press, 2002).

3. Elijah Adiv Edelman, "Why We Forget the Pulse Nightclub Murders: Bodies That (Never) Matter and a Call for Coalitional Models of Queer and Trans Social Justice," *GLQ: A Journal of Lesbian and Gay Studies* 24, no. 1 (2018).

4. Dean Mathiowetz, "Gay Love Conquers All," *The Contemporary Condition*, July 14, 2013.

5. Fatima El-Tayeb, "Time Travelers and Queer Heterotopias: Narratives from the Muslim Underground," *The Germanic Review: Literature, Culture, Theory* 88, no. 3 (2013), 307.

6. Cathy Cohen, "Punks, Bulldaggers, and Welfare Queens: The Radical Potential of Queer Politics?," in Mae G. Henderson and E. Patrick Johnson, eds., *Black Queer Studies: A Critical Anthology* (Durham NC: Duke University Press, 2005); Roderick A. Ferguson, *Aberrations in Black: Toward a Queer of Color Critique* (Minneapolis: University of Minnesota Press, 2003); Phillip Brian Harper, "The Evidence of Felt Intuition: Minority Experience, Everyday Life, and Critical Speculative Knowledge," in Mae G. Henderson and E. Patrick Johnson, eds., *Black Queer Studies: A Critical Anthology* (Durham NC: Duke University Press, 2005); and José Esteban Muñoz, *Disidentifications: Queers of Color and the Performance of Politics* (Minneapolis: University of Minnesota Press, 1999). Revisiting the Pulse nightclub shooting, for example, Edelman argues that the Pulse murders have been forgotten because so many of the victims were poor or working class, Latinx, Black, and/or gender nonconforming, and that even within queer communities, "these are bodies that never mattered." Edelman, "Why We Forget," 31.

7. On colonialism, see Scott Lauria Morgensen, "Theorizing Gender, Sexuality, and Settler Colonialism: An Introduction," *Settler Colonial Studies* 2, no. 2 (2012). For a critique of the idealization of the queer erotic, see Kadji Amin, "Racial Fetishism, Gay Liberation, and the Temporalities of the Erotic," in *Disturbing Attachments: Genet, Modern Pederasty, and Queer History* (Durham NC: Duke University Press, 2017).

8. Kai Green, "Troubling the Waters: Mobilizing A Trans* Analytic," in E. Patrick Johnson, ed., *No Tea, No Shade: New Writings in Black Queer Studies* (Durham NC: Duke University Press, 2016), 75.

9. Michael Warner, *The Trouble with Normal: Sex, Politics, and the Ethics of Queer Life* (Cambridge MA: Harvard University Press, 1999), 4 and 38–39.

10 Warner terms this "homonormativity," drawing from the argument about normative pressures within queer communities first developed by Adrienne Rich, "Compulsory Heterosexuality and Lesbian Existence," *Signs* 5, no. 5 (1980).

11 Warner, *The Trouble with Normal*, 4 and 38–39.

12 Ibid., 25–26.

13 On the politics of shame, see ,for instance ,Jack Halberstam, "Shame and White Gay Masculinity," *Social Text* 84–85, nos 3–4 (2005); David Halperin and Valerie Traub, *Gay Shame* (University of Chicago Press, 2009); Sally Munt, *Queer Attachments: The Cultural Politics of Shame* (Hampshire UK: Ashgate, 2008); and Eve Kosofsky Sedgwick, *Touching, Feeling: Affect, Pedagogy, Performativity* (Durham NC: Duke University Press, 2003).

14 Warner, *The Trouble with Normal*, 36.

15 Ibid., 133.

16 Ibid., 8.

17 Ibid., 6 and 74.

18 Ibid., 114.

19 Ibid., 65 and 71.

20 Ibid., 35 and 71.

21 Ibid., 108.

22 Ibid., 117–121.

23 Ibid., 129–130.

24 Ibid., 150.

25 Ibid., 149.

26 Ibid.

27 Ibid., 161.

28 Ibid., 152.

29 Ibid., 153.

30 Ibid.

31 This was in the years before applications such as Grindr, so physical spaces such as these were essential for aspects and segments of gay socializing.

32 Ibid., 162. Notably, he does not link this targeting of gay people and gay sex to the targeting of other already marginalized communities in New York City.

33 He does not attend to the ways that poor neighborhoods becoming gay neighborhoods has historically paved the way for gentrification. However, I will return to the fraught intersectionality in his approach later.

34 Ibid., 160.

35 Ibid., 151.

36 Ibid., 162. Interestingly enough, he does not offer examples of gay activists who do not want assimilation and normalization but do want the economic benefits of the market—benefits such as wealth, and high property values.

37 Ibid., 153 and 164.

38 Ibid., 151.

39 Ibid.

40 That some of the queer businesses were relocated to Chelsea rather than closed altogether is further evidence for Warner's point about the demands of market capital being the most significant catalyst for these changes to the West Village.

41 Ibid., 151.

42 Ibid., 150.

43 Ibid., 153–159.

44 Ibid., 153.

45 Ibid., 159.
46 Ibid., 154.
47 Ibid., 170.
48 Ibid., 171.
49 Ibid., 169.
50 Ibid.
51 Ibid., 170.
52 Ibid., 173.
53 Ibid., 179 and 178.
54 Ibid., 177.
55 Ibid., 178.
56 Ibid., 171.
57 Ibid., 152.
58 Ibid., 171.
59 Ibid., 183.
60 Ibid.
61 Ibid., emphasis added.
62 Ibid., 171.
63 Ibid.
64 Ibid., 167, emphasis added.
65 Ibid.
66 Jack Halberstam, for instance, cautions that the dominant narratives about shame are constructed by, for, and about white gay men, and includes Warner as a key perpetrator of this logic. Halberstam, "Shame and White Gay Masculinity," 221–222.
67 For one example of these statistics, see "LGBT Families of Color: Facts at a Glance," National Black Justice Coalition, January 2012. http://www.nbjc. org/sites/default/files/lgbt-families-of-color-facts-at-a-glance.pdf. For a discussion of this report by the Executive Director and CEO of the National Black Justice Coalition, see Sharon. J. Lettman-Hicks, "The State of Black LGBT People and Their Families," *Huffington Post*, May 13, 2014. https:// www.huffingtonpost.com/sharon-j-lettmanhicks/the-state-of-black-lgbt-p_b_4949992.html. As I will demonstrate in Chapter 6, this way of handling the tensions of value discourse has important implications when we take Warner's insights into an analysis of present-day struggles for racial equality. I will discuss how the Black Lives Matter movement and the communities they advocate for do not have the luxury of disavowing certain forms of material redistribution in favor of a particular set of ideals. The Black Lives Matter movement's core goals of revaluing and re-centering Black life in American politics and policy have been articulated in an array of policy platforms and local candidacies. Its radical, sweeping visions for a socially and institutionally transformed society are not perceived as contradictory with reforms targeted at transferring resources, such as stronger policing review boards, the abolition of cash bail, or mandatory body cameras. Forgoing these interventions is not an option, despite their not being a substantial or appropriately designed form of reparations. See, for instance, Campaign Zero "Solutions." https:// www.joincampaignzero.org/solutions/#contracts and Movement for Black Lives "Platform." https://policy.m4bl.org/platform/.
68 For one example, see Kara Cutruzzula, *What Does Consent Look Like in the #MeToo Era,* Women in the World Media, April 14, 2018. https://womenintheworld. com/2018/04/14/what-does-consent-look-like-in-the-metoo-era/.
69 This perspective comes through most thoroughly in Michael Warner, *Publics and Counterpublics* (Brooklyn NY: Zone Books, 2005).

70 Supreme Court of the United States, "584 U.S. (2018): Masterpiece Cakeshop Ltd. et al. *v.* Colorado Civil Rights Commission et al." (Washington DC, 2018), 9. All emphases added.

71 Obviously, such determinations about value can easily become quite complicated. The Court ultimately sidestepped the issue by ruling that the original case made against Masterpiece owner Jack Phillips by the Colorado Court of Appeals had been conducted unfairly. Rather than arbitrate between competing values, or else navigate the treacherous waters of determining a relationship between economic value and moral or ethical values, Justice Kennedy took the safe route and concluded that the case had been tainted from the beginning.

72 Implicitly, there is also a tension here between different conceptions of what it would mean to have a free economy—one in which all purchasers are guaranteed absolute freedom to buy whatever they want, or one in which all sellers are guaranteed absolute freedom to sell whatever they want, and to whomever they want. In either case, state intervention is presumably needed—either to protect religious shopkeepers or to protect gay consumers.

73 Ibid., 12.

6 Black Lives Matter and the Politics of Value

Although both Cooper's and Warner's arguments rely heavily on particular conceptualizations of value, the problem of recognition also lurks a hair below the surface in both of their writing. For instance, in one of the few lines in which Cooper directly addresses her Black readers, she warns that value is something that is "acknowledged."[1] Warner, meanwhile, describes the value of Christopher Street as a type of value that is "traded in recognition."[2] Evident in both of these statements is the importance of recognizing (and admitting to) unequal distributions of value as a necessary precursor for redistributing value.

These statements are evidence of some of the ways that many political claims rest on the unsteady ground of recognition politics. Recognition is treated by proponents of multicultural representation as the key mechanism for the protection of minority cultural rights and identities.[3] Critics of liberalism, by contrast, argue that conceding the power to recognize to the state is to treat identities as pre-given, and thus to erase the contestation behind their composition.[4] From the point of view of Indigenous studies, recognition discourse also reifies the settler state's logic and premises.[5] Following Franz Fanon's demonstration of the double binds recognition-based politics can place on people of color, adherents of Black Power have instead argued for an expression of Black identity that altogether rejects recognition.[6] In critical race theory, the tendency has frequently been to expose the liberal recognition-as-rights framework as a way of establishing dependence and coloniality in the name of accommodation, or else as a way of upholding a superficial leveling discourse that actually perpetuates inequality.[7] Yet despite anxiety about recognition, the Black Lives Matter movement, emergent in 2014, has been consistently and uncritically cast as a movement that is primarily focused on seeking it.[8]

The movement's efforts to draw attention and concern to the devastating losses of Black lives and livelihood in the face of police brutality and white supremacy indicates a need for a conceptualization of recognition that rests on firmer ground. Consistent with this broader goal, some have sought to extend the promise of recognition beyond the state and have argued that recognition be reframed as a process of mutually constitutive

DOI: 10.4324/9781003304302-6

identity formation or acknowledgment.[9] These perspectives uphold the importance of recognition as a useful space for intervening in racialized violence. Yet, as I argue, the Black Lives Matter movement engages in an innovative form of recognition politics. This movement is indeed making demands of the state, albeit not exclusively; at the same time, they are not seeking recognition in the usual ways—i.e., for an identity, whether that identity be an individual or group identity. Instead, they are demanding a broad recognition of the ways that value is political.

The Black Lives Matter movement's central contention—that "Black Lives Matter"—foregrounds tensions between different discourses of value. This dimension to their argument becomes apparent if one thinks about the distinctive use of the language of 'mattering' in the phrase mobilizing this movement and the things this word contains. Whereas 'matter' invokes an image of something physical and material, 'matters' denote how we value said objects or substances and our relationships with them.[10] Perhaps for this reason, the Black Lives Matter movement has been understood as taking up a politics of care and concern.[11] While this interpretation captures some dimensions of their argument, I argue that the lens of claiming value offers more insight into their work.

Though I nod to some of the ways that this movement syncretizes many elements of Black radical traditions (including abolitionist, Black feminist, and anti-capitalist thought), I focus primarily on how activists build upon these traditions by pulling the concept of value into the center of discourses about Black liberation. I argue that doing so enables activists to enact a deeply intersectional politics of prioritization. Toward this end, I read Patrisse Khan-Cullors's *When They Call You a Terrorist: A Black Lives Matter Memoir* [2018] as a text that articulates the political vision of this movement by drawing from a larger tradition of Black radical political thought, while building upon this tradition in significant ways. I also draw from Alicia Garza's "A Herstory of the Black Lives Matter Movement" [2014] and the platform of the Movement for Black Lives—and in both I find fidelity to the expanded project and perspective that Khan-Cullors articulates.

Khan-Cullors's memoir is divided into two parts: the first contains a personal narrative of growing up a Black, queer woman in Los Angeles, and the second is an origin story of the Black Lives Matter movement. These two developmental stories are deeply intertwined. In the first part of the book, Khan-Cullors assesses the myriad experiences of devaluation she experienced over the course of her lifetime as a way of contextualizing the mobilization she describes undertaking in the second part of the book. This approach fits into a broader tradition of political theorizing that conjoins diagnoses of political problems with calls to action.[12] Yet Khan-Cullors's specific linking of the reality of Black devaluation with the political project of ensuring that Black lives "matter" also demonstrates a unique perspective on value discourse.

My own narrative in this chapter proceeds in three parts. In the first part of the chapter I draw from Khan-Cullors's memoir to provide a brief overview of the emergence of this movement from the vantage point of one of its founders, pausing to situate it in a broader tradition of political theorizing whenever Khan-Cullors herself expresses such a connection. I foreground the careful thinking behind the development of this movement's mobilizing hashtag, slogan, and ultimately, name. In the second part of the chapter I show that the concept of value, expressed primarily in the language of mattering, plays a key role in the agenda of this movement, and discuss some of the ways that the thinkers at the helm of this movement draw out a politics of value that has much in common with the agonist democratic means of asserting priority that is my focus throughout this book. I further argue that Black Lives Matter activists mobilize both economic and moral logics of value to show that moral priorities must go hand in hand with economic investment. I conclude by arguing that the movement mobilizes the concept of value in a way that simultaneously argues for a valuation of Black lives in the world, and of women, queer people, and disabled people within the movement. I call this multilayered intervention *distinction without,* and *prioritization within.* I argue that although the controversial language of 'mattering' has led to troubling appropriation of this same language of mattering—both in the racially charged claims that "Blue (and/or) White Lives Matter" and in the willfully ignorant argument that "All Lives Matter"—these responses actually reveal the power of the claim that "Black Lives Matter." Moreover, the Black Lives Matter movement's emphasis on distinction and prioritization counterintuitively lends itself to a politics that can uplift the most vulnerable people within already marginalized communities.

More than a Hashtag: A Brief Herstory of the Movement

Pinning down the Black Lives Matter movement's intellectual interventions can be tricky. As a decentralized movement with localized leadership and without a ratified manifesto, the movement's political agenda of upending racialized state violence has been tethered to a variety of imaginations of equality, justice, and freedom by writers and activists, allies and critics.[13] Nevertheless, theorists have begun to uncover a rich intellectual history of Black political thought invoked by the movement's messaging and core platform, including key figures like James Baldwin, W. E. B. Du Bois, Audre Lorde, and Anna Julia Cooper.[14] Movement leaders are explicit about these connections. Patrisse Khan-Cullors, one of the founders of this movement, cites an extensive legacy of intellectual thought centered on Black social movements and an eclectic group of philosophers and feminists.[15] She recalls, for instance, reading Karl Marx and Emma Goldman alongside Audre Lorde, David Walker, and Ida B. Wells.[16] Alicia Garza, another founder, writes that Black feminist thinkers, including Barbara Smith, bell hooks, and Patricia Hill Collins, had deep influences on her own organizing work.[17] Khan-Cullors also describes numerous ways that her thinking is influenced by a larger history of Black struggle, connecting her political awakening to reading about the Civil Rights movement and the struggle to end apartheid.[18] She argues that Mandela's "I am prepared to die" speech could easily have been the statement of one of the leaders in the 1992 Los Angeles uprising.[19] She also names the Deacons for Defense and Justice and the Black Panthers as progenitors, and describes the Black Lives Matter movement as picking up their torch.[20]

Black Lives Matter first rose to national prominence following the murder of Trayvon Martin. Founding organizers Alicia Garza, Patrisse Khan-Cullors, and Opal Tometi supported a White House petition calling for George Zimmerman's prosecution and circulated a Facebook post presented as a "love letter" to Black people that affirmed their value.[21] The movement gained ground in July 2016 amid protests of killings of Alton Sterling in Baton Rouge and Philando Castile in Minneapolis.[22] Its first high-profile action was a nationally coordinated bussing of activists into Ferguson to support and sustain protest about the murder of Michael Brown. While in Ferguson, activists began to build a network of affiliate organizations, organized around the central mission of making Black lives matter.[23]

The mythology surrounding this movement often casts protests as a spontaneous response to police violence in Ferguson.[24] However, the movement's leading figures had already been doing much of the work that is now encompassed by this broader umbrella for many years. Before the "Black Lives Matter" banner began to appear at marches in white neighborhoods, die-ins, and highway blockages, and before white brunches in gentrified neighborhoods were interrupted by activists listing the names of Black people slain by police, these activists had been honing a strategy that Khan-Cullors describes as "how to launch, execute and win campaigns by building power among those the world considers powerless."[25] Khan-Cullors, for instance, had been organizing in her hometown of Los Angeles since the age of 17. While in high school she had mobilized her community to stop fines associated with truancy, and she later co-created a coalition to end police violence, which in 2016 installed the first civilian oversight board of the Los Angeles County Sheriff's Department.[26] She spent years mobilizing people to call out racialized media biases, and was a longtime member of the Los Angeles organization Dignity and Power Now.[27] Alicia Garza and Opal Tometi had led similar work in their own communities.[28]

Though the murder of Trayvon Martin and the Ferguson protests are often represented as the beginning of this movement, they are actually the movement's first manifestation on a national scale. Prior to Ferguson, the movement's three founders had met at a nationwide summit of Black activists and had spent years developing "Black Lives Matter" as a discourse to unify and draw connections between the political energies they saw in their otherwise disparate organizations. This point will become critical later, when I discuss the ways that this movement's revaluation of Black life hinges on a politics of non-erasure. However, for now it is important to note that before the movement that is now called "Black Lives Matter" ever assisted demonstrations in Ferguson, its activists had been coordinating protests and sit-ins across the nation for decades.[29] The movement was a carefully planned and coordinated political movement with years of local victories behind it, rather than a spontaneous hashtag.[30]

The Black Lives Matter movement has gained national prominence not only for its controversial slogan, but also for its unconventional tactics and inclusivity. Barnor Hesse and Juliet Hooker explain that the movement, which is often "viewed as a new civil rights movement for the twenty-first century," has "borrowed tactics from earlier protest movements (e.g., black power, black feminism), particularly the emphasis on publicly disruptive demonstrations and expositional uses of popular culture."[31] Yet as they further explain, "it has also pioneered new strategies, such as the use of social media to organize, heighten immediacy, and widen the scope of the public that acts as witness to the disposability of black lives."[32] Angela Davis argues that the movement pushes not only Black and left, but also feminist and queer movements to a new level in its use of art and activism to transform state violence, and offers a fresh perspective on some of the contradictions with which earlier iterations of these movements wrestled.[33] Likewise, as Keeanga-Yamahtta Taylor shows, the movement has played an undeniable role in shifting public discourse, and this is at least in part because it has had Black women (particularly queer ones) as its face.[34]

At times, the movement's tactics have not been received well by a white-dominated society.[35] The movement's tactics, Debra Thompson shows, are disruptive—activists "organize protests and marches, stage die-ins in public spaces, shut down highways and busy intersections, use direct action to target and block access to hubs of transportation and commerce, and provide instructions for white people on how to be good allies."[36] However, she argues, although the movement is considered by some to be violent and even blamed for incitement of anger, these perceptions are borne out of anti-Black racism, and are a form of backlash against the movement for its refusal to adhere to a respectability politics of "soothing and alleviating" white anxiety and quietly calling for diversity.[37]

Black Lives Matter" is the rallying cry uniting all these efforts and actions. Yet this language of mattering contains within it a much more complex and significant set of premises, assertions, and agendas than is immediately apparent. As Christopher Lebron puts it, "there is something undeniably powerful about those three words: black lives matter" and their role in "the struggle to insist that black lives are indeed lives."[38] The movement's slogan is presented as a lamentation—Alicia Garza's original post coining this phrase came in the wake of the George Zimmerman acquittal, and was intended to show "how little black lives matter."[39] But the language is also an ironic attempt to expose how Black people have been subject to systematized gaslighting about their worth. As Khan-Cullors writes, the hashtag is intended to show the way that harm to Black people is consistently framed "as our own doing."[40] The slogan thus echoes a longer tradition of Black political thought about the politics of value. For instance, I have already shown that Anna Julia Cooper uses similar language in her discussions of Black worth and material.[41] The slogan also calls attention to systems of structural inequality, and seeks to expose the numerous ways that society shows that Black lives do not matter, evident in such diverse manifestations as whitewashed history books, food deserts, healthcare and education disparities, popular media, and arbitrary arrests.[42] Finally, the language offers a normative political agenda to re-value Black lives—to make Black lives matter.

That the language "Black Lives Matter" is simultaneously a lamentation, an ironic twist, a historical reference, an exposure of political-economic structures, and a call to action says much about the multifaceted nature of the movement's broader mobilizing strategies. Minkah Makalani argues that Black Lives Matter is first and foremost:

> A political language capturing the queer, the trans, the convicted, the disabled, the undocumented, and the gender nonconforming, actually insists on a radical transformation. Put differently, the statement "Black lives matter" operates through its acknowledgment of the racial reality that black lives *do not* matter. This is not to impugn or dismiss the claim as such but to underscore that its demand for black lives *to* matter involves an indictment of the sociopolitical order in which black people's incorporation into white racial democracy occurs through their marginalization, exploitation, and exclusion.[43]

The language demands changes to the current systems, which, its organizers argue, "place profit over people."[44] As Makalani writes, "what is key in the declaration 'Black lives matter' is that it refuses any simplistic call for increased electoral participation, policy proposals, and the expansion of democratic protections."[45] The operative word here is "simplistic"— the movement does not ignore formal channels of political participation. However, activists show that structural change must include and transcend elections and policy, and that change requires significant shifts in political discourse.

Since this language of mattering is what connects the disparate activists and organizations that compose this movement, it is also in many ways constitutive of the movement itself. Eschewing traditional hierarchies,

Black Lives Matter has no single group of leaders—the hashtag instead functions, as Lebron argues, as an open-source brand that can be taken up by anyone, much like corporate branding but without the profit motive.[46] Hesse and Hooker discuss how this language works as a "political slogan" that has the effect of enacting a "creative disembedding of particular meanings of black solidarity from local events and settings, where these meanings become transferable to other places, linking previously disparate black communities in affinity and dialogical networks of discourses and activities."[47] Perhaps this general applicability is why the language has stuck—in addition to its resonance, it has functioned as a sort of glue for otherwise localized anti-racist movements.

This distinct choice of language mirrors activists' main commitments. As Khan-Cullors explains, the use of this particular language was a carefully considered choice made with Opal Tometi, a communications professional. This choice of phrase, Khan-Cullors elaborates, was made in full awareness that there would be many people who would feel the words to be "separatist" and "isolating."[48] As Khan-Cullors writes, "there are people close to us who are worried that the very term, Black Lives Matter, is too radical to use, alienating, even as we all are standing in the blood of Black children and adults."[49] She even explains that part of the aim was to try "to get people to see that as much as there is a progressive movement for justice, here are those working just as hard for the opposite outcome, an outcome where only the fewest of lives matter at all."[50] In addition to being a lamentation, an ironic twist, a historical reference, an exposure of political-economic structures, and a call to action, the language "Black Lives Matter" is carefully separatist. This dimension of the slogan is seemingly at odds with some of this movement's broader efforts, since the movement is also admired for being especially inclusive. However, as I will show, looking more closely at how the politics of value animates this movement's claim resolves this apparent contradiction.

Black Lives Matter's Value Politics

The Black Lives Matter movement invites a reinvestigation of the role of value in political discourse through their use of this concept to gain recognition of and redress the precarious position of Black life.[51] Developed by activists demanding an end to decades of systematic anti-Black oppression, the movement's catchphrase has become a globally resonant rallying cry against police brutality and vigilante violence. The movement declares that "Black Lives Matter" because the value of these lives has consistently been denied.[52] As movement co-founder Alicia Garza puts it:

> We've said from the very beginning Black Lives Matter is [sic] a network, and also as a broad set of individuals, is an organization moving to transform the way our society *values* black lives.[53]

Or, as co-founder Patrisse Khan-Cullors explains:

> This is a much broader conversation and the conversation around state
> violence isn't just about the act of murdering a black person, but rather
> how this country, at every level of government, at every moment, has
> *devalued* black lives, whether that's by putting black folks in ghettos,
> defunding our school systems, over-policing our communities.

"I think the hashtag #BlackLivesMatter," she continues, "was about trying to heal from my own grief as a black person and my life and other
black people's lives constantly being devalued."[54] Mwende Katwiwa of
the Black Lives Matter affiliate Black Youth Project 100 explains that "the
relationship between economic and racial justice" is ultimately about "a
recognition that Black life is *valuable* while it is still being lived."[55] Meanwhile, Garza writes that "#BlackLivesMatter doesn't mean your life isn't
important—it means that Black lives, which are seen as without *value* within
White supremacy, are important to your liberation."[56]

Activists argue that society has systemically devalued Black lives
through targeted exploitation and violence, legal and political neglect, and
a lack of media and political attention.[57] Their response is to attempt to
return attention to both Black lives and Black livelihood by promoting the
value of ignored past and present achievements and by mourning the lost
value of lives taken by anti-Black violence. In doing so, the Black Lives
Matter movement demands that we rethink value as a category of political
analysis.

Yet seeing how the movement's value claims are political requires revisiting some of the dimensions of value discourse that I have analyzed.
Though value discourse is often framed in terms of economic and moral
abstractions, I have argued that valuation is essentially a logic of prioritization, and thus of politics. In Chapter 2, I genealogically traced the
concept along this neglected path. I drew from Aristotle to argue that the
transmutation of needs discourse into value discourse during the handover
of political-economic thought from Ancient Greece to Ancient Rome
represents a missed opportunity to keep the politics of needs at the front
and center of political discourse.

The Black Lives Matter movement echoes Aristotle when its activists
self-consciously put needs at the center of their efforts even as they engage
in contestation about the boundaries of those needs. Though mobilization
against police violence has gained the most media attention, the movement has also made living wages, shelter, and access to quality food and
grocery stores key demands of its platform.[58] In order for Black lives to
matter, its founders are clear, significant efforts must be made to remedy
wealth inequality, and to resolve the contradiction between the wealth
of the United States and the widespread lack of basic opportunity and
livable wages for many who reside within its territories.[59] Khan-Cullors

rhetorically asks, "what is the impact of not being valued? how do you measure the loss of what a human being does not receive?"[60] Khan-Cullors builds this perspective from a description of her own experience of persistently facing a shortage of food as a child.[61] She writes that she made it through childhood alive because of "the Black Panthers, who made Breakfast for Children a thing."[62] She also explains that because the budget for education was so limited and the policy that set standards for the quality of that food was so morally bankrupt, those who depended on the food provided at school for meals could only count on ketchup for their daily source of vegetables.[63] The full realization of the claim that "Black Lives Matter" depends, as Khan-Cullors explains, upon tangible investment in Black life, beginning with basic food provision.

Just like Aristotle, Khan-Cullors and her fellow organizers also imagine an array of needs that go beyond these rudimentary requirements, and that include such goals as living well. An expansive vision of human needs influences the way that activists pursue the goals of food, wage, and housing security. Explaining that organizers of the movement make significant efforts to be inclusive and to recognize an array of experiences of oppression, Khan-Cullors describes conscious efforts to create a space for generative community-building that refuses to deplete the time and energy of its members. She writes, "in the fullness of our humanity we need this too...a place to rest, to renew. A place to restore."[64] Khan-Cullors thus broadens needs beyond economic investment, to encompass things like emotional support. This perspective is evident in her argument that the movement attempts to build "intentional family," to center healing and care, and to make sure it is restorative, not exploitative.[65] That many of the movement's protests also end in celebratory and tension-releasing actions like block parties is emblematic of this effort.[66] Activists establish a valuation of deliberation and public life by linking demands for safety in their communities and ownership thereof, and in their use of protests which culminate in the celebration of life and joy in public spaces.

There are also parallels between Black Lives Matter and Aristotelian freedom in this movement's centering of deliberation and action as essential activities of politics. The movement's platform emerged from a long, deliberative process between the numerous activists that comprise the movement, making it clear that collective decision-making is not only the method but also the end goal. For instance, the Movement for Black Lives also lists the acquisition of "political power" and "community control" as key priorities in its platform alongside "reparations and targeted long-term investments."[67] Although some argue that the Black Lives Matter movement has been hindered by its efforts to support specific campaigns for political office, Khan-Cullors is clear that this representation misconstrues what the movement most stands for. She explains, "I really don't give a fuck about shiny, polished candidates...if we do what we are called to do, curate events and conversations that lead to actions that lead to decisions about how we should and would live, we will win."[68] Herein lies a republican image of citizenship and freedom, in which coming together as a community and taking action in support of an ever-evolving understanding of justice is a central aim. Candidate victories are viewed as important when they facilitate these deeper and more expansive goals of collectively making decisions about how to live and acting to realize these goals and decisions.

As I also showed in Chapter 2, the democratic potential of needs discourse is not only in its attention to resource distribution, but also in how this discourse lends itself to contestation over the boundaries of political community. Khan-Cullors's perspective on the primacy of deliberation and communal self-determination also animates her imagination of alternatives to a world in which Black lives do not matter. While navigating her brother's struggles with mental health and the ways that police presence would always worsen any situation in which his psychosis was activated, Khan-Cullors imagines a way of enacting community control that does not rely upon police and instead stems from deliberation and mutual support. She argues that this is what a Black future must look like, and in doing so argues that political boundaries must be redrawn.[69] Moreover, reading Aristotle's discussions of needs, I showed that needs and the activities of meeting them are never fully private. Khan-Cullors is also clear that framing issues of poverty as matters of personal responsibility denies and erases the distribution of resources that undergirds them—as she explains, poverty is a problem of state budget priorities rather than individual efforts.[70]

The Black Lives Matter movement thus represents a way of bringing a contingent perspective on needs into discussions about value, and in a way that re-grounds value more firmly in politics. Seeing how activists' perspectives on needs and community self-actualization enact this radicalization of value discourse also requires a revisiting of the concept's modern uses. In Chapter 3, I looked at the origin of modern value discourse in Ancient Rome and argued that the concept of value is at its root biopolitical, in that it implicates and produces bodies and people. I also traced the emergence of liberal discourses about value and showed how they represented a significant departure from the just price debates that were a central focus of medieval political-economic thought. The logic of value as deeply personal that animated Roman and medieval European laws of sale persists today, yet this quality of value is visible only in glimpses behind the abstractions of liberal economic theory. Khan-Cullors also shows valuation to be personal rather than abstract—and she makes this point across numerous examples and contexts. In doing so, she identifies political processes of valuation that are often construed as impersonal economic necessities.

This perspective comes through most clearly in Khan-Cullors's discussions of disposability. She explains that by the time Black Lives Matter was created, Black disposability was something that she knew both through statistics and lived experience.[71] She describes the transition to her teenage years as "the year we become a thing to be discarded" and the one in which she and her siblings and began a process of "learning that they did not matter, that they were expendable."[72] She decries the constant patrolling of her childhood neighborhood by police and their harassment of her preteen brothers as of a piece with the untimely deaths of Freddie Gray, 12-year-old Tamir Rice, and even the media denunciation of Mike Brown's character to justify his murder.[73] That Black Lives Matter protesters are met with violence, even though their claim is merely that "we have a right to live," is evidence for Khan-Cullors of the significant uphill battle required to get white people to recognize their investment in the disposability of Black life.[74]

Showing that Black devaluation is political, for Khan-Cullors, requires recognizing that white supremacy is built by expropriating Black resources. Neighborhood segregation, she argues, has always been about white people not wanting "to be reminded of what it took to keep themselves rich."[75] In other words, coming into contact with visibly deprived Black people would force white people to confront how the economic value invested in their homes conflicts with their professed values of justice and equality. Khan-Cullors further argues that the extensive police presence in her neighborhood originates in a drug war aimed specifically at Black people.[76] She describes the war as a "forced migration project," and as the legal response to gains made by the Civil Rights Movement and Black Power movements.[77] As a consequence of this war, she elaborates, "literally breathing while Black became cause for arrest—or worse."[78] A similar perspective comes through in her comment about the irony that it is those who have been harmed, rather than those who harm, who are viewed as "disposable."[79] Across all of these examples it is apparent that Khan-Cullors is fully aware of the political nature of Black valuation, and of how value is historically grounded not in abstract economic theory or moral ideals, but in force and violence. When she argues that police budgets should be slashed, and investments instead made into what actually keeps communities safe—the communities themselves—it is clear that she has in mind not merely a redistribution of economic resources, but also a wholesale political prioritization of Black communities.[80]

Khan-Cullors does not stop short at just pointing out the political nature of Black devaluation—she also discusses how the politics of value actually function. In Chapter 4, I argued that Anna Julia Cooper shows that economic and moral logics of value work together to deprioritize Black life. Khan-Cullors's identification of the connection between economic extraction and moralization around "safety" supports this argument, and she also draws out some idiosyncrasies within value's material manifestations. On the one hand, Khan-Cullors draws from a history of Black Marxism and identifies examples of a particular type of economic valuation placed on Black labor. She argues, for instance, that mass incarceration is "valuable" to white people as a means of replacing jobs lost to economic disinvestment in their rural communities, as well as to companies with stock in private prisons and for states and private companies that extract free labor from incarcerated populations.[81] On the other hand, she decries a mass devaluation of Black lives and livelihoods. She describes watching family members struggle to achieve steady employment and a livable wage while being pushed out of stable industries, and sent to prison rather than supported with treatment for mental illness and addiction.[82] She similarly recounts seeing resources diverted to fighting gangs that could instead be placed into improving schools and investing in arts and athletics.[83] These disparate points reveal the apparent contradiction of Black people being highly valued for the labor and resources that can be extracted from them, while their lives and livelihoods are deprioritized and treated as expendable. Yet this contradiction is resolvable, Khan-Cullors shows, when we realize that valuation is first and foremost a political valuation of white life over Black life—and thus an extension of racialized violence.

In Chapter 4 I also showed that Cooper presents the supposed tension between economic and moral discourses of value as a distraction from the way that Black women have been a particular target of political devaluations. Like Cooper, Khan-Cullors also shows the politics of value to be contingently racialized, gendered, and sexualized. Khan-Cullors extends her perspective on Black devaluation to include the ways that she is especially devalued as a woman by both white and Black men. She describes, for instance, the intergenerational harm wreaked upon her family by her grandmother's rape by a white man.[84] She also details how her mother faced rejection, judgment, and punishment from the male leaders of her own Jehovah's Witness community, describing these punishments as "particularly aimed at women and our bodies, our sexuality."[85] As Khan-Cullors shows, political devaluation is magnified for Black women, as they are doubly devalued by the white-dominated world and within Black communities.

Khan-Cullors uses similar language to describe her experiences of devaluation as a queer person. She notes the high depression and suicide rates for queer people and writes about how during her childhood a student group organized to support students with depression functioned as a de facto LGBTQIA+ community group because "depression is the predictable outcome when people are forced to deny their humanity."[86] While describing her early days of involvement in community organizing and advocacy, she writes about a friend who was HIV positive, and the way that his experience was immediately discernible to her as connected to the devaluation of Black life that she is organizing against.[87] She explains:

> [W]e who...are Queer...learn in the harshest of ways that this is what it means to be young and Queer: you can do nothing wrong

whatsoever, you can just be alive and yourself, and that is enough to have the whole of your life smashed to the ground and swept away.[88]

She also describes her experiences of shaming from her own queer Black peers over her leaving a nonbinary partner and beginning a relationship with a cis-gendered man, despite the abusive behavior of the former partner.[89] In Khan-Cullors's description of the politics of intersectional devaluation she does not exempt oppressed people from culpability in these projects of devaluation.

In addition to drawing attention to the ways that the politics of value are based in extraction, violence, and intersectional oppression, the Black Lives Matter movement also foregrounds the material dimensions of revaluing Black life and shows how economic redistribution is necessary but not sufficient for changing broader political structures. In Chapter 5, I showed that Michael Warner's writing at its best carves out a space for valuing queer livelihoods and cultures. Writing against heteronormativity (and homonormativity), Warner champions a public sexual culture that can improve the lives of some of the most vulnerable people in the United States. As he shows, this alternative culture has the potential to replace a culture of repression with a radical politics of safety and community, and with a political culture that celebrates experimentation, perspective-taking, and diversity. However, because of the unacknowledged tension in his writing between material and aspirational life, as I argued, Warner's treatise on the cultural politics of queer unity implicitly excludes many people within queer communities.

The Black Lives Matter movement's perspective on Black devaluation also relies on a complex understanding of the relationship between material and aspirational politics. Garza describes the movement as centered on shared "aspirations."[90] In addition to the material values of food, shelter, and livable wages, this movement's central argument engages in an ideological struggle about the highest values according to which we should live. This perspective is evident in the way that the movement, like Warner, works to shift the valence of values from economic priorities to alternative values in community self-actualization. In Garza's words, "Black Lives Matter is an ideological and political intervention in a world where Black lives are systematically and intentionally targeted for demise."[91] According to this logic, this movement's political (or material) intervention can be seen in the way activists focus on redistributing wealth and meeting material needs. The movement's ideological (or aspirational) interventions are evident in the way activists emphasize the ambiguous relationship between material and aspirational politics by shifting the valence of value to mattering.

This multivalent politics of 'mattering' is perhaps most evident in Khan-Cullors's discussions of public love as an alternative value to mobilize around, thus mirroring Warner's own efforts to shift the central values for queer activism. As Khan-Cullors argues, for Black people there is "no city, no block where what they [Black communities] know, all they know, is that their lives matter, that they are loved."[92] However Khan-Cullors's appeal to love as an alternative value is not idealistic, but complex and ambivalent. Discussing the flaws of 12-step programs and the ways such programs ignore structural causes of addiction in favor of a logic of individuation, she writes that these programs at their best focus on public accountability, which she sees as akin to a kind of public love.[93] Honesty, she explains, can be life-giving, as she positions this kind of public sharing as in implicit contrast to a politics of denial or repression.[94] From this point, she develops an argument that open expressions of love, in families but also in politics, are not only a means to an end, but also an essential end in their own right.[95] In fact, she explains, her childhood activism was actually the first way she was able to be in public space with both of her parents, just like white kids could.[96] She then details the way that celebrating love in public space plays a key role in Black Lives Matter activism.[97] The primary function of the movement's demonstrations is, as she writes, to call community "together to acknowledge a life."[98] Though the movement has been labeled by detractors as disruptive, these efforts demonstrate a priority in restoration and joy.

Just as Warner showed that the values of Christopher Street surpassed economic investment and included things like visibility, safety, community, and self-actualization, Khan-Cullors discusses how meeting the material demands of life (in the form of shifting economic value) will support other possible values, like love, public accountability, and celebrations of life itself. At the same time, the Black Lives Matter movement's use of the concept of value is more self-conscious than Warner's, and thus less vulnerable to the types of exclusions that he slips into his own political vision. Moreover, as I will show later, this movement's emphases on non-erasure and on an intersectional approach to Black activism use the tension between material and aspirational politics to enact the opposite effect.

On Mattering

To understand Black Lives Matter's claim about the political nature of value, it is necessary to pause on one more quality of the distinctive language mobilizing this movement. Black Lives Matter activists, in their claim that Black lives *matter*, foreground the intrinsic importance of Black life as a moral priority. Yet they also make specific demands to set a firm baseline of material resources necessary for survival. The movement responded to early critiques about a lack of clarity in their message by developing a detailed policy platform housed under an umbrella organization, the Movement for Black Lives (M4BL).[99] This platform consists of a strategic set of demands—activists are clear that these demands do not entail all of their "collective needs and visions," but nevertheless include a far-reaching policy agenda including "calls for reparations, an end to state killings of black people, social justice, and political power for black people."[100] Other organizations under this umbrella are similarly strategic. Campaign Zero's list of objectives provides a detailed accounting of the material resources necessary for surviving police encounters—including body cameras, the use of mental health professionals for crisis response, independent investigative and prosecutor bodies, and funding for these and many other policies and judicial reforms across multiple levels of governance.[101] Black Youth Project 100 meanwhile "calls for defunding police departments, and it also calls on the state to 'fund Black futures' by investing in education, healthcare, job creation and other vital needs in Black communities."[102] Importantly, each of these political demands brings material and moral claims together.

Black Lives Matter activists frame their problem as one of maintaining a delicate balance between two very different logics of value, calling attention to the ways that they have been complementarily disposed to the devaluation of Black life. The movement champions "a wide-reaching and in-depth platform" listing concrete economic demands, including reparations.[103] They do not wish to merely *assert* that Black lives matter, but to remedy a material disinvestment in Black life, and activists recognize that doing so requires a redistribution of economic resources. For instance, Garza explains that, during a survey she conducted, "over 60 percent of black domestic workers that we talked to said that they didn't have [reliable access to] food in the last month. Many are also spending way more of their income than they should on rent or mortgage."[104] Garza's statement on racialized income disparities makes it clear that a key aim of the Black Lives Matter movement is to reclaim material resources for Black people. But activists are equally firm that being actively engaged in a project of revaluing must go beyond redressing economic injuries, which they make clear through frequent condemnations of capitalism and economism.[105] From some perspectives, this would read as a contradiction—the Movement for Black Lives' platform specifically calls for material resources in the form of reinvestment and empowerment, even as they argue for a set of values that is not evaluated in material resources.[106] But the contradiction vanishes upon moving beyond a vision of politics that assumes material and aspirational life can be cleanly divided. Moreover, this movement's use of the language of mattering, I will now argue, mobilizes the tension between material and aspirational life with the purpose of prioritizing the voices of queer and trans people, women, young people, and disabled people within the movement even as it calls for a prioritization of Black lives in society at large.

Distinction Without, Prioritization Within

The Black Lives Matter movement's central contention—that #BlackLivesMatter—brings to the surface tensions between different discourses of value, as well as tensions between different political communities, or visions of political community. Yet this movement is ultimately more intent on thinking about new ways of holding collective power and different ways that political institutions should work than it is in receiving recognition from pre-existing political collectivities and institutions. This perspective is evident in activists' use of the concept of value to enact logics of prioritization and distinction. Attention to priority and distinction, activists show, is a critical political endeavor simply because if we look at how priorities develop and shift we are more likely to see violence.[107]

The claim that "Black Lives Matter" relies upon a logic of distinction—the focus is not on the value of any lives, but on the value of Black lives. Of course, groups opposing the Black Lives Matter movement have also seized upon the language of mattering, treating the claims of Black Lives Matter activists as illusory through attempts to disperse value in the claim that "all lives matter," or actively re-concentrate it with claims that "white lives matter" or "blue lives matter."[108] The counter-claims of "blue lives matter" and "white lives matter" appropriate the Black Lives Matter movement's contention that value is unevenly distributed between groups in order to assert that, despite appearances, it is white people, or their police protectors, whose lives are devalued by the very claim that *Black* lives matter.[109] The discourse of "all lives matter," meanwhile, seeks to shore up the status quo, where both the additional value attached to white lives through privilege and the devaluation of Black lives are hidden by a presumption of colorblindness.[110] This latter claim's willful naïveté also indicates that discourses of value and equality cannot be easily disentangled. This claim conceals its racism in a vision of universal equality by arguing that the best way for equality to be realized is through the uncritical valorization of all people—rather than through a particular focus on elevating those who have been systematically devalued.

Black Lives Matter activists, by contrast, are clear that their priority is specifically in Black lives.[111] Garza writes that appropriations of this movement's language and the replacement of the 'Black' in Black Lives Matter by other groups (even well-meaning allies) engages in a type of erasure that amounts to anti-Blackness.[112] As Garza elaborates, "when we deploy 'All Lives Matter' as if to correct an intervention specifically created to address anti-blackness, we lose the ways in which the state apparatus has built a program of genocide and repression mostly on the backs of Black people."[113] Her alternative is to "lift up Black lives as an opportunity to connect struggles across race, class, gender, nationality, sexuality and disability."[114] This is why the Black Lives Matter movement calls "to defund the police and invest in black communities instead."[115] Achieving a true valuation of Black communities, activists argue, means deprioritizing police.

Black Lives Matter activists consequently show that achieving substantive equality counterintuitively requires a politics of distinction.[116]

While the language of equality can be mobilized against redistributive policies like reparations and affirmative action, the language of value cannot do so without revealing racial prioritization.[117] In this way, the issue with "all lives matter" may not be that value discourse enables such a claim, but that equality discourse does.[118] Were value discourse deployed on its own here, the claim that "all lives matter" is meaningfully distinct from "white lives matter" would be a tougher sell. The "Black Lives Matter" claim, by contrast, is open to a dynamic and even dialectical relationship between equality and value. Indeed, every claim to equality *is* also a claim to a certain value or set of values. For instance, as I showed in Chapter 5, the argument for marriage equality is also a way into valuation of queer relationships (and at the expense of other possible values in building and sustaining queer community). Value claims can therefore buttress, support, and even enhance the force of equality claims.[119] The language of equality needs the language of values in order to maintain its status as a discourse that is distinctly about justice rather than leveling.

Herein lies the power of this movement's means of claiming value. Recall again Khan-Cullors's description of the aim of the movement as getting "people to see that as much as there is a progressive movement for justice, here are those working just as hard for the opposite outcome, an outcome where only the fewest of lives matter at all."[120] From this perspective, racist appropriations of the Black Lives Matter slogan are examples of the movement's very point about Black devaluation. Contested as it may be, the argument that Black lives "matter" must merely raise the possibility that Black lives have been and continue to be devalued in order to be effective. The claim that "all lives matter" is exposed as disingenuous whenever a life of *any* color is taken by police brutality. For this very reason, the Black Lives Matter movement has subverted and reclaimed the language of "all lives matter" in the 2020 slogan "All Black Lives Matter," as a call for recognition of the particular vulnerability of Black trans people.[121]

Prioritizing Intersectionality

In ongoing efforts to combat intersectional erasures, Black Lives Matter activists turn this logic of prioritization within. Movement leaders describe a distinct relationship between working to recognize the value of Black lives and identifying women and queer people whose lives and contributions otherwise go unacknowledged. The "Say Their Name" campaign was one such effort. Activists publicly pushed to share the names of Black people killed by state violence so that they could not be forgotten.[122] The movement made special efforts to list the names of Black women (and especially trans women) killed by police, to highlight the fact that the names most aired by the media were predominantly male and cis-gendered.[123]

Where this action dovetails with a politics of valuation is in these activists' demonstration that erasure and devaluation are sides of the same
coin—that even if some names of men murdered by police officers are
remembered, few know the names of the Black trans women killed during
the same years.[124] Despite being founded by Black queer women, activists
note that the movement still faces the problem not only of white people
caring less about Black deaths, but also of Black men and women caring
less about the deaths of Black women and trans people. For instance, while
many people recognize the name of George Floyd following the eruption
of massive-scale Black Lives Matter protests across the United States in
mid-2020, fewer know the names of Tony McDade or Breonna Taylor, or
even Iyonna Dior, a Black trans woman who was beaten by a mob at one
of the protests in Minneapolis.[125]

This priority of anti-erasure accounts for many of the careful decisions in the way that the movement is organized. For instance, activists
make a concerted effort to recognize the fact that Black women are on
the frontlines of all of its actions.[126] This composition of protests is not
obvious, Khan-Cullors explains, because the media focuses primarily on
the men in the movement.[127] Organizers also highlight the fact that the
work of this movement is lifted up by an extraordinary number of trans
people.[128] In fact, Khan-Cullors writes that women (including many
trans women) constituted around 80 percent of the protesters bussed in
to Ferguson.[129]

Activists developed these means of combatting erasure in response to
gendered silences and hostility against women and queer people in activist
spaces dominated by Black men and their agendas.[130] As Garza explains,
the movement actually grew not only out of a response to white supremacy, but also as a response to "people of color who erase the labor of black
queer women."[131] She writes:

> Black Lives Matter is a unique contribution that goes beyond extraju-
> dicial killings of Black people by police and vigilantes. It goes beyond
> the narrow nationalism that can be prevalent within some Black com-
> munities, which merely call on Black people to love Black, live Black
> and buy Black, keeping straight cis Black men in the front of the move-
> ment while our sisters, queer and trans and disabled folk take up roles
> in the background or not at all. Black Lives Matter affirms the lives
> of Black queer and trans folks, disabled folks, Black-undocumented
> folks, folks with records, women and all Black lives along the gender
> spectrum. It centers those that have been marginalized within Black
> liberation movements. It is a tactic to (re)build the Black liberation
> movement.[132]

The movement, in other words, is about making Black lives matter in
Black spaces, rather than only in white spaces. This requires attention to

the experiences of Black people who are intersectionally marginalized. Yet these people and their experiences are often erased by Black movements that seek a unity in Blackness at the expense of paying adequate attention to the differences and divides within their communities. Garza elaborates: "perhaps if we were the charismatic Black men many are rallying around these days, it would have been a different story, but being Black queer women in this society (and apparently within these movements) tends to equal invisibility and non-relevancy."[133] This erasure echoes the invisibility of "the woman who organized, strategized, marched, cooked, typed up and did the work to ensure the Civil Rights Movement, women whose names," Khan-Cullors also writes, "go unspoken, unknown."[134] Black Lives Matter activists' refusal of erasure therefore honors not only the work of present-day women and queer activists, but also those whose legacy they build upon.

Beyond merely identifying the hidden contributions of women and queer people, the movement also makes a careful effort to ensure that intersectionally marginalized people continue to be at its center of its leadership and advocacy. As Khan-Cullors explains, the coordinated efforts that we now think of as the Black Lives Matter movement grew out of conversations following the Ferguson protests which were carried out mostly by women, many of whom are queer and trans.[135] Organizers are careful to ensure that their organization continues to be a space centered on Black women, defined by its freedom from male centeredness.[136] Khan-Cullors explains that the goal is to make "everyday people feel part of a push for change," and as she pointedly specifies, by "ordinary people" she means "people like Sandra Bland."[137] In their ongoing organizing efforts, Black Lives Matter activists pay special attention to the precarity of Black trans and nonbinary people.[138] They also describe working to make sure that both their organization and their advocacy are non-heteronormative and non-ageist.[139] These priorities reflect activists' own experiences living at these intersections. For instance, Khan-Cullors's memoir is filled with stories and discussions of friends and family living with HIV, depression and suicide, mental illness, and addiction, all of which draw out the importance she sees in anti-ableist politics.

In each of these ways, the Black Lives Matter movement calls out devaluations of women and queer, disabled, and otherwise marginalized lives within Black communities. But in ongoing efforts to include people who are intersectionally devalued, activists also move beyond merely identifying devaluations, and advance a project of revaluing these lives and contributions. The movement's efforts to champion women leaders such as those behind the Civil Rights Movement enact a rewriting of history that valorizes people who have played an underacknowledged role in shaping it. Activists' focus on prioritizing the most vulnerable voices within their organization repeatedly transfers power and ownership to people who are consistently pushed to its margins.

Notes

1 Anna Julia Cooper, *A Voice from the South* (New York NY: Oxford University Press, 2008), 285. This sort of address from Cooper is extremely rare, according to Mary Helen Washington, "Anna Julia Cooper: The Black Feminist Voice of the 1890s," *Legacy* 4, no. 2 (1987).

2 Michael Warner, *The Trouble with Normal: Sex, Politics, and the Ethics of Queer Life* (Cambridge MA: Harvard University Press, 1999), 184–185.

3 Charles Taylor, *Multiculturalism: Examining the Politics of Recognition* (Princeton University Press, 1992).

4 Wendy Brown, *States of Injury: Power and Freedom in Late Modernity* (Princeton University Press, 1995), and Nancy Fraser and Axel Honneth, *Redistribution or Recognition? A Political–Philosophical Exchange* (New York NY: Verso, 2004).

5 Robert Nichols, "Theft Is Property! The Recursive Logic of Dispossession," *Political Theory* 46, no. 1 (2018), 3–28.

6 Frantz Fanon, *The Wretched of the Earth* (New York NY: Grove Press, 2005), and Kwame Ture, "Toward Black Liberation," *The Massachusetts Review* (1966).

7 Glen Sean Coulthard, *Red Skin White Masks: Rejecting the Colonial Politics of Recognition* 2 (Minneapolis MN: University of Minnesota Press, 2014).

8 Tommy J. Curry, "Michael Brown and the Need for a Genre Study of Black Male Death and Dying," *Theory & Event* 17, no. 3 (2014); Patrice Douglass, "Black Feminist Theory for the Dead and Dying," *Theory & Event* 21, no. 1 (2018), Jonathan Havercroft and David Owen, "Soul-Blindness, Police Orders and Black Lives Matter: Wittgenstein, Cavell, and Rancière," *Political Theory* 44, no. 6 (2016); Juliet Hooker, "Black Lives Matter and the Paradoxes of U.S. Black Politics: From Democratic Sacrifice to Democratic Repair," *Political Theory* 44, no. 4 (2016); Glenn Mackin. "Black Lives Matter and the Concept of the Counterworld," *Philosophy and Rhetoric* 49 no. 4 (2016); David W. McIvor, *Mourning in America: Race and the Politics of Loss* (Ithaca NY: Cornell University Press, 2016); See also Russell Rickford, "Black Lives Matter: Toward a Modern Practice of Mass Struggle," *New Labor Forum* 25 no. 1 (2016).

9 Patchen Markell, *Bound by Recognition* (Princeton: Princeton University Press, 2003).

10 Bonnie Washick, Elizabeth Wingrove, Kathy E. Ferguson, and Jane Bennett, "Politics that Matter: Thinking About Power and Justice with the New Materialists," *Contemporary Political Theory* 14, no. 1 (2015).

11 For examples of Black feminist theorizations of the politics of care and concern, see Audre Lorde, *A Burst of Light* (Mineola NY: Dover Publications, 1988), and Patricia Hill Collins, *Black Feminist Thought: Knowledge, Consciousness, and the Politics of Empowerment* (New York NY: Routledge 2000). For examples of this language in descriptions of the Black Lives Matter movement, see Hooker, "Black Lives Matter"; Utz Lars McKnight, "Where Is The Love That You Promised?," *Theory & Event* 17, no. 3 (2014); Melvin Rogers, "Introduction: Disposable Lives," *Theory & Event* 17, no. 3 (2014).

12 On thinking of political theory as both diagnostic and prescriptive, see Mary Dietz, "Between Polis and Empire: Aristotle's Politics," *American Political Science Review* 106, no. 2 (2012), 275–293. See also Hanna Fenichel Pitkin, *The Attack of the Blob: Hannah Arendt's Concept of the Social* (University of Chicago Press, 1998).

13 Christopher Lebron, *The Making of Black Lives Matter: A Brief History of an Idea* (Oxford University Press, 2017), xv and 72. For a deep engagement with the decentralized nature of this movement, see Barbara Ransby, *Making*

All Black Lives Matter: Reimagining Freedom in the 21st Century (Berkeley CA: University of California Press, 2018).

14 For instance, Lebron locates much evidence of Audre Lorde's influence in the movement's central priorities.

15 Patrisse Khan-Cullors and asha bandele, *When They Call You a Terrorist: A Black Lives Matter Memoir* (New York NY: St. Martin's Press, 2017).

16 Ibid., 88, 111, and 148.

17 Keeanga-Yamahtta Taylor, *How We Get Free: Black Feminism and the Combahee River Collective* (Chicago IL: Haymarket Books, 2017), 147–148.

18 Khan-Cullors and bandele, *When They Call*, 21; 50–51. Later in Khan-Cullors's life, she connects her advocacy for justice for her brother to lunch counter sit-ins and pushes for voting rights. Ibid., 127.

19 Ibid., 52.

20 Ibid., 186.

21 Barnor Hesse and Juliet Hooker, "Introduction: On Black Political Thought inside Global Black Protest," *The South Atlantic Quarterly* 116, no. 3 (2017), 451; Lebron, *The Making of*, xi; and Angela Davis, "Foreword," in Patrisse Khan-Cullors and asha bandele, *When They Call You a Terrorist: A Black Lives Matter Memoir* (New York NY: St. Martin's Press, 2017), xi. As Alicia Garza writes, "I created #BlackLivesMatter with Patrisse Cullors and Opal Tometi, two of my sisters, as a call to action for Black people after 17-year-old Trayvon Martin was posthumously placed on trial for his own murder and the killer, George Zimmerman, was not held accountable for the crime he committed." Alicia Gaza, "A Herstory of the #BlackLivesMatter Movement," *Feminist Wire,* October 7, 2014, https://thefeministwire.com/2014/10/blacklivesmatter-2/.

22 Khan-Cullors and bandele, *When They Call*, 6.

23 Ibid., 223.

24 There is some truth to this claim to the extent that the Ferguson protests helped the movement gain national (and even international) attention. See, for instance, Keeanga-Yamahtta Taylor, *From #BlackLivesMatter to Black Liberation* (Chicago IL: Haymarket Books, 2016). However, the argument that these protests were spontaneous is overstated.

25 Khan-Cullors and bandele, *When They Call*, 164, 198, and 201.

26 Ibid., 164–165.

27 Ibid., 174 and 167.

28 Garza had begun her activism with tenant rights organizing in West Oakland and San Francisco. See Taylor, *How We Get Free*, 152.

29 Khan-Cullors and bandele, *When They Call*, 184.

30 Khan-Cullors and Garza had met at a conference in 2005, while both women were organizing for employment rights. Taylor, *How We Get Free*, 156.

31 Hesse and Hooker, "Introduction: On Black Political," 452.

32 Ibid.

33 Davis, "Foreword," xi–xii.

34 Taylor, *From #BlackLivesMatter to Black*.

35 Despite this reception, Debra Thompson argues for the importance of public displays of affect by Black communities and explains that the movement's language and protests reflect "grief, anger, fury, rage, terror, and exasperation" as police killings of Black people have meant that "heartbroken families are forced to mourn in public." Debra Thompson, "An Exoneration of Black Rage," *The South Atlantic Quarterly* 116, no. 3 (2017), 458–459.

36 Ibid., 475.

37 Ibid.

38 Lebron, *The Making of*, xii.

39 Khan-Cullors and bandele, *When They Call*, 180; Lebron, *The Making of*, xiv.

40 Khan-Cullors and bandele, *When They Call*, 145.

41 Likewise, James Baldwin describes Black people as "a people from whom everything has been taken away, including, most crucially, their sense of their own worth." As he elaborates, "people cannot live without this sense; they will do anything whatever to regain it." James Baldwin, *The Fire Next Time* (New York NY: Vintage International, 1991), 48.

42 Ibid., 148–149.

43 Minkah Makalani, "Black Lives Matter and the Limits of Formal Black Politics," *The South Atlantic Quarterly* 116, no. 3 (2017), 532–533.

44 Ibid., 532.

45 Ibid., 531.

46 Lebron, *The Making of*, xi–xii.

47 Hesse and Hooker, "Introduction: On Black Political," 444.

48 Khan-Cullors and bandele, *When They Call*, 180.

49 Ibid., 197.

50 Ibid., 205.

51 In doing so, activists draw from a legacy of Black feminist theorizing about the devaluation of Black lives. See, for example, Taylor, *How We Get Free*, 18.

52 Liz Pleasant, "Meet the Woman Behind #BlackLivesMatter – The Hashtag That Became a Civil Rights Movement," *YES! Magazine*, May 1, 2015.

53 Racahell Davis, "Black Lives Matter Co-Founder Alicia Garza Talks Philando Castile, Alton Sterling and How You Can Get Involved in Fighting Injustice," *Essence*, July 8, 2016, http://www.essence.com/2016/07/08/black-lives-matter-co-founder-alicia-garza-philando-castile-alton-sterling, emphasis added.

54 Corinne Gaston, "On Black Lives Matter: An Interview With Patrisse Cullors," *Neon Tommy: Annenberg Media Center*, January 7, 2015, http://www.neontommy.com/news/2015/01/black-lives-matter-interview-patrisse-cullors, emphasis added.

55 Taylor, *From #BlackLivesMatter to Black*, 183, emphasis added.

56 Alicia Garza, "A Herstory of the #BlackLivesMatter Movement," emphasis added.

57 Ibid. October 7, 2014. http://www.thefeministwire.com/2014/10/blacklivesmatter-2/.

58 Khan-Cullors and bandele, *When They Call*, 124 and 200.

59 Ibid., 5.

60 Ibid., 108.

61 Ibid., 11–12.

62 Ibid., 21.

63 Ibid., 54.

64 Ibid., 222.

65 Ibid., 129, 250–251.

66 The Anti Police-Terror Project, an Oakland-based Black Lives Matter affiliate, for instance, conducted a protest in which chants were made about reclaiming local streets with a barbecue in a park located in the center of the city. Western Regional Advocacy Project, "Recap of MLK JR. Days of Action 2017 BY WRAP Members, Allies & Friends!!!!," http://wraphome.org/2017/01/24/recap-mlk-jr-days-action-2017-wrap-members-allies-friends/.

67 Movement for Black Lives, "Platform," https://policy.m4bl.org/platform/.

68 Khan-Cullors and bandele, *When They Call*, 249.

69 Ibid., 138.

70 Ibid., 124.

71 Ibid., 27.

72 Ibid., 25.

73 Ibid.,14, 16, 28, and 15–16, respectively.

74 Ibid., 6.

75 Ibid., 46 and 54. For discussions of police brutality in response to protesters, see Li Zhou, " 'The Protesters Had to De-escalate the Police': Demonstrators Are the Ones Defusing Violence at Protests," *Vox*, June 12, 2020, https://www.vox.com/2020/6/12/21279619/protesters-police-violence-philadelphia-los-angeles-washington-dc.

76 Khan-Cullors and bandele, *When They Call*, 26.

77 Ibid., 134 and 144.

78 Ibid., 8.

79 Ibid., 120.

80 Ibid., 203.

81 Ibid., 44–45, and 55. Khan-Cullors is drawing from work like that of Ruth Wilson Gilmore, *Golden Gulag: Prisons, Surplus, Crisis, and Opposition in Globalizing California* (Berkeley CA: University of California Press, 2007).

82 Khan-Cullors and bandele, *When They Call*, 50.

83 Ibid., 58. These sorts of programs, she argues, provide creative outlets that would prevent gangs from developing in the first place.

84 Ibid., 36.

85 Ibid., 70–72.

86 Ibid., 82, 75.

87 Ibid., 87.

88 Ibid., 77.

89 Ibid., 152. This criticism in many ways mirrors Cooper's condemnation of white feminist movements for their racialized oversights—having had the experience of oppression, Khan-Cullors shows, does not mean that one is never oneself culpable for similar exclusions.

90 Taylor, *How We Get Free*, 168. As Lebron explains, the movement's central slogan represents "an ideal." Lebron, *The Making of*, xii. Davis argues that the framing forces a confrontation between Western logic—a logic which, she elaborates, "expresses itself through philosophical certainties and ideological presuppositions"—and reparative efforts at racialized justice. Davis, "Foreword," xiii.

91 Garza, "A Herstory of."

92 Khan-Cullors and bandele, *When They Call*, 16.

93 Ibid., 37–38.

94 Ibid., 40.

95 Ibid., 90.

96 Ibid., 89.

97 Ibid., 90. Whether intentionally or not, this effort echoes Martin Luther King, Jr.'s theorizations of the role of love in the movement for racial justice.

98 Ibid., 106.

99 Makalani, "Black Lives Matter," 530.

100 Ibid., 532.

101 Campaign Zero, "Solutions," https://www.joincampaignzero.org/solutions/#contracts.

102 Martha Biondi, "The Radicalism of Black Lives Matter," *In These Times*, August 15, 2016, http://inthesetimes.com/features/black-lives-matter-history-police-brutality.html.

103 According to *The Atlantic*:

The "Vision 4 Black Lives," as the platform has been known on social media, lays out six core planks around criminal justice, reparations, investment and divestment, economic justice, community control, and political power. Some of these items, including the criminal-justice components of the platform's demands to "end the war on black people," are likely familiar to anyone who has followed the development of Black Lives Matter. But other ideas, including demands to add special protections for trans, queer, and gender-nonconforming people to anti-discrimination laws, a call for free education for black people, and a proposal to implement black economic cooperatives, haven't previously been spelled out quite this clearly. The demands are certainly controversial, but they are clearly the result of considered and methodical decision-making.

> (Vann R. Newkirk II, "The Permanence of Black Lives Matter," *The Atlantic*, August 3, 2016, https://www.theatlantic.com/politics/ archive/2016/08/movement-black-lives-platform/494309/. See also Biondi, "The Radicalism of Black Lives Matter").

104 Alicia Garza and Mychal Denzel Smith, "A Q&A With Alicia Garza, Co-Founder of #BlackLivesMatter," March 24, 2015, https://www.thenation. com/article/qa-alicia-garza-co-founder-blacklivesmatter/.

105 "In Honor of Our Dead: Latinx, Queer, Trans, Muslim, Black—We Will Be Free," http://blacklivesmatter.com/in-honor-of-our-dead-queer-trans-muslim-black-we-will-be-free/.

106 Movement for Black Lives, "Platform," https://policy.m4bl.org/platform/.

107 When this movement argues that "Black Lives Matter" they are pointing out political divides in valuation by saying that they value Black people, and that what activists value should be valued by the society in which they live.

108 George Yancy and Judith Butler, "What's Wrong With 'All Lives Matter'?," *New York Times*, January 12, 2015, https://opinionator.blogs.nytimes. com/2015/01/12/whats-wrong-with-all-lives-matter/?_r=0.

109 This distortion raises tactical concerns about the efficacy of rational dialogue, non-violence, and other forms of "appropriate" political action. Hooker, "Black Lives Matter," 2016.

110 Catherine L. Langford and Montené Speight, "#BlackLivesMatter: Epistemic Positioning, Challenges, and Possibilities," *Journal of Contemporary Rhetoric* 5, nos. 3/4 (2015).

111 Juliet Hooker argues that the Black Lives Matter movement ultimately challenges the very value of whiteness. As Hooker explains, "distinguishing between material and symbolic loss...has normative implications for how we assess different forms of white grievance." For example, she continues, "it is undeniable that the white working class has suffered significant material losses in recent decades." But she further argues that white supremacy is also predicated on an evasion of symbolic loss. She writes, "that the response to a movement created to bring attention to the disproportionate violence faced by black people should be the slogan 'All lives matter'...reveals how white grievance is in many ways constituted in response to symbolic losses." As Hooker shows, "the symbolic decentering of whiteness implied by saying #BlackLivesMatter could only be taken as a devaluation of white lives by those who believe that politics should always center the concerns of whites as a group." Here it is notable for Hooker that the Black Lives Matter movement centers tangible losses rather than symbolic ones, and that their language of mattering is connected to extended conversations about material redistribution. Juliet Hooker, "Black Protest/White Grievance: On the Problem of White Political Imaginations Not Shaped by Loss," *The South Atlantic Quarterly* 116, no. 3 (2017), 492–494.

112 Ibid.

113 As Garza elaborates, "given the disproportionate impact state violence has on Black lives, we understand that when Black people in this country get free, the benefits will be wide reaching and transformative for society as a whole. When we are able to end hyper-criminalization and sexualization of Black people and end the poverty, control, and surveillance of Black people, every single person in this world has a better shot at getting and staying free. When Black people get free, everybody gets free." Garza, "A Herstory of."

114 Garza, "A Herstory of."

115 Hooker, "Black Protest/White Grievance."

116 As Angela Davis explains, "the seemingly simple phrase 'Black Lives Matter' has disrupted undisputed assumptions about the logic of equality, justice, and human freedom in the United States and all over the world." Davis, "Foreword," xiii.

117 When the bad faith pretense of agreement in the phrase "All Lives Matter" appeals to equality in its replacement of 'Black' with 'all' they emphasize the distinction inherent in the Black Lives Matter movement's central claim. After all, 'all' implies equivalence, whereas 'Black' is specific. Yet the Black Lives Matter movement's use of the language of mattering also sneaks value discourse into the equation, and value implies importance.

118 To the extent that I am critical of equality discourse, my point is akin to Martin Luther King, Jr.'s worry by 1967/1968 that the Civil Rights Movement might be seeking to integrate into a burning house.

119 This is not to say that value claims are a substitute for equality claims. Value discourse needs equality discourse in order to avoid the value relativism upon which movements like the evangelical right's "values voters" defend their racism and homophobia. Priority on its own could cause a lot of political problems, absent a long history of treating equality as an unqualified good. Part of my argument about the importance of the language of value and values in political discourse is that false universalism is harder to hide in this vocabulary simply because this language forces a way of being more explicit about the people with whom our true sympathies lie.

120 Khan-Cullors and bandele, *When They Call*, 205.

121 See Hailey Branson-Potts and Matt Stiles, "All Black Lives Matter March Calls for LGBTQ Rights and Racial Justice," *Los Angeles Times*, June 15, 2020, https://www.latimes.com/california/story/2020-06-15/lgbtq-pride-black-lives-controversy.

122 Khan-Cullors and bandele, *When They Call*, 204, and Lebron, *The Making of*, x.

123 Khan-Cullors and bandele, *When They Call*, 227–228. See also Shatema Threadcraft, "North American Necropolitics and Gender: On #BlackLivesMatter and Black Femicide," *The South Atlantic Quarterly* 116, no. 3 (2017), 568–570.

124 As Lebron puts it, this reveals the "hypocrisy" of the claim that "All Lives Matter." Lebron, *The Making of*, 95.

125 On Tony McDade, see Gwen Aviles, "Black Transgender Man Fatally Shot by Florida Police," *NBC News*, May 29, 2020, https://www.nbcnews.com/feature/nbc-out/black-transgender-man-fatally-shot-florida-police-n1218156. On Breonna Taylor, see "LMPD Releases Nearly Blank Report from The Night of Breonna Taylor's Killing." *NPR*, June 11, 2020, https://www.npr.org/2020/06/11/875311065/lmpd-releases-nearly-blank-report-from-the-night-of-breonna-taylors-killing. For an all-too-brief mention of Iyonna Dior, see Siobhan Burke, "Dancing Bodies That Proclaim: Black Lives Matter," June 9, 2020, https://www.nytimes.com/2020/06/09/arts/dance/dancing-protests-george-floyd.html.

126 Khan-Cullors and bandele, *When They Call*, 249.

127 Ibid., 218.
128 Ibid., 216.
129 Ibid., 218–219.
130 Taylor, *How We Get Free*, 157–159.
131 Garza, "A Herstory of."
132 Ibid.
133 Ibid.
134 Khan-Cullors and bandele, *When They Call*, 219–221.
135 Ibid., 202.
136 Khan-Cullors and bandele, *When They Call*, 203.
137 Ibid., 250. Sandra Bland was a 28-year-old woman who, inspired by the Black Lives Matter movement's message, had begun posting videos detailing police abuses before she was suspiciously found hanged in a jail cell after being stopped for a minor traffic violation, so Khan-Cullors's point is that both the brave contributions and brutal murders of Black women like Bland are underacknowledged.
138 Ibid., 202.
139 Ibid., 203.

7 Conclusion

Centering Value in Political Praxis

Pundits and newscasters were bewildered by the 2016 U.S. Presidential Election results, and much of the debate in the months that followed this election echoed the old "What's the Matter with Kansas?" debate about interest-based voting, but from within a slightly different frame—namely the extent to which moral commitments or economic hardship had secured Trump's victory.[1] The question most often posed by pundits was whether Rust Belt voters had fallen in line with the evangelical right and acted on their ideas of what society should look like—their *values*—or whether their vote had instead sought to bring economic *value* to depressed communities.[2] Though appeals to identity were certainly at play, parsing them—and especially identifying their precise connection to Trump's racist rhetoric—was difficult, and that was because of a disagreement about which logic of value took precedence in this moment, and for which communities.

My argument is that unresolved conceptual tensions like these can obscure prejudice and oppression. Centering the political dimensions of value, by contrast, reveals the values these voters supported to be neither economic nor moral, but white ones. After all, as I have tried to show throughout this book, opacity around which logic of value is at play in various political considerations can conceal a de facto prioritization of select communities.

By contrast, the Black Lives Matter movement mobilizes the language of value and values as political concepts to redraw the boundaries of political community, and to reimagine distributions of material resources and priorities. As the Black Lives Matter movement shows us, when someone claims value they are distinctly not articulating a politics of equality, but of priority and distinction—of what, above other things, matters. Value claims can therefore be mobilized as agonist democratic claims that do not cover their tracks behind a leveling discourse that comes at the expense of real equality. In claiming priority, these activists do not erase political contestation, but instead encourage judgments about what (and who) takes precedence, and on what basis.

For this reason, I argue that the tensions at the heart of value discourse can be useful for democratic practice. To see how this could be the case,

DOI: 10.4324/9781003304302-7

we need only look at the example of the ways anti-racism is often presented in the terms of moral values. Yet anti-racism could also be framed as a means to attaining economic value. Eliminating racial hierarchies could unlock the undervalued wealth of human creativity and talent of those currently oppressed by these hierarchies. There is also a very real possibility that structural racism does not derive value for anyone. Indeed, with the proper frame of reference, many "selfless" actions can readily be demonstrated to align with a particular set of personal (or even shareholder) values. In each of these cases, what is really being prioritized is not the ingrained economic or moral values of a situation, but an expression of who "the people" really are and what concerns them.

Value and value claims therefore have the potential to enable the exercising, both in the sense of building capacity for and of executing a kind of paradoxical democratic agency, wherein the process of drawing boundaries can undermine them. This potential is why I argue that neither collapsing value and values into one nor setting them as distinct fully captures the politics at work in navigations of material and aspirational life. Instead, I argue from the perspective of radical democratic theory, that moments of reformulation of the ways we understand value assist the construction of boundaries placed around the body politic, and the very making of the political.

Understanding and maintaining the tension between value and values rather than collapsing these two valences into one or insisting on a radical separation suggests something prescriptive in terms of how to engage in the study and praxis of political theory, as well as for how to engage in political life. If we adhere to a clean divide between material and aspirational life, then we might miss the ways that value, expressed in our material interests and conditioning, plays into the political problems we attempt to address or the systems we seek to create. If we treat value and values as indistinct, then we might overlook the way that our aspirations and our vested interests can be at odds—and lose sight of the range of political perspectives and actions available to us. But if we treat the two types of value as in tension, then we can approach voting, activism, and even public discourse with a mindful awareness of the ways that our values and our value can be deeply intertwined, without treating their connection as predetermined or outside of our control. Like tuning an instrument, the tension between value and values can be carefully adjusted—and, if we want our politics to sing, must be.

Claiming Value as Democratic Agonism

Thinking about value in the way this book does has important stakes for political praxis. My engagement with value discourses demonstrates the importance of critically engaging political-economic theory without discarding the concept of value as irredeemably tainted by recent capitalist transformations. I also show that the position of pure moralism is always deeply enmeshed in material interests. Moreover, I argue that the tension between different discourses of value is a democratic resource for navigating the complexities of identity, overcoming internal fractures without erasing them, and enacting an agonist politics based in concerns about priority.

First, value claims, at their core, offer a means of putting identity at the center of our analyses, but doing so in a way that acknowledges the complications of such a project. Attention to value discourse requires analysis of the various communities that are subject to devaluations, and the particular ways they are devalued. At the same time, claiming value for marginalized communities does not require that we collapse social categories into individualized identity expression. Value claims can acknowledge that the composition and intersections of identities cannot be understood at the exclusion or implicit de-prioritization of fighting against systems of economic stratification. Put simply: if we think about value primarily as political, then we can deny hard distinctions between identity politics and anti-capitalist politics, while at the same time avoiding collapsing identity politics *into* anti-capitalist projects. In short, value discourse enables us to call attention to various modes of intersectional disadvantage while keeping their entanglements with capitalism front and center.

Second, the most compelling role for claiming value as an agonist mode of political agency is in how doing so offers a tool for talking about diverse modes of subjection and the means of overcoming them in a combined— but no less fractured—political voice. By keeping the tensions of value discourse alive while still pushing forward and articulating particular claims about value, we can find ways to achieve unity *in* our disagreements and various intersections rather than despite them. For left activism, this means that internal divides can be used as sources of strength rather than abjured as debilitating weaknesses. Claiming value, we can avoid papering over internal divisions in order to present a fictional unity that incidentally reproduces the homogenizing discourses it seeks to overcome. Because value claims are about priorities, but priorities that are always contingent and contestable, value discourse enables unique forms of dispossession to find shared expression in a way that keeps internal logics of distinction and prioritization at the fore.

Finally, throughout this book I have sought to explore value claims as an agonist form of political action. The tension between different discourses of value is a reminder that there are numerous possibilities for reshaping our understanding of the relationship between material and aspirational politics. It is for this reason that I argue that the language of value is an important channel for making political demands and articulating experiences of injustice in a way that centers contestation. Like equality claims, value discourse can be a tool for the production and subversion of hierarchy. However, unlike equality claims, value claims establish difference and distinction. I therefore offer value claims as actions that importantly highlight the political–economic dimensions of political life and offer alternative organizations of material life.

Put simply, claims to value are about priority; they reveal tensions between different communities (or visions of community). Often, implicit prioritizations are troubling for those of us committed to diversity and inclusion. But in another sense, the exclusive nature of value claims is why they have agonist democratic potential. A claim to value, when made in a way that does not deny internal tensions, can highlight some of the problems of defining and constituting a democratic populace without eliminating diversity. The tension between economic and moral discourses of value hides in plain view an array of people and things we could value, what it would mean to value them, and who would benefit or suffer as a consequence. These different discourses of value serve as a signal that valuation is historically constituted, and that communities are continuously being refashioned according to particular material processes and aspirations.

We ultimately should not want to resolve the tension between value and values, as this tension betrays an ambiguous relationship between material and aspirational life. Dilemmas about value and values, in addition to causing problems, are also opportunities for democratic politics. If the relationship between material and aspirational life is not clear-cut, then this means that how to delineate this boundary remains open for us to decide.

Notes

1 For examples of the debate (not the bewilderment), see Tobita Chow, "Thomas Frank on How Democrats Went From Being the 'Party of the People' to the Party of Rich Elites," *In these Times*, April 26, 2016, http:// inthesetimes.com/features/listen-liberal-thomas-frank-democratic-party-elites-inequality.html, and Seth Masket, "What's the Matter With Kansas? aptly describes the 2016 election—but was written in 2004," *Vox*, December 1, 2016, https://www.vox.com/mischiefs-of-faction/2016/12/1/13807382/thomas-frank-kansas-2016-election. I also have in mind Ella Myers's discussion of Du Bois's "psychological wage" thesis alongside her reading of his *Darkwater*. Ella Myers, "Beyond the Wages of Whiteness: Du Bois on the Irrationality of Anti-Black Racism," *Social Science Research Council*, Reading Racial Conflict Series, 2017, and Ella Myers, "Beyond the Psychological Wage: Du Bois on White Dominion," *Political Theory* 47, no. 1 (2019). Here I am especially intrigued by Ella Myers's connection between Du Bois's concept of the psychological wage of whiteness and the racial politics of the 2016 election. As she writes, "the claims embedded in this thesis—that whiteness provides meaningful "compensation" (Du Bois's term) for citizens otherwise exploited by the organization of capitalism; that the value of whiteness depends on the devaluation of black existence; and that the benefits enjoyed by whites are not strictly monetary—shaped subsequent efforts to theorize white identity and to grasp the (non)formation of political coalitions in the United States. The lasting impact of Du Bois's thinking was evident most recently

in debates surrounding the 2016 presidential election, in which the category of the "white working class" featured prominently. Commentators wrestled with whether the actions of this demographic could be best explained by feelings of economic insecurity, racial animus, or, in a more Du Boisean vein, some potent alchemy between the two." Myers, "Beyond the Wages."

2 See Sarah Pulliam Bailey, "White Evangelicals Voted Overwhelmingly for Donald Trump, Exit Polls Show," *Washington Post*, November 9, 2016, https://www.washingtonpost.com/news/acts-of-faith/wp/2016/11/09/exit-polls-show-white-evangelicals-voted-overwhelmingly-for-donald-trump/?utm_term=.238ba86c5852; Nate Cohen, "Donald Trump Can't Count on Those 'Missing White Voters'," *New York Times*, November 3, 2016, https://www.nytimes.com/2016/11/04/upshot/donald-trump-cant-count-on-those-missing-white-voters.html?_r=0; D. Sunshine Hillygus and Todd G. Shields, "Moral Issues and Voter Decision Making in the 2004 Presidential Election," *PS: Political Science and Politics* 38, no. 2 (2005); Gary Langer and Jon Cohen, "Voters and Values in the 2004 Election," *Public Opinion Quarterly* 69 no. 5 (2005); Sarah Posner, *God's Profits: Faith, Fraud, and the Republican Crusade for Values Voters* (Sausalito CA: Polipoint Press, 2008); Gregory A. Smith and Jessica Martínez. "How the Faithful Voted: A Preliminary 2016 Analysis," Pew Research Center, November 9, 2016, http://www.pewresearch.org/fact-tank/2016/11/09/how-the-faithful-voted-a-preliminary-2016-analysis/; and Daniel K. Williams. "Why Values Voters Value Donald Trump," *New York Times*, August 20, 2016, http://www.nytimes.com/2016/08/21/opinion/sunday/why-values-voters-value-donald-trump.html?_r=0. For an example of this kind of language, see Tom Gjelten, "Evangelicals Consider Whether God Really Cares How They Vote," National Public Radio, November 1, 2016, http://www.npr.org/2016/11/01/500105245/evangelicals-consider-whether-god-really-cares-how-they-vote.

Bibliography

Alexander, Elizabeth. "'We Must Be About Our Father's Business': Anna Julia Cooper and the In-Corporation of the Nineteenth-Century African American Woman Intellectual." *Signs* 20, no. 2 (1995), 336–356.

Ambler, Wayne. "Aristotle on Nature and Politics: The Case of Slavery." *Political Theory* 15, no. 3 (1987), 390–410.

Amin, Kadji. "Racial Fetishism, Gay Liberation, and the Temporalities of the Erotic." In *Disturbing Attachments: Genet, Modern Pederasty, and Queer History*. Durham NC: Duke University Press, 2017.

Appleby, Andrew. *Famine in Tudor and Stuart England*. Stanford University Press, 1978.

Aquinas, Thomas. *Summa Theologiae* (1485).

Arendt, Hannah. *The Human Condition*. University of Chicago Press, 1958.

Arendt, Hannah. *Between Past and Future*. London: Random House, 2006.

Aristotle. *The Nicomachean Ethics*. Trans. David Ross. Oxford University Press, 2009.

Aristotle. *Politics*. Trans. Carnes Lord. Chicago University Press, 2013.

Baeck, Louis. *The Mediterranean Tradition in Economic Thought*. London: Routledge, 1994.

Baker-Fletcher, Karen. *A Singing Something: Womanist Reflections on Anna Julia Cooper*. New York NY: The Crossroad Publishing Company, 1994.

Baldwin, James. *The Fire Next Time*. New York NY: Vintage International, 1991.

Baldwin, John W. "The Medieval Theories of the Just Price: Romanists, Canonists, and Theologians in the Twelfth and Thirteenth Centuries." *Transactions of the American Philosophical Society*, New Series 49, no. 4 (1959), 1–92.

Balot, Ryan. *Greed and Injustice in Classical Athens*. Princeton University Press, 2001.

Bassichis, Morgan, Alexander Lee, and Dean Spade. "Building an Abolitionist Trans and Queer Movement with Everything We've Got." In Eric Stanley and Nat Smith, eds., *Captive Genders: Trans Embodiment and the Prison Industrial Complex*. Chico CA: AK Press, 2015.

Belle, Kathryn. "Black Feminism and Intersectional Analyses: A Defense of Intersectionality." *Philosophy Today* 55 (2011).

Belle, Kathryn. "Race Women, Race Men and Early Expressions of Proto-Intersectionality, 1830s–1930s." In Namita Goswami, Maeve M. O'Donovan, and Lisa Yount, eds., *Why Race and Gender Still Matter: An Intersectional Approach*. London: Pickering & Chatto (Publishers), 2014.

Belle, Kathryn. "Anna Julia Cooper." *Stanford Encyclopedia of Philosophy* (2015).

Belsey, Catherine. *Critical Practice*. Abingdon UK: Routledge, 1980.

Benians, E. A. "Adam Smith's Project of an Empire." *The Cambridge Historical Journal* 1, no. 3. (1925), 249–283.

Bentham, Jeremy. *An Introduction to the Principles of Morals and Legislation*. Kitchener: Batoche Books, 1781.

Berger, Harry. *The Perils of Uglytown: Studies in Structural Misanthropology from Plato to Rembrandt*. New York NY: Fordham University Press, 2015.

Bernal, Angélica M. *Beyond Origins: Rethinking Founding in a Time of Constitutional Democracy*. New York NY: Oxford University Press, 2017.

Bernstein, Michael. "A Brief History of the American Economic Association." *The American Journal of Economics and Sociology* 67, no. 5 (2008), 1007–1024.

Berry, Christopher J. *The Idea of Luxury: A Conceptual and Historical Investigation*. New York NY: Cambridge University Press, 1994.

Bickford, Susan. "Beyond Friendship: Aristotle on Conflict, Deliberation, and Attention." *The Journal of Politics* 58 no. 2 (1986), 398–421.

Blank, Andrea. "Value, Justice, and Presumption in the Late Scholastic Controversy over Price Regulation." *Journal of the History of Ideas* 80, no.2 (2019), 183–202.

Brenner, Neil. Jamie Peck, and Nik Theodore. "Variegated Neoliberalization: Geographies, Modalities, Pathways." *Global Networks* (2010), 182–222.

Brenner, Robert. "Agrarian Class Structure and Economic Development in Pre-Industrial Europe." In T. H. Aston and C. H. E. Philpin, eds., *The Brenner Debate: Agrarian Class Structure and Economic Development in Pre-Industrial Europe*. New York NY: Cambridge University Press, 1985.

Brown, Wendy. *States of Injury: Power and Freedom in Late Modernity*. Princeton University Press, 1995.

Brown, Wendy and Janet Halley. *Left Legalism/Left Critique*. Durham NC: Duke University Press, 2002.

Brown, Wendy. *Undoing the Demos: Neoliberalism's Stealth Revolution*. Cambridge MA: MIT Press, 2014.

Brown, Wendy. *In the Ruins of Neoliberalism: The Rise of Anti-Democratic Politics in the West*. New York NY: Columbia University Press, 2019.

Caffentzis, Constantine G. *Clipped Coins, Abused Words, and Civil Government: John Locke's Philosophy of Money*. Brooklyn NY: Autonomedia, 1989.

Cahn, Kenneth S. "The Roman and Frankish Roots of the Just Price of Medieval Canon Law." In William M. Bowsky, ed., *Studies in Medieval and Renaissance History Volume VI*. Lincoln NE: University of Nebraska Press, 1969.

Cammack, Daniela. "Aristotle on the Virtue of the Multitude." *Political Theory* 41, no. 2 (2013), 175–202.

Cassin, Barbara. *Dictionary of Untranslatables: A Philosophical Lexicon*. Princeton University Press, 2014.

Cohen, Cathy. "Punks, Bulldaggers, and Welfare Queens: The Radical Potential of Queer Politics?" In Mae G. Henderson and E. Patrick Johnson, eds., *Black Queer Studies: A Critical Anthology*. Durham NC: Duke University Press, 2005.

Collins, Patricia H. *Black Feminist Thought: Knowledge, Consciousness, and the Politics of Empowerment*. New York NY: Routledge, 2000.

Connolly, William. *The Terms of Political Discourse*. Princeton University Press, 1993.

Cooper, Anna J. *The Voice of Anna Julia Cooper.* Edited by Charles Lemert and Esme Bhan. Lanham MD: Rowman & Littlefield Publishers, 1998.

Cooper, Anna J. *Slavery and the French and Haitian Revolutionists.* Lanham MD: Rowman & Littlefield Publishers, 2006.

Cooper, Anna J. *A Voice from the South.* New York NY: Oxford University Press, 2008.

Cooper, Brittney C. *Beyond Respectability: The Intellectual Thought of Race Women.* Champaign IL: University of Illinois Press, 2017.

Cooper, Melinda. *Family Values: Between Neoliberalism and the New Social Conservatism.* New York NY: Zone Books, 2017.

Coulthard, Glen. *Red Skin White Masks: Rejecting the Colonial Politics of Recognition.* Minneapolis MN: University of Minnesota Press, 2014.

Curry, Tommy J. "Michael Brown and the Need for a Genre Study of Black Male Death and Dying." *Theory & Event* 17, no. 3 (2014).

Cusick, Carolyn. "Anna Julia Cooper, Worth, and Public Intellectuals." *Philosophia Africana* 12, no. 1 (2009), 21–40.

Dagger, Richard. "Republican Citizenship." In Engin Isin and Bryan Turner, eds., *Handbook of Citizenship Studies.* Thousand Oaks CA: Sage Publications, 2003.

Davidson, James N. *Courtesans and Fishcakes: The Consuming Passions of Classical Athens.* London: Harper Collins Publishers, 1997.

Davis, Angela. "Foreword." In Patrisse Khan-Cullors and asha bandele, *When They Call You a Terrorist: A Black Lives Matter Memoir.* New York NY: St. Martin's Press, 2017.

De Roover, Raymond. "The Concept of the Just Price: Theory and Economic Policy." *The Journal of Economic History* 18 no. 4 (1958), 418–434.

De Villiers, Melius. "The Roman Contract According to Labeo." *The Yale Law Journal* 35, no. 3 (1926), 292–295.

Dean, Jodi. *Democracy and Other Neoliberal Fantasies: Communicative Capitalism and Left Politics.* Durham NC: Duke University Press, 2007.

Decock, Wim. "Introduction." *Journal of Markets & Morality* 10, no. 2 (2007).

Dermot, Ryan. "'The Beauty of That Arrangement': Adam Smith Imagines Empire." *Studies in Romanticism* 48 no. 1 (2009), 543–554.

Derrida, Jacques. "Signature Event Context." In *Limited Inc.* Chicago IL: Northwestern University, 1988.

Deslauriers, Marguerite. "Political Rule Over Women in *Politics* I." In Thornton Lockwood and Thanassis Samaras, eds., *Aristotle's Politics: A Critical Guide.* New York NY: Cambridge University Press, 2015.

Dewey, John. *Democracy and Education: An Introduction to the Philosophy of Education.* New York NY: Macmillan Company, 1916.

Dietz, Mary. "Between Polis and Empire: Aristotle's Politics." *American Political Science Review* 106, no. 2 (2012), 275–293.

Douglass, Patrice. "Black Feminist Theory for the Dead and Dying." *Theory & Event* 21, no. 1 (2018).

Dowland, Seth. *Family Values and the Rise of the Christian Right.* Philadelphia PA: University of Pennsylvania Press, 2015.

Edelman, Elijah A. "Why We Forget the Pulse Nightclub Murders: Bodies That (Never) Matter and a Call for Coalitional Models of Queer and Trans Social Justice." *GLQ: A Journal of Lesbian and Gay Studies* 24, no. 1 (2018).

El-Tayeb, Fatima. "Time Travelers and Queer Heterotopias: Narratives from the Muslim Underground." *The Germanic Review: Literature, Culture, Theory* 88, no. 3 (2013).

Ely, Richard T. "The Founding and Early History of the American Economic Association." *The American Economic Review* 26, 1 (1936), 141–150.

Engelmann, Stephen G. *Imagining Interest in Political Thought: Origins of Economic Rationality.* Durham NC: Duke University Press, 2003.

Evans, Peter and William H. Sewell, Jr. "The Neoliberal Era: Ideology, Policy, and Social Effects." In Peter Hall and Michele Lamont, eds., *Social Resilience in the Neoliberal Era.* New York NY: Cambridge University Press, 2013.

Evans, Stephanie Y. *Black Women in the Ivory Tower, 1850–1954: An Intellectual History.* Gainesville FL: University Press of Florida, 2007.

Fanon, Frantz. *The Wretched of the Earth.* New York NY: Grove Press, 2005.

Ferguson, Roderick A. *Aberrations in Black: Toward a Queer of Color Critique.* Minneapolis MN: University of Minnesota Press, 2003.

Fernheimer, Janice W. "Arguing from Difference: Cooper, Emerson, Guizot, and a More Harmonious America." In Kristin Waters and Carol B. Conaway, eds., *Black Women's Intellectual Traditions: Speaking Their Minds.* Burlington VT: University of Vermont Press, 2007.

Finley, M. I. "Aristotle and Economic Analysis." *Past & Present* 47 (1970), 3–25.

Foley, Duncan K. *Notes on the Theoretical Foundations of Political Economy.* Universidad Nacional Autónoma de México, 1999.

Foucault, Michel. "Nietzsche, Genealogy, History." In Donald F. Bouchard, ed., *Language, Counter Memory, Practice: Selected Essays and Interviews.* Trans. Donald F. Bouchard and Sherry Simon. Ithaca NY: Cornell University Press, 1977.

Foucault, Michel. *Discipline and Punish: The Birth of the Prison.* New York NY: Vintage Books, 1991.

Foucault, Michel. *The Order of Things: An Archaeology of the Human Sciences.* Abingdon UK: Routledge, 1994.

Foucault, Michel. *Society Must Be Defended: Lectures at the Collège de France 1975–1976.* New York NY: Picador, 2003.

Foucault, Michel. *The Birth of Biopolitics: Lectures at the College de France, 1978–1979.* New York NY: Palgrave, 2008.

Frank, Jill. "Democracy and Distinction: Aristotle on Just Desert." *Political Theory* 26, no. 6 (1998), 784–802.

Frank, Jill. "Citizens, Slaves, and Foreigners: Aristotle on Human Nature." *American Political Science Review* 98, no. 1 (2004), 91–104.

Frank, Jill. *A Democracy of Distinction: Aristotle and the Work of Politics.* University of Chicago Press, 2005.

Frankena, William. "Value." In P. Edwards, ed., *The Encyclopedia of Philosophy.* New York NY: Macmillan, 1967.

Fraser, Nancy and Axel Honneth. *Redistribution or Recognition? A Political-Philosophical Exchange.* New York NY: Verso, 2004.

Freeden, Michael. *The Political Theory of Political Thinking.* Oxford: Oxford University Press, 2013.

Fritsch, Kelly, Clare O'Connor, and A. K. Thompson. *Keywords for Radicals: The Contested Vocabulary of Late Capitalist Struggle.* Oakland CA: AK Press, 2016.

Gabel, Leona C. *From Slavery to the Sorbonne and Beyond: The Life and Writings of Anna J. Cooper.* Smith College Studies in History, 1982.

Gadamer, Hans-Georg. *Truth and Method*. New York NY and London: Continuum, 1989.

Gallagher, Catherine. "The Body Versus the Social Body in the Works of Thomas Malthus and Henry Mayhew." *Representations* no. 14 (1986), 83–106.

Gallagher, Catherine. *The Body Economic: Life, Death, and Sensation in Political Economy and the Victorian Novel*. Princeton University Press, 2005.

Geuss, Raymond. *Reality and Its Dreams*. Cambridge MA: Harvard University Press, 2016.

Gibson-Graham, J. K. *The End of Capitalism (As We Knew It): A Feminist Critique of Political Economy*. Minneapolis MN: University of Minnesota Press, 1996.

Giddings, F. H. "The Concepts of Utility, Value, and Cost." *Publications of the American Economic Association* 6, nos. 1/2 (1891), 41–43.

Gillespie, Michael A. *The Theological Origins of Modernity*. University of Chicago Press, 2009.

Glass, Kathy L. "Tending to the Roots: Anna Julia Cooper's Sociopolitical Thought and Activism." *Meridians* 6, no. 1 (2005), 23–55.

Gordon, Barry. "Aristotle, Schumpeter, and the Metalist Tradition." *The Quarterly Journal of Economics* 75, no. 4 (1961), 608–614.

Gordon, Barry. *Economic Analysis Before Adam Smith: Hesiod to Lessius*. London: The MacMillan Press, 1975, 608–614.

Gordon, Jane A. *Creolizing Political Theory: Reading Rousseau Through Fanon*. New York NY: Fordham University Press, 2014.

Gordon, Jane A. "Unmasking the *Big Bluff* of Legitimate Governance and So-Called Independence: Creolizing Rousseau through the Reflections of Anna Julia Cooper." Critical *Philosophy of Race* 6, no. 1 (2018), 1–25.

Gordon, Lewis. "Anna Julia Cooper and the Problem of Value." In Lewis Gordon, ed., *An Introduction to Africana Philosophy*. New York NY: Cambridge University Press, 2008.

Gower, John. *The English Works of John Gower*. Edited by G. C. Macaulay, Vol. 1. Early English Text Society, 1900.

Graeber, David. *Debt: The First 5,000 Years*. Brooklyn NY: Melville House, 2012.

Green, Kai. "Troubling the Waters: Mobilizing A Trans* Analytic." In E. Patrick Johnson, ed., *No Tea, No Shade: New Writings in Black Queer Studies*. Durham NC: Duke University Press, 2016.

Grotius, Hugo. *The Rights of War and Peace, Book II*. Indianapolis IN: Liberty Fund 2005.

Halberstam, Jack. "Shame and White Gay Masculinity." *Social Text* 84–85, nos. 3–4 (2005), 219–233.

Halperin, David and Valerie Traub. *Gay Shame*. University of Chicago Press, 2009.

Harpam, Geoffrey. *Language Alone: The Critical Fetish of Modernity*. Abingdon UK: Routledge, 2002.

Harper, Phillip B. "The Evidence of Felt Intuition: Minority Experience, Everyday Life, and Critical Speculative Knowledge." In Mae G. Henderson and E. Patrick Johnson, eds., *Black Queer Studies: A Critical Anthology*.Durham NC: Duke University Press, 2005.

Hartman, Saidiya. *Lose Your Mother: A Journey Along the Atlantic Slave Route*. New York NY: Farrar, Straus and Giroux, 2008.

Harvey, David. *A Brief History of Neoliberalism*. New York NY: Oxford University Press, 2007.

Havercroft, Jonathan and David Owen. "Soul-Blindness, Police Orders and Black Lives Matter: Wittgenstein, Cavell, and Rancière." *Political Theory* 44, no. 6 (2016), 739–763.

Heller, Agnes. *The Theory of Need in Marx*. London: Allison & Busby, 1974.

Henderson, George. *Value in Marx: The Persistence of Value in a More-Than-Capitalist World*. Minneapolis MN: University of Minnesota Press, 2013.

Hesse, Barnor and Juliet Hooker. "Introduction: On Black Political Thought inside Global Black Protest." *The South Atlantic Quarterly* 116, no. 3 (2017).

Hill, Mike and Warren Montag. *The Other Adam Smith*. Stanford University Press, 2015.

Hirschman, Albert O. *The Passions and the Interests: Political Arguments for Capitalism Before Its Triumph*. Princeton University Press, 1977.

Hirschmann, Nancy J. and Kirstie M. McClure. *Feminist Interpretations of John Locke*. University Park PA: The Pennsylvania State University Press, 2007.

Hobbes, Thomas. *Leviathan*. Edited by Richard Tuck. Cambridge UK: Cambridge University Press, 1991.

Hont, Istvan and Michael Ignatieff. "Needs and Justice in the Wealth of Nations." In Istvan Hont and Michael Ignatieff, eds., *Wealth and Virtue: The Shaping of Political Economy in the Scottish Enlightenment*. New York NY: Cambridge University Press, 1983.

Hooker, Juliet. "Black Lives Matter and the Paradoxes of U.S. Black Politics: From Democratic Sacrifice to Democratic Repair." *Political Theory* 44, no. 4 (2016), 448–469.

Hooker, Juliet. "Black Protest/White Grievance: On the Problem of White Political Imaginations Not Shaped by Loss." *The South Atlantic Quarterly* 116, no. 3 (2017).

Hubbard, LaRese. "When and Where I Enter: Anna Julia Cooper, Afrocentric Theory, and Africana Studies." *Journal of Black Studies* 40, no. 2 (2009), 283–295.

Hubbard, LaRese. "Anna Julia Cooper and Africana Womanism: Some Early Conceptual Contributions." *Black Women, Gender, + Families* 2, no. 4 (2010), 31–43.

Hunt, Alan. *Governance of the Consuming Passions: A History of Sumptuary Law*. New York NY: St. Martin's Press 1996.

Khalil, Elias. "What Determines the Boundary of Civil Society? Hume, Smith, and the Justification of European Exploitation of Non-Europeans." *Theoria: A Journal of Social and Political Theory* 60, no. 134 (2013), 26–49.

Khan-Cullors, Patrisse and asha bandele. *When They Call You a Terrorist: A Black Lives Matter Memoir*. New York NY: St. Martin's Press, 2017.

Koselleck, Reinhardt. "Begriffsgeschichte and Social History." In *Futures Past: On the Semantics of Historical Time*. New York NY: Columbia University Press, 2004.

Laclau, Ernesto and Chantal Mouffe. *Hegemony and Socialist Strategy: Towards a Radical Democratic Politics*. New York NY: Verso, 2001.

Laclau, Ernesto. *On Populist Reason*. London: Verso, 2007.

Langford, Catherine L. and Montené Speight. "#BlackLivesMatter: Epistemic Positioning, Challenges, and Possibilities." *Journal of Contemporary Rhetoric* 5, nos. 3/4 (2015), 78–89.

Langholm, Odd. *Price and Value in the Aristotelian Tradition: A Study in Scholastic Economic Sources.* Oslo Norway: The Norwegian Research Council for Science and the Humanities, 1979.

Langholm, Odd. *Economics in the Medieval Schools: Wealth, Exchange, Value, Money, and Usury According to the Paris Theological Tradition 1200–1305.* Leiden NL: Brill, 1992.

Langholm, Odd. *The Merchant in the Confessional: Trade and Price in the Pre-Reformation Penitential Handbooks.* Leiden NL: Brill, 2002.

Lebron, Christopher. *The Making of Black Lives Matter: A Brief History of an Idea.* New York NY: Oxford University Press, 2017.

Lemert, Charles. "Anna Julia Cooper: The Colored Woman's Office." In *The Voice of Anna Julia Cooper.* Lanham MD: Rowman & Littlefield Publishers, 1998.

Lessius, Leonardus. "On Buying and Selling." Trans. Wim Decock. 2007.

Lindsay, Thomas. "Was Aristotle Racist, Sexist, and Anti-Democratic? A Review Essay." *The Review of Politics* 56, no. 1 (1994), 127–151.

Lipson, E. *The Economic History of England Volume 2: The Age of Mercantilism.* London: A & C Black, 1934.

Locke, John. *Two Treatises of Government.* Cambridge University Press, 1960.

Lockwood, Thornton. "*Politics II:* Political Critique, Political Theorizing, Political Innovation." In Thornton Lockwood and Thanassis Samaras, eds., *Aristotle's Politics: A Critical Guide.* Cambridge UK: Cambridge University Press, 2015.

Lorde, Audre. *A Burst of Light.* Mineola NY: Dover Publications, 1988.

MacGilvray, Eric. *The Invention of Market Freedom.* Cambridge University Press, 2011.

Mackin. Glenn. "Black Lives Matter and the Concept of the Counterworld." *Philosophy and Rhetoric* 49 no. 4, (2016), 459–481.

Makalani, Minkah. "Black Lives Matter and the Limits of Formal Black Politics." *The South Atlantic Quarterly* 116, no. 3 (2017).

Maniatis, G. C. "Operationalization of the Concept of Just Price in the Byzantine Legal, Economic and Political System." *Byzantion* 71, no. 1 (2001), 131–193.

Marcuse, Hermann. "Unbalanced Transactions Under Common and Civil Law." *Columbia Law Review* 43, no. 7 (1943).

Markell, Patchen. *Bound by Recognition.* Princeton University Press, 2003.

Marx, Karl. "Economic and Philosophic Manuscripts of 1844." In Robert C. Tucker, ed., *The Marx-Engels Reader 2nd Edition.* W.W. Norton & Company, 1978.

Marx, Karl. "The German Ideology." In Robert C. Tucker, ed., *The Marx-Engels Reader 2nd Edition.* W.W. Norton & Company, 1978.

Mathie, William. "Political and Distributive Justice in the Political Science of Aristotle." *The Review of Politics* 49, no. 1 (1987), 59–84.

Mathiowetz, Dean. "Feeling Luxury: Invidious Political Pleasures and the Sense of Touch." *Theory & Event* 13, no. 4 (2010), 1–31.

Mathiowetz, Dean. *Appeals to Interest: Language, Contestation, and the Shaping of Political Agency.* University Park PA: The Pennsylvania State University Press, 2011.

Mathiowetz, Dean. "Gay Love Conquers All." *The Contemporary Condition*, July 14, 2013.

Mathiowetz, Dean "'Meditation is Good for Nothing': Leisure as a Democratic Practice." *New Political Science* 38, no. 2 (2016), 1–15.

May, Vivian. "Thinking from the Margins, Acting at the Intersections: Anna Julia Cooper's A Voice from the South." *Hypatia* 19, no. 2 (2004), 74–91.

May, Vivian. *Anna Julia Cooper: Visionary Black Feminist.* New York NY: Routledge, 2007.

May, Vivian. "'It is Never a Question of the Slaves': Anna Julia Cooper's Challenge to History's Silences in Her 1925 Sorbonne Thesis." *Callaloo* 31, no. 3 (2008), 903–918.

May, Vivian. "Anna Julia Cooper's Philosophy of Resistance." *Philosophia Africana* 12, no. 1 (2009), 41–65.

May, Vivian. "Writing the Self into Being: Anna Julia Cooper's Textual Politics." *African American Review* 43, no. 1 (2009), 17–34.

Mazzucato, Mariana. *The Value of Everything: Making and Taking in the Global Economy.* New York NY: PublicAffairs, 2018.

McIvor, David W. *Mourning in America: Race and the Politics of Loss.* Ithaca NY: Cornell University Press, 2016.

McKnight, Utz Lars. "Where Is The Love That You Promised?" *Theory & Event* 17, no. 3 (2014).

McMillan Cottom, Tressie. *Lower Ed: The Troubling Rise of For-Profit Colleges in the New Economy.* New York NY: The New Press, 2018.

Meagher, Thomas. "Black Issues in Philosophy: On Teaching Anna Julia Cooper's 'What Are We Worth' in Introductory Courses." *American Philosophical Association*, May 30, 2018.

Meikle, Scott. "Aristotle and the Political Economy of the Polis." *The Journal of Hellenic Studies* 99, no. (1979), 57–73.

Mitchell, W. J. T. "Value." In Tony Bennett, Lawrence Grossberg, and Meaghan Morris, eds., *New Keywords: A Revised Vocabulary of Culture and Society.* Malden MA: Blackwell Publishing, 2005.

Moody-Turner, Shirley. "A Voice Beyond the South: Resituating the Locus of Cultural Representation in the Later Writings of Anna Julia Cooper." *African American Review* 43 (2009), 57–67.

Moody-Turner, Shirley and James Stewart. "Gendering Africana Studies: Insights from Anna Julia Cooper." *African American Review* 43, no. 1 (2009), 35–44.

Morgensen, Scott Lauria. "Theorizing Gender, Sexuality, and Settler Colonialism: An Introduction." *Settler Colonial Studies* 2, no. 2 (2012).

Mulgan, Richard. "Aristotle and the Value of Political Participation." *Political Theory* 18, no. 2 (1990), 195–215.

Muñoz, José Esteban. *Disidentifications: Queers of Color and the Performance of Politics.* Minneapolis MN: University of Minnesota Press, 1999.

Munt, Sally. *Queer Attachments: The Cultural Politics of Shame.* Hampshire, UK: Ashgate, 2008.

Myers, Ella. "Beyond the Wages of Whiteness: Du Bois on the Irrationality of Anti-Black Racism." *Social Science Research Council*, Reading Racial Conflict Series, 2017.

Myers, Ella. "Beyond the Psychological Wage: Du Bois on White Dominion." *Political Theory* 47, no. 1 (2019), 6–31.

Nacol, Emily. *An Age of Risk: Politics and Economy in Early Modern Britain.* Princeton University Press, 2016.

Nancy, Jean-Luc. *The Truth of Democracy*. New York NY: Fordham University Press, 2010.

Nichols, Mary P. *Citizens and Statesmen: A Study of Aristotle's Politics*. Lanham MD: Rowman & Littlefield Publishers, 1992.

Nichols, Robert. "Theft Is Property! The Recursive Logic of Dispossession." *Political Theory* 46, no. 1 (2018), 3–28.

Nietzsche, Friedrich. *On the Genealogy of Morals* and *Ecce Homo*. New York NY: Vintage, 1967.

Palen, Marc William. "Adam Smith as Advocate of Empire." *The History Journal* 1, no. 57 (2014), 179–198.

Palliser, D. M. *The Age of Elizabeth: England Under the Later Tudors 1547–1603*. Harlow UK: Longman Group, 1983.

Peck, Jamie. *Constructions of Neoliberal Reason*. Oxford University Press, 2010.

Perelman, Michael. *The Invention of Capitalism: Classical Political Economy and the Secret History of Primitive Accumulation*. Durham NC: Duke University Press, 2000.

Pitkin, Hanna Fenichel. "Obligation and Consent." *The American Political Science Review* 59, no. 4 (1965), 39–52.

Pitkin, Hanna Fenichel. "Justice: On Relating Private and Public." *Political Theory* 9, no. 3 (1981), 327–352.

Pitkin, Hanna Fenichel. "Slippery Bentham: Some Neglected Cracks in the Foundation of Utilitarianism." *Political Theory* 18, no. 1 (1990), 104–131.

Pitkin, Hanna Fenichel. *The Attack of the Blob: Hannah Arendt's Concept of the Social*. University of Chicago Press, 1998.

Pocock, J. G. A. *Politics and Time: Essays on Political Thought and History*. University of Chicago Press, 1989.

Polanyi, Karl. "Aristotle Discovers the Economy." In *Trade and Market in the Early Empires: Economies in History and Theory*. New York NY: The Free Press, 1957.

Poovey, Mary. *A History of the Modern Fact: Problems of Knowledge in the Sciences of Wealth and Society*. University of Chicago Press, 1998.

Posner, Sarah. *God's Profits: Faith, Fraud, and the Republican Crusade for Values Voters*. Sausalito CA: Polipoint Press, 2008.

Ransby, Barbara. *Making All Black Lives Matter: Reimagining Freedom in the 21st Century*. Berkeley CA: University of California Press, 2018.

Rich, Adrienne. "Compulsory Heterosexuality and Lesbian Existence." *Signs* 5, no. 5 (1980).

Richter, Melvin. *The History of Social and Political Concepts*. Oxford University Press, 1995.

Rickford, Russell. "Black Lives Matter: Toward a Modern Practice of Mass Struggle." *New Labor Forum* 25 no. 1 (2016), 34–42.

Salkever, Stephen. "Whose Prayer? The Best Regime of Book 7 and the Lessons of Aristotle's *Politics*." *Political Theory* 35, no. 1 (2007), 29–46.

Samaras, Thanassis. "Aristotle and the Question of Citizenship." In Thornton Lockwood and Thanassis Samaras, eds., *Aristotle's Politics: A Critical Guide*. Cambridge UK: Cambridge University Press, 2015.

Saxonhouse, Arlene. "Family, Polity & Unity: Aristotle on Socrates' Community of Wives." *Polity* 15, no. 2 (1982), 202–219.

Schuck, Peter. "Liberal Citizenship." In Engin Isin and Bryan Turner, eds., *Handbook of Citizenship Studies*. Thousand Oaks CA: Sage Publications, 2003.

Schumpeter, Joseph. "On the Concept of Social Value." *The Quarterly Journal of Economics* 23, no. 2 (1909), 213–232.

Schütrumpf, Eckart. "Little to Do with Justice: Aristotle on Distributing Political Power." In Thornton Lockwood and Thanassis Samaras, eds., *Aristotle's Politics: A Critical Guide.* Cambridge UK: Cambridge University Press, 2015.

Sedgwick, Eve K. *Touching, Feeling: Affect, Pedagogy, Performativity.* Durham NC: Duke University Press, 2003.

Sekora, John. *Luxury: The Concept in Western Thought, Eden to Smollett.* Baltimore MD: The Johns Hopkins University Press, 1977.

Seneca, Lucius. *On Benefits.* Trans. Thomas Lodge (1614).

Seth, Vanita. *Europe's Indians: Producing Racial Difference, 1500–1900.* Durham NC: Duke University Press, 2010.

Shakhsari, Sima. "Killing Me Softly with Your Rights: Queer Death and the Politics of Rightful Killing." In Jin Haritaworn, Adi Kuntsman, and Silvia Posocco, eds., *Queer Necropolitics.* Abingdon UK: Routledge, 2015.

Shepard, Alexandra. *Accounting for Oneself: Worth, Status, and the Social Order in Early Modern England.* Oxford University Press, 2015.

Shklar, Judith. *Political Theory and Ideology.* New York NY: The Macmillan Company, 1966.

Shklar, Judith. *American Citizenship: The Quest for Inclusion.* Cambridge MA: Harvard University Press, 1998.

Skinner, Quentin. "'Social Meaning' and the Explanation of Social Action." In James Tully, ed., *Meaning & Context: Quentin Skinner and his Critics.* Princeton University Press, 1988.

Skinner, Quentin. *Liberty Before Liberalism.* Cambridge University Press, 1998.

Slack, Paul. *Poverty and Policy in Tudor and Stuart England.* Harlow UK: Longman Group UK, 1988.

Smith, Adam. *An Inquiry into the Nature and Causes of the Wealth of Nations.* New York NY: Oxford University Press, 1993.

Smith, Adam. *The Theory of Moral Sentiments.* Cambridge University Press, 2002.

Sombart, Werner and Philip Siegelman. *Luxury and Capitalism.* Ann Arbor MI: University of Michigan Press, 1967.

Springborg, Patricia. "Aristotle and the Problem of Needs." *History of Political Thought* 5, no. 3 (1984), 393–424.

Strohm, Paul. *England's Empty Throne: Usurpation and the Language of Legitimation 1399–1422.* New Haven CT: Yale University Press, 1998.

Stuard, Susan Mosher. *Gilding the Market: Luxury and Fashion in Fourteenth-Century Italy.* Philadelphia PA: University of Pennsylvania Press, 2006.

Sulé, V. Thandi. "Intellectual Activism: The Praxis of Dr. Anna Julia Cooper as a Blueprint for Equity-Based Pedagogy." *Feminist Teacher* 23, no. 3 (2013), 211–229.

Swanson, Judith. *The Public and the Private in Aristotle's Political Philosophy.* Ithaca NY: Cornell University Press, 1992.

Swinburne, Henry. *A Briefe Treatise of Testaments and Last Willes iii.* London: John Windet, 1590.

Tawney, R. H. *The Agrarian Problem in the Sixteenth Century.* New York NY: Burt Franklin, 1912.

Taylor, Charles. *Human Agency and Language.* Cambridge University Press, 1985.

Taylor, Charles. "The Hermeneutics of Conflict." In James Tully, ed., *Meaning and Context: Quentin Skinner and His Critics*. Princeton University Press, 1988.

Taylor, Charles. *Multiculturalism: Examining the Politics of Recognition*. Princeton University Press, 1992.

Taylor, Keeanga-Yamahtta. *From #BlackLivesMatter to Black Liberation*. Chicago IL: Haymarket Books, 2016.

Taylor, Keeanga-Yamahtta. *How We Get Free: Black Feminism and the Combahee River Collective*. Chicago IL: Haymarket Books, 2017.

Tellmann, Ute. *Life and Money: The Genealogy of the Liberal Economy and the Displacement of Politics*. New York NY: Columbia University Press, 2018.

Temin, Peter. *The Roman Market Economy*. Princeton University Press, 2013.

Thompson, Debra. "An Exoneration of Black Rage." *The South Atlantic Quarterly* 116, no. 3 (2017).

Threadcraft, Shatema. "North American Necropolitics and Gender: On #Black-LivesMatter and Black Femicide." *The South Atlantic Quarterly* 116, no. 3 (2017).

Trott, Adriel M. "Rancière and Aristotle: Parapolitics, Party Politics, and the Institution of Perpetual Politics." *The Journal of Speculative Philosophy* 26, no. 4 (2012), 627–646.

Trott, Adriel M. *Aristotle on the Nature of Community*. New York NY: Cambridge University Press, 2014.

Tully, James. *A Discourse on Property: John Locke and his Adversaries*. Cambridge UK: Cambridge University Press, 1980.

Ture, Kwame. "Toward Black Liberation." *The Massachusetts Review* (1966).

Van Houdt, Toon. "Tradition and Renewal in Late Scholastic Economic Thought: The Case of Leonardus Lessius." *Journal of Medieval and Early Modern Studies* 28, no. 1 (1998), 51–73.

Van Houdt, Toon. "Just Pricing and Profit Making in Late Scholastic Economic Thought." *Supplementa Humnnistica Lovaniens* 16 (2000).

Vilar, Pierre. *A History of Gold and Money 1450–1920*. New York NY: Verso, 1991.

Warner, Michael. *The Trouble with Normal: Sex, Politics, and the Ethics of Queer Life*. Cambridge MA: Harvard University Press, 1999.

Warner, Michael. *Publics and Counterpublics*. Brooklyn NY: Zone Books, 2005.

Washick, Bonnie, Elizabeth Wingrove, Kathy E. Ferguson, and Jane Bennett. "Politics that Matter: Thinking About Power and Justice with the New Materialists." *Contemporary Political Theory* 14, no. 1 (2015), 63–89.

Wayne White, Carol. "One and All: Anna Julia Cooper's Romantic Feminist Vision." *Philosophia Africana* 12, no. 1 (2009), 83–106.

Weiss, Penny A. *Canon Fodder: Historical Women Political Thinkers*. University Park PA: Pennsylvania State University Press, 2009.

Whelan, Frederick G. "Population and Ideology in the Enlightenment." *History of Political Thought* 12, no. 1 (1991), 35–72.

Williams, Eric. *Capitalism and Slavery*. Chapel Hill NC: University of North Carolina Press, 1994.

Williams, Patricia. "On Being the Object of Property." *Signs* 14, no.1 (1988).

Williams, Raymond. *Keywords: A Vocabulary of Culture and Society*. Oxford University Press, 1985.

Wilson Gilmore, Ruth. *Golden Gulag: Prisons, Surplus, Crisis, and Opposition in Globalizing California*. Berkeley CA: University of California Press, 2007.

Winch, David. *Adam Smith's Politics: An Essay in Historiographic Revision.* Cambridge UK: Cambridge University Press, 1978.

Wittgenstein, Ludwig. *The Philosophical Investigations.* Trans. G. E. M. Anscombe. Hoboken NJ: Blackwell Publishers, 1953.

Wood, Ellen M. *Class Ideology and Ancient Political Theory: Socrates, Plato, and Aristotle in Social Context.* New York NY: Oxford University Press, 1978.

Wood, Ellen M. *The Origin of Capitalism: A Longer View.* Brooklyn NY: Verso, 2002.

Wordie, J. R. "Deflationary Factors in the Tudor Price Rise." *Past & Present* no. 154 (1997), 32–70.

Worland, Stephen. "Aristotle and the Neoclassical Tradition: The Shifting Ground of Complementarity." *History of Political Economy* 16, no. 1 (1984), 107–134.

Zerilli, Linda. *A Democratic Theory of Judgment.* University of Chicago Press, 2016.

Ziff, Paul. *Semantic Analysis.* Ithaca NY: Cornell University Press, 1960.

Zivi, Karen. *Making Rights Claims: A Practice of Democratic Citizenship.* New York NY: Oxford University Press, 2011.

Index

Note: Page numbers followed by "n" denote endnotes.